REDBONE

The True Story of a Native American Rock Band

IDW

Facebook: **facebook.com/idwpublishing**
Twitter: **@idwpublishing**
YouTube: **youtube.com/idwpublishing**
Tumblr: **tumblr.idwpublishing.com**
Instagram: **instagram.com/idwpublishing**

ISBN: 978-1-68405-714-6   23 22 21 20   1 2 3 4

Translated by
Edward Gauvin

Lettering by
Frank Cvetkovic

Edits by
Justin Eisinger and
Alonzo Simon

Design by
Maqsimum Creation

Production by
Ron Estevez

REDBONE: THE TRUE STORY OF A NATIVE AMERICAN ROCK BAND.
SEPTEMBER 2020. FIRST PRINTING. Redbone © Steinkis 2019.
© 2020 Idea and Design Works, LLC. The IDW logo is registered in
the U.S. Patent and Trademark Office. IDW Publishing, a division of
Idea and Design Works, LLC. Editorial offices: 2765 Truxtun Road, San
Diego, CA 92106. Any similarities to persons living or dead are purely
coincidental. With the exception of artwork used for review purposes,
none of the contents of this publication may be reprinted without the
permission of Idea and Design Works, LLC. Printed in Korea.

IDW Publishing does not read or accept unsolicited submissions of
ideas, stories, or artwork.

NOTICE FROM THE PUBLISHER: This book is an English language version of the original publication by
Steinkis Groupe. It is a work of nonfiction and based upon the personal and professional experiences as well
as observations of Pat Vegas, founding member of Redbone. To this extent, while it is intended to provide as
accurate information as possible, certain recollections may differ from those of others, and the authors and
publisher accept no responsibility for inaccuracies or omissions, and specifically disclaim any liability for loss
of any nature incurred as a result thereof.

Chris Ryall, President & Publisher/CCO
Cara Morrison, Chief Financial Officer
Matthew Ruzicka, Chief Accounting Officer
John Barber, Editor-in-Chief
Justin Eisinger, Editorial Director, Graphic Novels and Collections
Scott Dunbier, Director, Special Projects
Jerry Bennington, VP of New Product Development
Lorelei Bunjes, VP of Technology & Information Services
Jud Meyers, Sales Director
Anna Morrow, Marketing Director
Tara McCrillis, Director of Design & Production
Mike Ford, Director of Operations
Shauna Monteforte, Manufacturing Operations Director
Rebekah Cahalin, General Manager

Ted Adams and Robbie Robbins, IDW Founders

Written by
Christian Staebler & Sonia Paoloni

Art by
Thibault Balahy

Inspired by the music of Redbone and the friendship of Pat Vegas.

FOREWORD

The story of Pat and Lolly Vegas is not easily told but is undoubtedly understood through the soul. The story of Redbone is equally as significant, as it changed the lives of Pat, Lolly, Tony, Pete, and Butch. Along with all those who took a chance to listen to their message.

The Native American community went through a lot of trials and tribulations, with losses and gains, and peace pipes in between. From the loss of many lives, (up to 100 million in genocide), to Wounded Knee, segregation, and more... all the way to transformation, there are many instances where the strength of the Native community was tested. But through it all we prevailed.

I am honored to introduce the story of my father and uncle's journey. Every day I sit in amazement for what they have accomplished, and how their ongoing ripple effect continues to elevate those around them. Pat and Lolly did not come from a financially wealthy family, but a family wealthy in love and communication. They were taught at a young age what hard work truly means and from that modality they built the foundation of success. They struggled, went hungry some nights, played their butts off, and lived with depth. Had the lowest of lows and the highest of highs!

Everywhere they went they stood for something and represented awareness in a time of serious conformity, especially through their music. This gave them a platform to become legendary, and boy did they! They are the faces of the community and the heart of the city and will continue to inspire all those around them.

This story goes into detail about the origin of Pat Vegas, Lolly Vegas, and the birth of Redbone.

It will take you through the history of our people and the future of our next generation. Whether Native American or not, this is an incredible story for everyone, and one that all can relate to. As we all have felt the tomahawk of struggle.

There is a beautiful aspect of realization to it... that through it all, if you remain true to your core and keep striving for all that moves you, your dreams surely will come true. I hope you enjoy this flashback journey into the history of my family! It's rich in knowledge, wisdom, truth, love, originality, and strength.

This is one story you will never forget.

_____

Remember.
We are all one race, the human race.
The more we understand that, the more we understand ourselves and
can come together to make a brighter future. This is your time now, to get
inspired and make a change! Don't wait.

Special Shoutout: PJ, Tobie, Sarah, Acela, Bianca, Dominic, Malia, River,
Sophia, Nikko, all of our family in Salinas and to you...
our REDBONE FAMILY!

Rest In Music: Lolly and Tony

Sending love and blessings to you all!

Enjoy it.

FRANKIE VEGAS

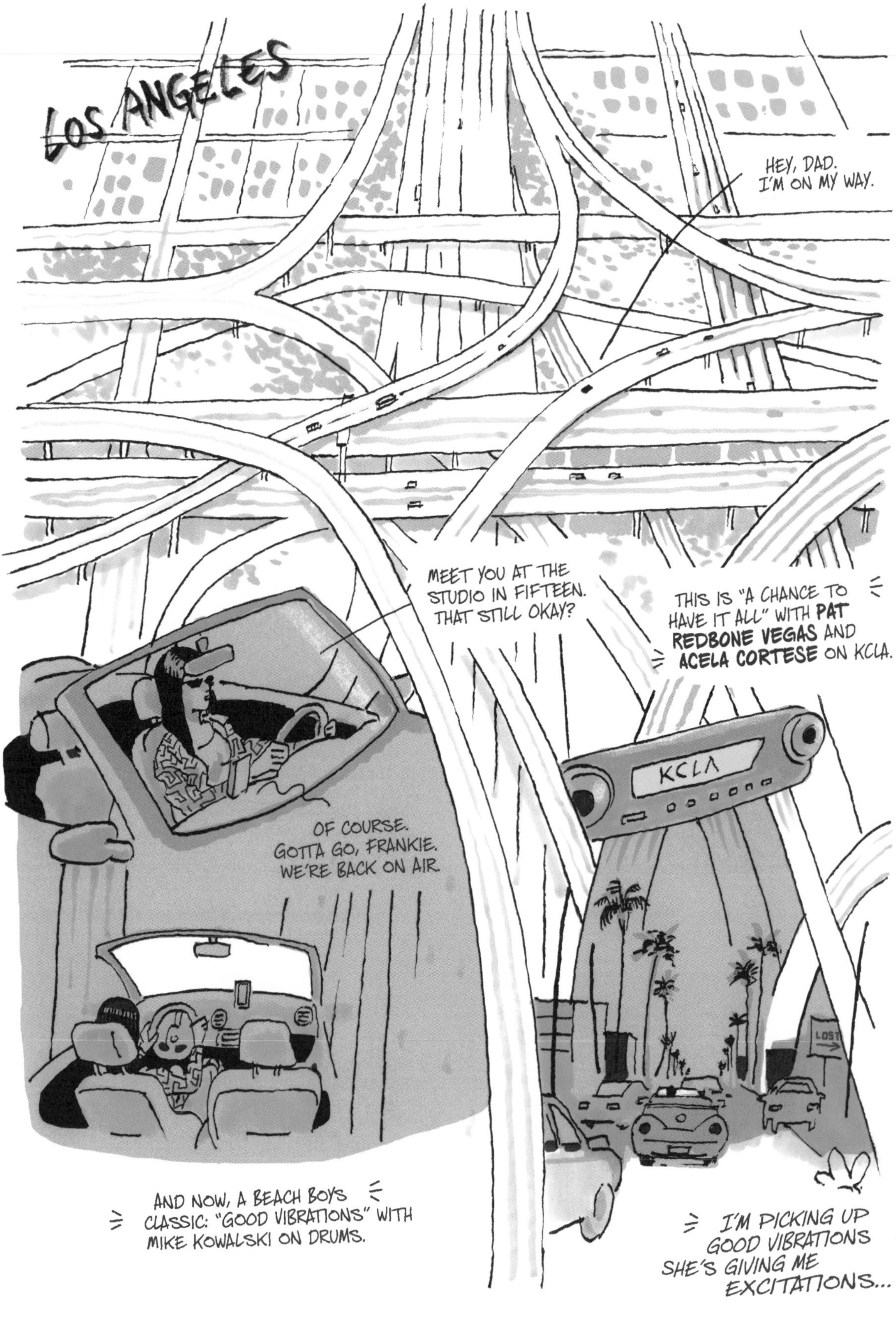
LOS ANGELES
HEY, DAD. I'M ON MY WAY.
MEET YOU AT THE STUDIO IN FIFTEEN. THAT STILL OKAY?
THIS IS "A CHANCE TO HAVE IT ALL" WITH PAT REDBONE VEGAS AND ACELA CORTESE ON KCLA.
KCLA
OF COURSE. GOTTA GO, FRANKIE. WE'RE BACK ON AIR.
LOST
AND NOW, A BEACH BOYS CLASSIC: "GOOD VIBRATIONS" WITH MIKE KOWALSKI ON DRUMS.
I'M PICKING UP GOOD VIBRATIONS SHE'S GIVING ME EXCITATIONS...

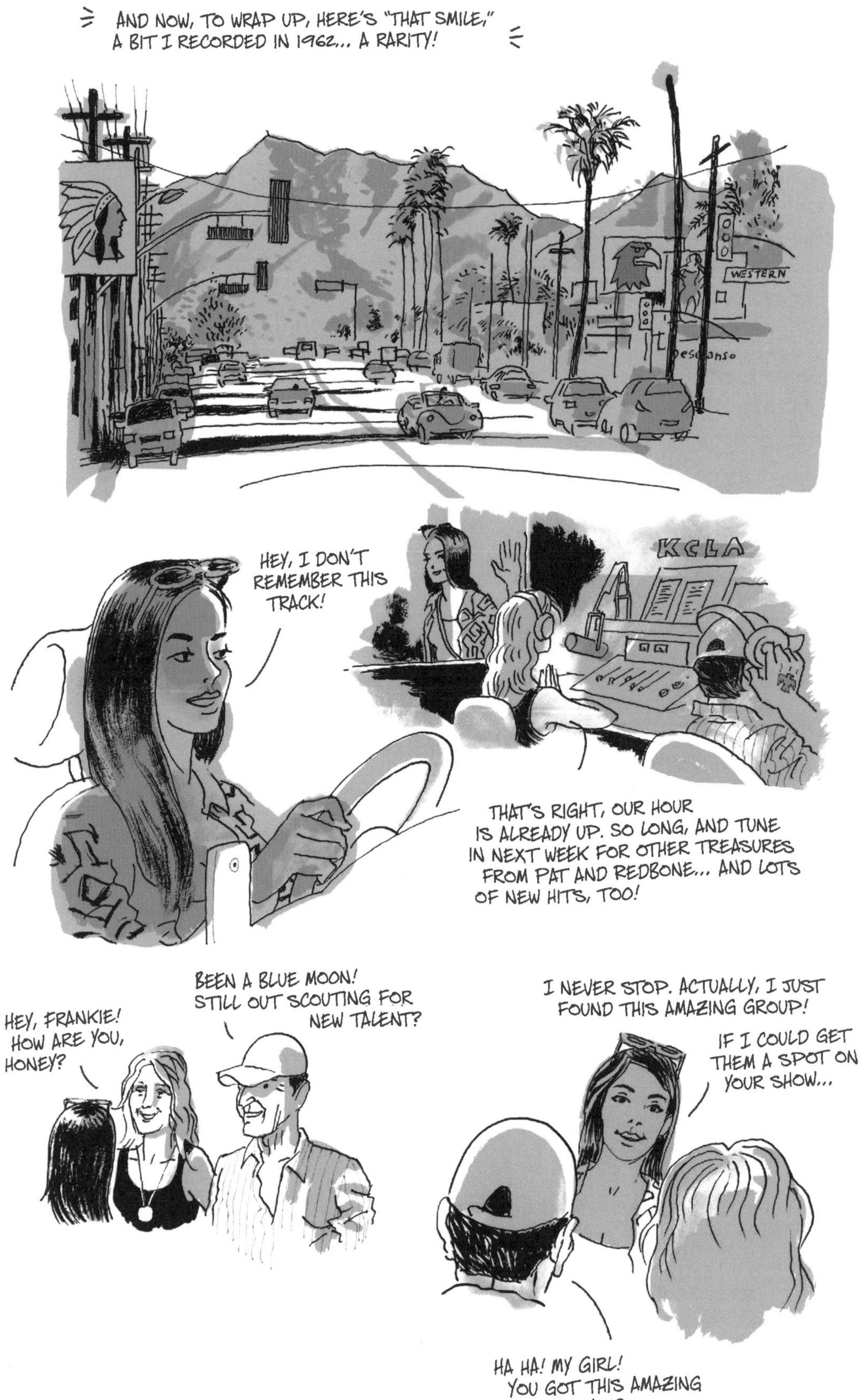
AND NOW, TO WRAP UP, HERE'S "THAT SMILE," A BIT I RECORDED IN 1962... A RARITY!
WESTERN
KCLA
HEY, I DON'T REMEMBER THIS TRACK!
THAT'S RIGHT, OUR HOUR IS ALREADY UP. SO LONG, AND TUNE IN NEXT WEEK FOR OTHER TREASURES FROM PAT AND REDBONE... AND LOTS OF NEW HITS, TOO!
HEY, FRANKIE! HOW ARE YOU, HONEY?
BEEN A BLUE MOON! STILL OUT SCOUTING FOR NEW TALENT?
I NEVER STOP. ACTUALLY, I JUST FOUND THIS AMAZING GROUP!
IF I COULD GET THEM A SPOT ON YOUR SHOW...
HA HA! MY GIRL! YOU GOT THIS AMAZING MUSIC ON YOU?

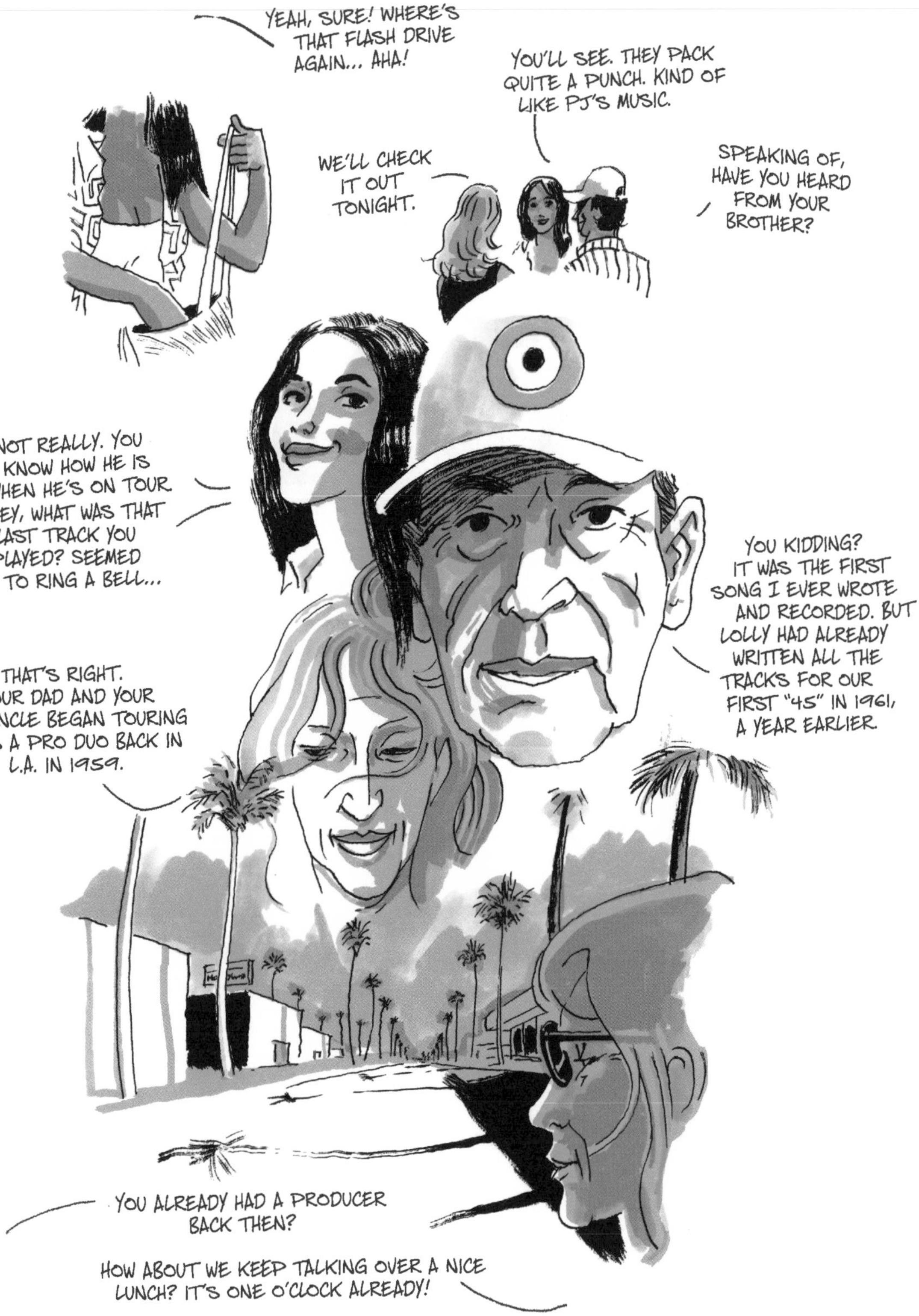
YEAH, SURE! WHERE'S THAT FLASH DRIVE AGAIN... AHA!
YOU'LL SEE. THEY PACK QUITE A PUNCH. KIND OF LIKE PJ'S MUSIC.
WE'LL CHECK IT OUT TONIGHT.
SPEAKING OF, HAVE YOU HEARD FROM YOUR BROTHER?
NOT REALLY. YOU KNOW HOW HE IS WHEN HE'S ON TOUR
HEY, WHAT WAS THAT LAST TRACK YOU PLAYED? SEEMED TO RING A BELL...
YOU KIDDING? IT WAS THE FIRST SONG I EVER WROTE AND RECORDED. BUT LOLLY HAD ALREADY WRITTEN ALL THE TRACKS FOR OUR FIRST "45" IN 1961, A YEAR EARLIER.
THAT'S RIGHT. YOUR DAD AND YOUR UNCLE BEGAN TOURING AS A PRO DUO BACK IN L.A. IN 1959.
YOU ALREADY HAD A PRODUCER BACK THEN?
HOW ABOUT WE KEEP TALKING OVER A NICE LUNCH? IT'S ONE O'CLOCK ALREADY!

I
PAT AND LOLLY VEGAS
(1960-1968)

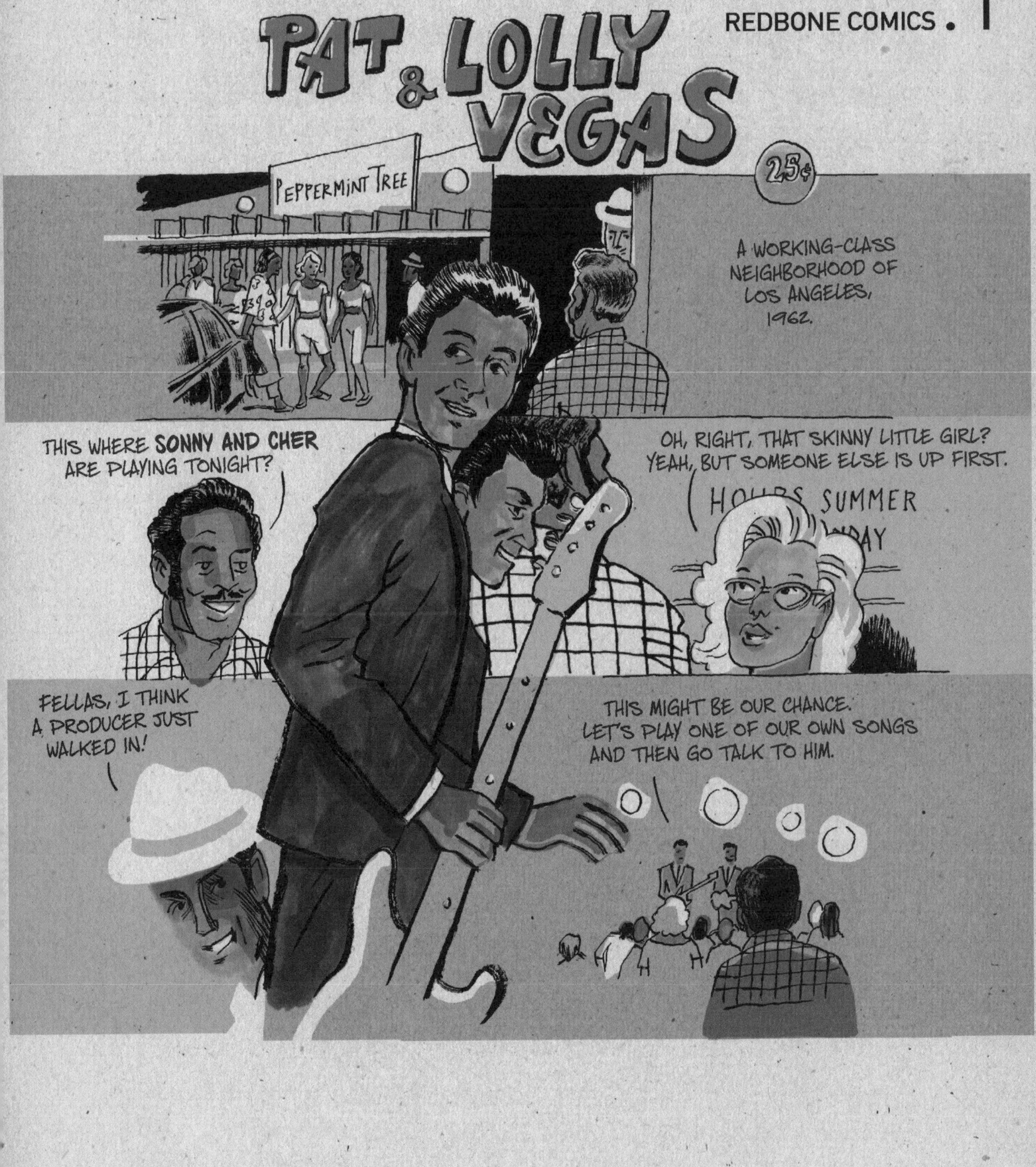
PAT & LOLLY VEGAS
REDBONE COMICS . 1
25¢
PEPPERMINT TREE
A WORKING-CLASS NEIGHBORHOOD OF LOS ANGELES, 1962.
THIS WHERE SONNY AND CHER ARE PLAYING TONIGHT?
OH, RIGHT, THAT SKINNY LITTLE GIRL? YEAH, BUT SOMEONE ELSE IS UP FIRST.
FELLAS, I THINK A PRODUCER JUST WALKED IN!
THIS MIGHT BE OUR CHANCE. LET'S PLAY ONE OF OUR OWN SONGS AND THEN GO TALK TO HIM.

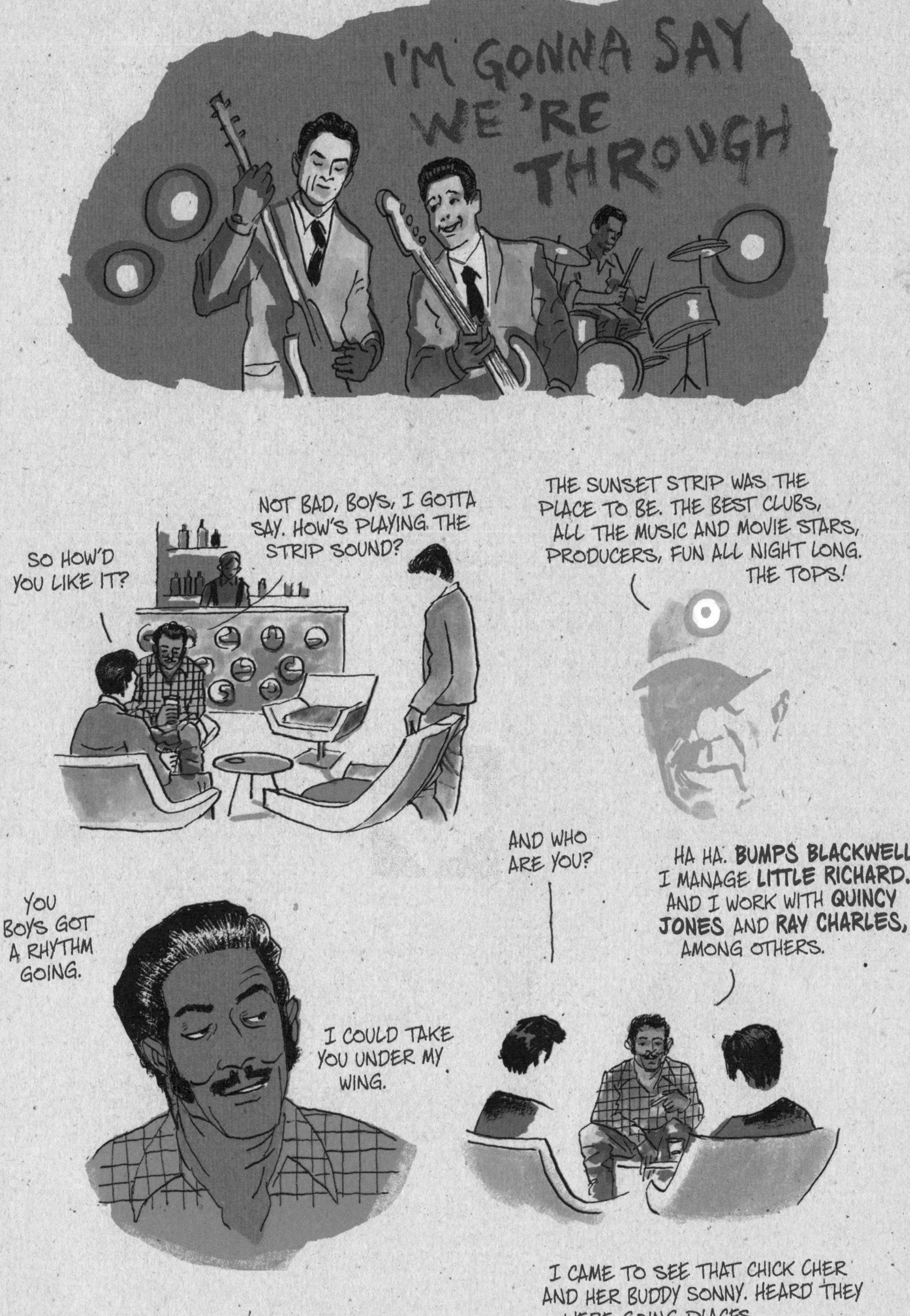

I'M GONNA SAY WE'RE THROUGH
SO HOW'D YOU LIKE IT?
NOT BAD, BOYS, I GOTTA SAY. HOW'S PLAYING THE STRIP SOUND?
THE SUNSET STRIP WAS THE PLACE TO BE. THE BEST CLUBS, ALL THE MUSIC AND MOVIE STARS, PRODUCERS, FUN ALL NIGHT LONG. THE TOPS!
YOU BOYS GOT A RHYTHM GOING.
I COULD TAKE YOU UNDER MY WING.
AND WHO ARE YOU?
HA HA. **BUMPS BLACKWELL.** I MANAGE **LITTLE RICHARD.** AND I WORK WITH **QUINCY JONES** AND **RAY CHARLES,** AMONG OTHERS.
I CAME TO SEE THAT CHICK CHER AND HER BUDDY SONNY. HEARD THEY WERE GOING PLACES.

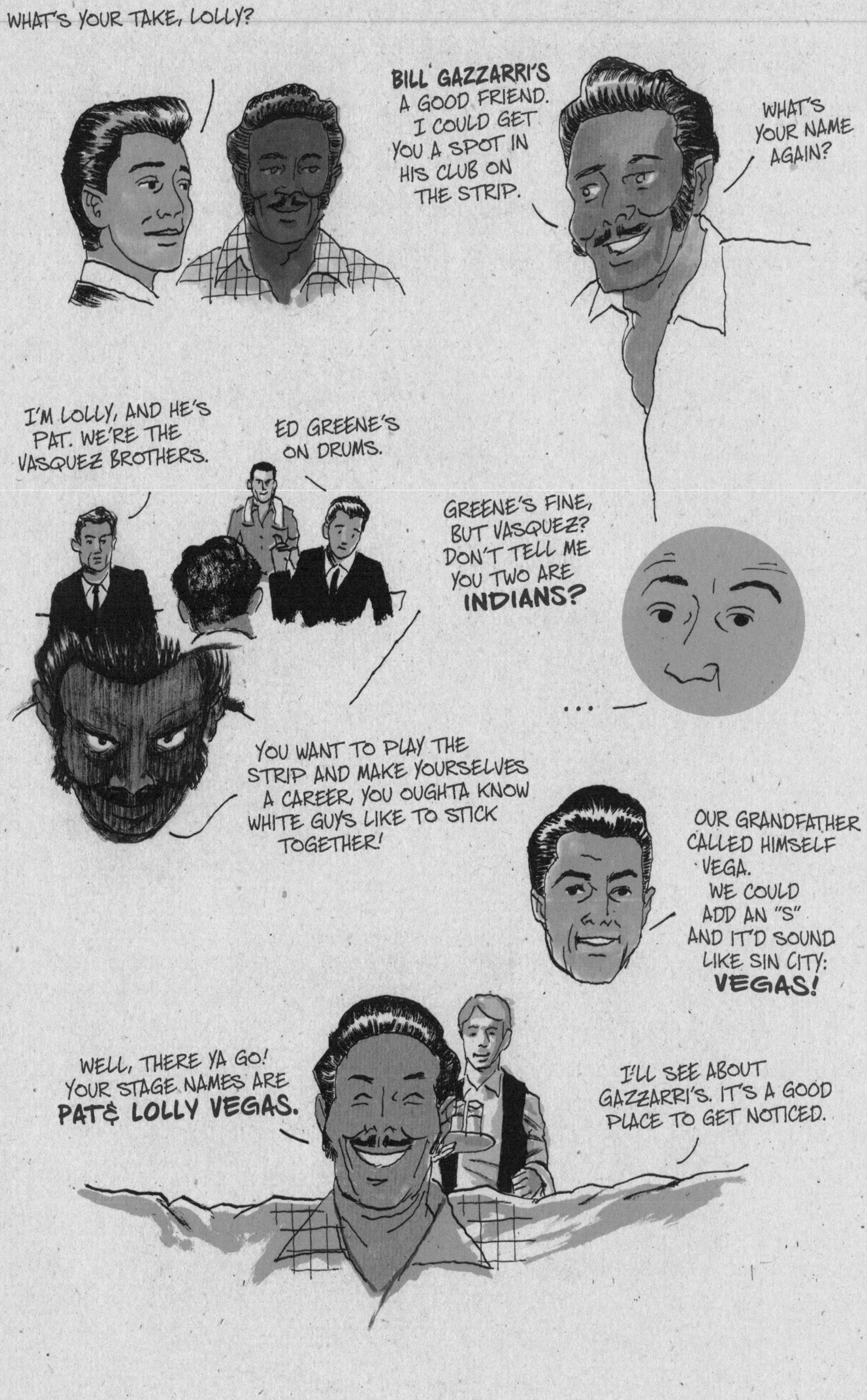
WHAT'S YOUR TAKE, LOLLY?
BILL GAZZARRI'S A GOOD FRIEND. I COULD GET YOU A SPOT IN HIS CLUB ON THE STRIP.
WHAT'S YOUR NAME AGAIN?
I'M LOLLY, AND HE'S PAT. WE'RE THE VASQUEZ BROTHERS.
ED GREENE'S ON DRUMS.
GREENE'S FINE, BUT VASQUEZ? DON'T TELL ME YOU TWO ARE INDIANS?
...
YOU WANT TO PLAY THE STRIP AND MAKE YOURSELVES A CAREER, YOU OUGHTA KNOW WHITE GUYS LIKE TO STICK TOGETHER!
OUR GRANDFATHER CALLED HIMSELF VEGA. WE COULD ADD AN "S" AND IT'D SOUND LIKE SIN CITY: VEGAS!
WELL, THERE YA GO! YOUR STAGE NAMES ARE PAT & LOLLY VEGAS.
I'LL SEE ABOUT GAZZARRI'S. IT'S A GOOD PLACE TO GET NOTICED.

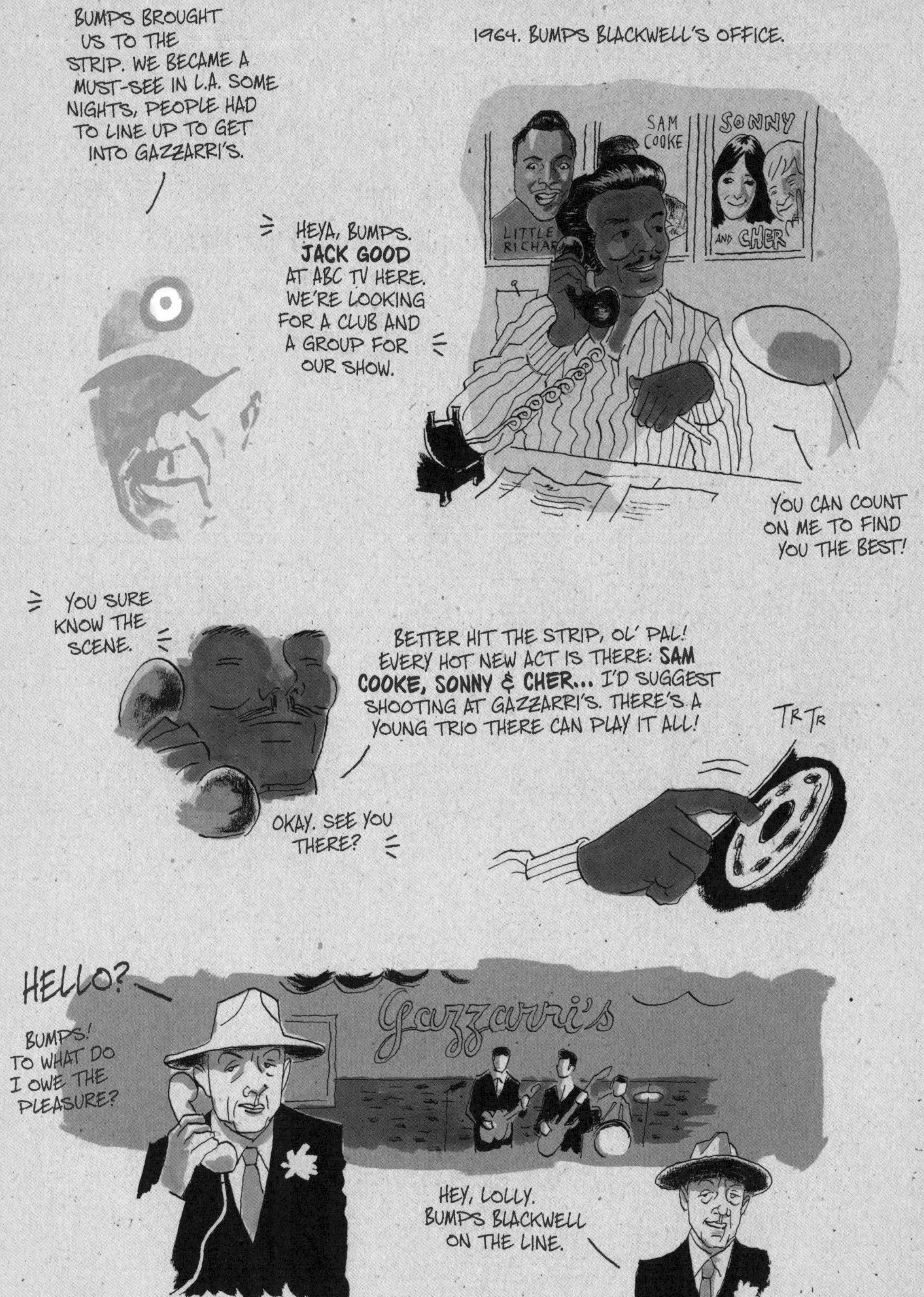
BUMPS BROUGHT US TO THE STRIP. WE BECAME A MUST-SEE IN L.A. SOME NIGHTS, PEOPLE HAD TO LINE UP TO GET INTO GAZZARRI'S.
1964. BUMPS BLACKWELL'S OFFICE.
SAM COOKE
SONNY AND CHER
HEYA, BUMPS. **JACK GOOD** AT ABC TV HERE. WE'RE LOOKING FOR A CLUB AND A GROUP FOR OUR SHOW.
YOU CAN COUNT ON ME TO FIND YOU THE BEST!
YOU SURE KNOW THE SCENE.
BETTER HIT THE STRIP, OL' PAL! EVERY HOT NEW ACT IS THERE: **SAM COOKE, SONNY & CHER...** I'D SUGGEST SHOOTING AT GAZZARRI'S. THERE'S A YOUNG TRIO THERE CAN PLAY IT ALL!
OKAY. SEE YOU THERE?
TR TR
HELLO?
Gazzarri's
BUMPS! TO WHAT DO I OWE THE PLEASURE?
HEY, LOLLY. BUMPS BLACKWELL ON THE LINE.

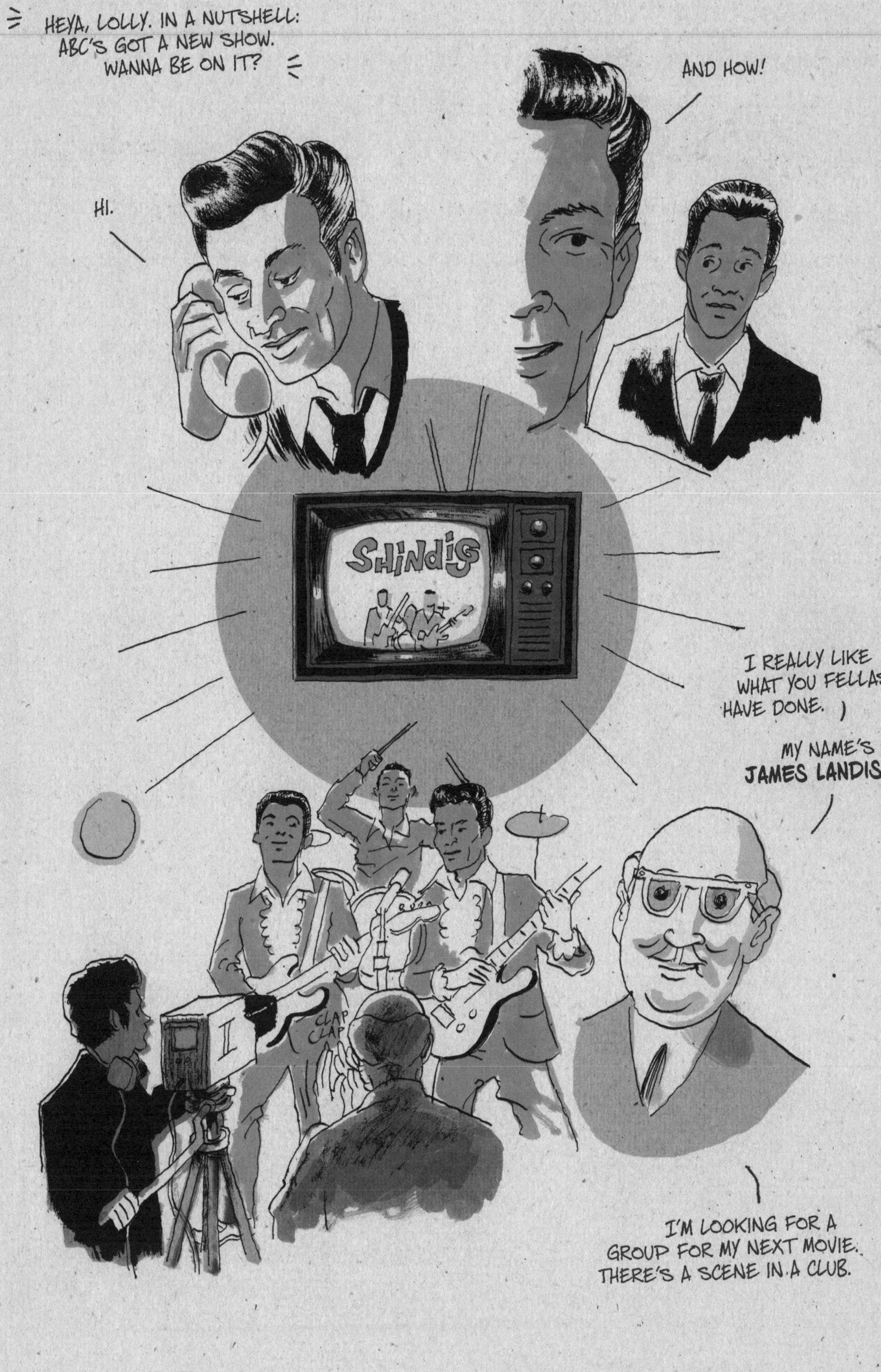
HEYA, LOLLY. IN A NUTSHELL: ABC'S GOT A NEW SHOW. WANNA BE ON IT?
HI.
AND HOW!
SHINDIG
I REALLY LIKE WHAT YOU FELLAS HAVE DONE.
MY NAME'S **JAMES LANDIS.**
CLAP CLAP
I'M LOOKING FOR A GROUP FOR MY NEXT MOVIE. THERE'S A SCENE IN A CLUB.

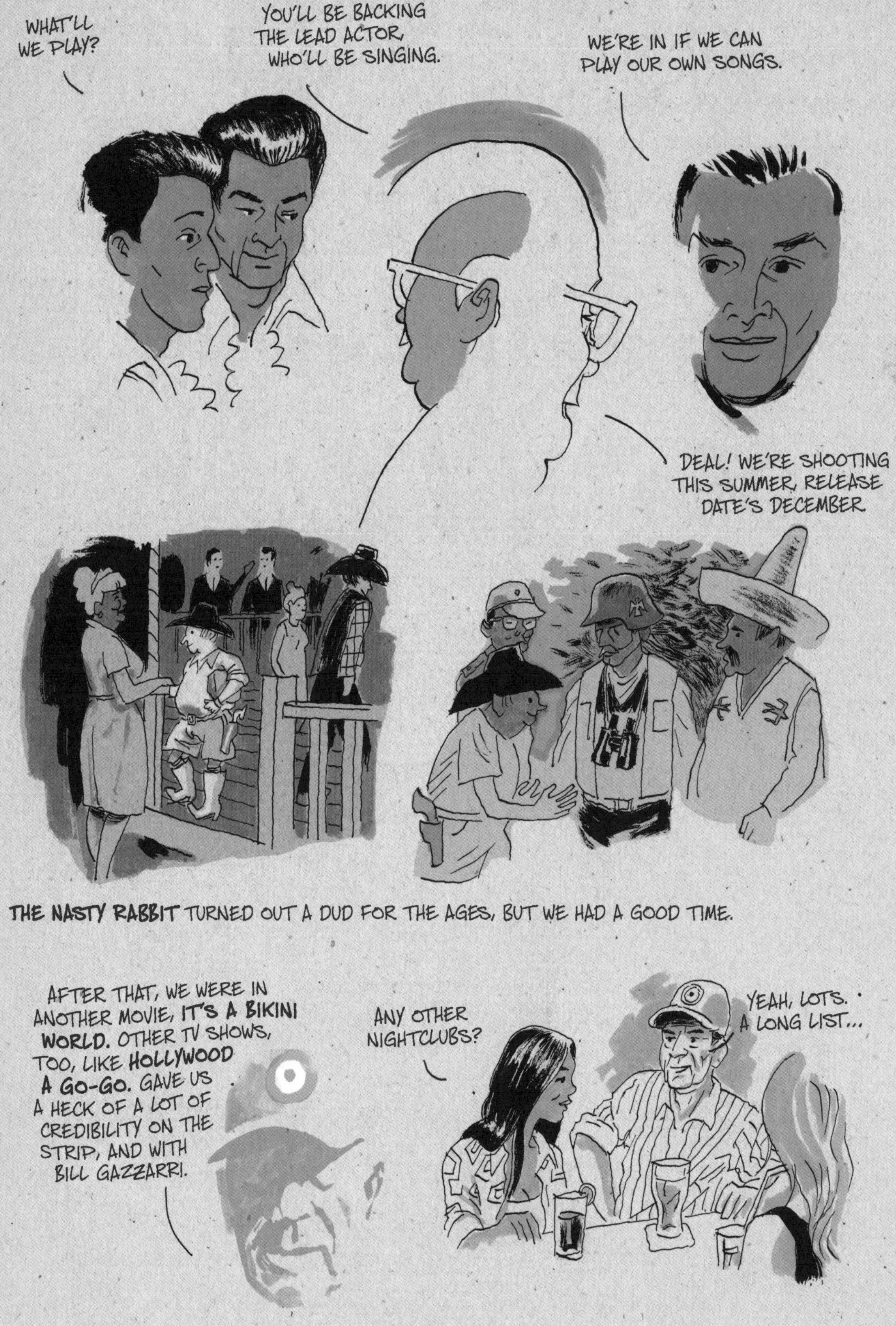
WHAT'LL WE PLAY?
YOU'LL BE BACKING THE LEAD ACTOR, WHO'LL BE SINGING.
WE'RE IN IF WE CAN PLAY OUR OWN SONGS.
DEAL! WE'RE SHOOTING THIS SUMMER, RELEASE DATE'S DECEMBER.
THE NASTY RABBIT TURNED OUT A DUD FOR THE AGES, BUT WE HAD A GOOD TIME.
AFTER THAT, WE WERE IN ANOTHER MOVIE, IT'S A BIKINI WORLD. OTHER TV SHOWS, TOO, LIKE HOLLYWOOD A GO-GO. GAVE US A HECK OF A LOT OF CREDIBILITY ON THE STRIP, AND WITH BILL GAZZARRI.
ANY OTHER NIGHTCLUBS?
YEAH, LOTS. A LONG LIST...

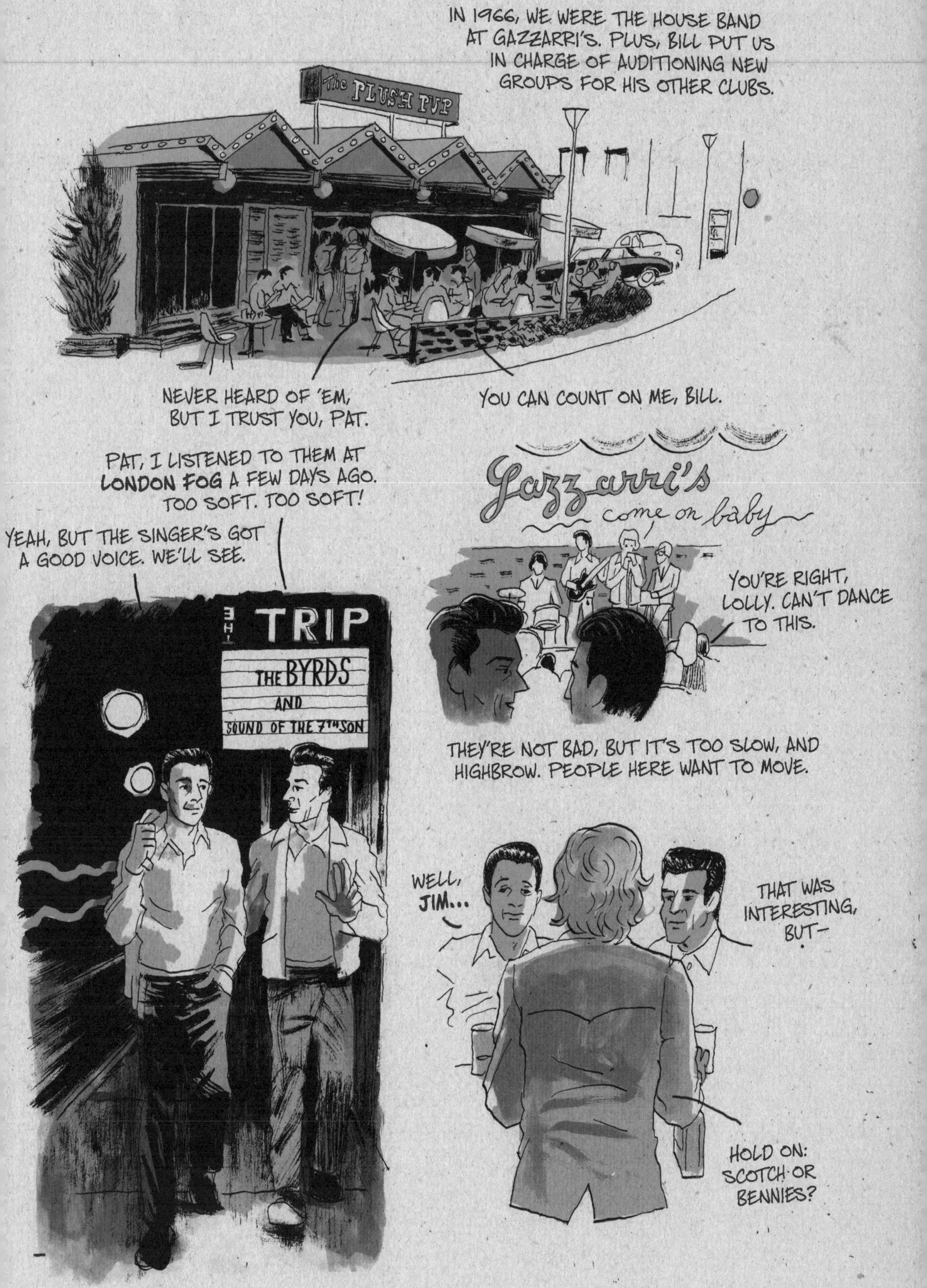
IN 1966, WE WERE THE HOUSE BAND AT GAZZARRI'S. PLUS, BILL PUT US IN CHARGE OF AUDITIONING NEW GROUPS FOR HIS OTHER CLUBS.
The PLUSH PUP
NEVER HEARD OF 'EM, BUT I TRUST YOU, PAT.
YOU CAN COUNT ON ME, BILL.
PAT, I LISTENED TO THEM AT LONDON FOG A FEW DAYS AGO. TOO SOFT. TOO SOFT!
YEAH, BUT THE SINGER'S GOT A GOOD VOICE. WE'LL SEE.
THE TRIP
THE BYRDS
AND
SOUND OF THE 7TH SON
Gazzarri's
come on baby
YOU'RE RIGHT, LOLLY. CAN'T DANCE TO THIS.
THEY'RE NOT BAD, BUT IT'S TOO SLOW, AND HIGHBROW. PEOPLE HERE WANT TO MOVE.
WELL, JIM...
THAT WAS INTERESTING, BUT–
HOLD ON: SCOTCH OR BENNIES?

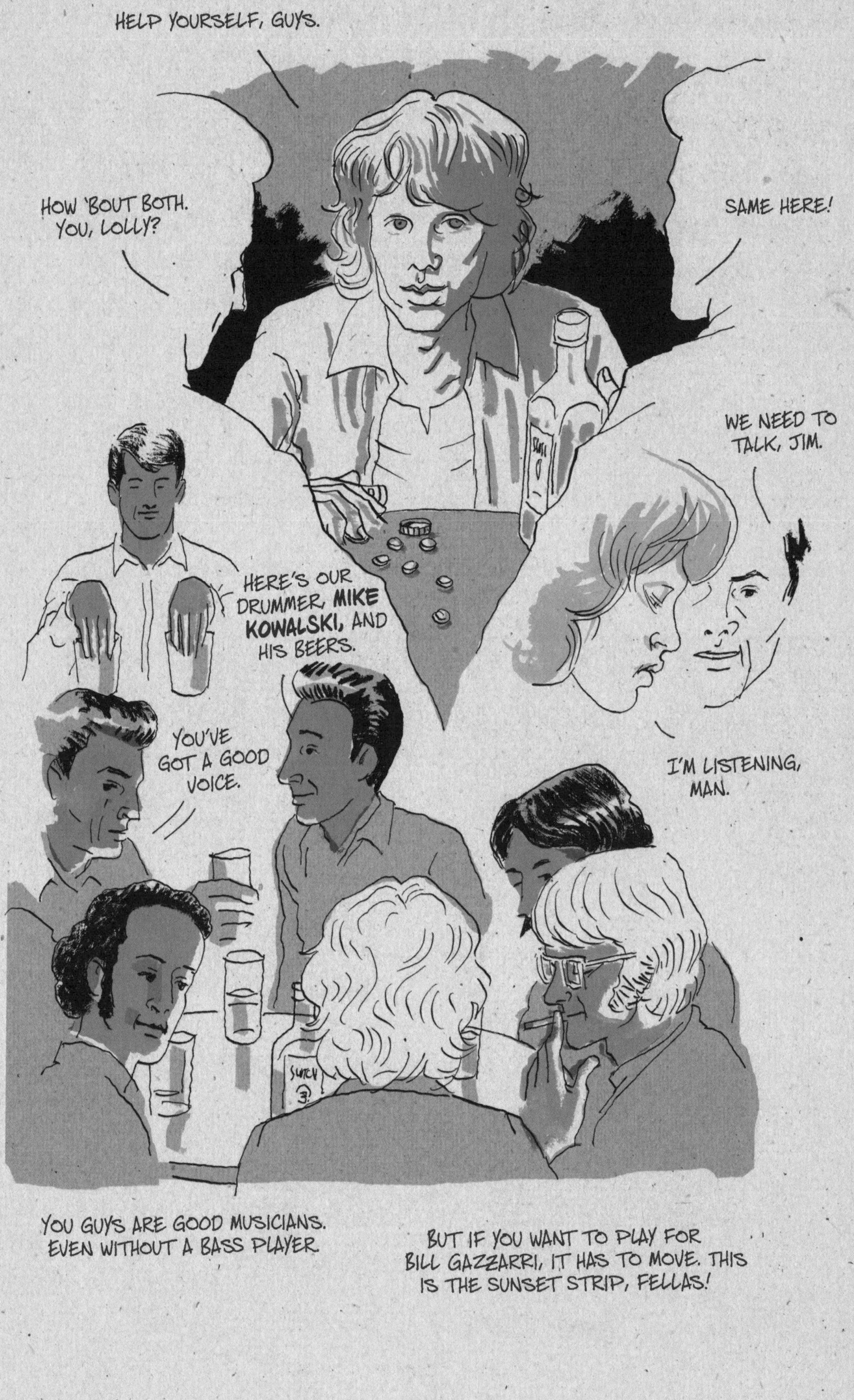
HELP YOURSELF, GUYS.
HOW 'BOUT BOTH. YOU, LOLLY?
SAME HERE!
WE NEED TO TALK, JIM.
HERE'S OUR DRUMMER, **MIKE KOWALSKI,** AND HIS BEERS.
YOU'VE GOT A GOOD VOICE.
I'M LISTENING, MAN.
YOU GUYS ARE GOOD MUSICIANS. EVEN WITHOUT A BASS PLAYER.
BUT IF YOU WANT TO PLAY FOR BILL GAZZARRI, IT HAS TO MOVE. THIS IS THE SUNSET STRIP, FELLAS!

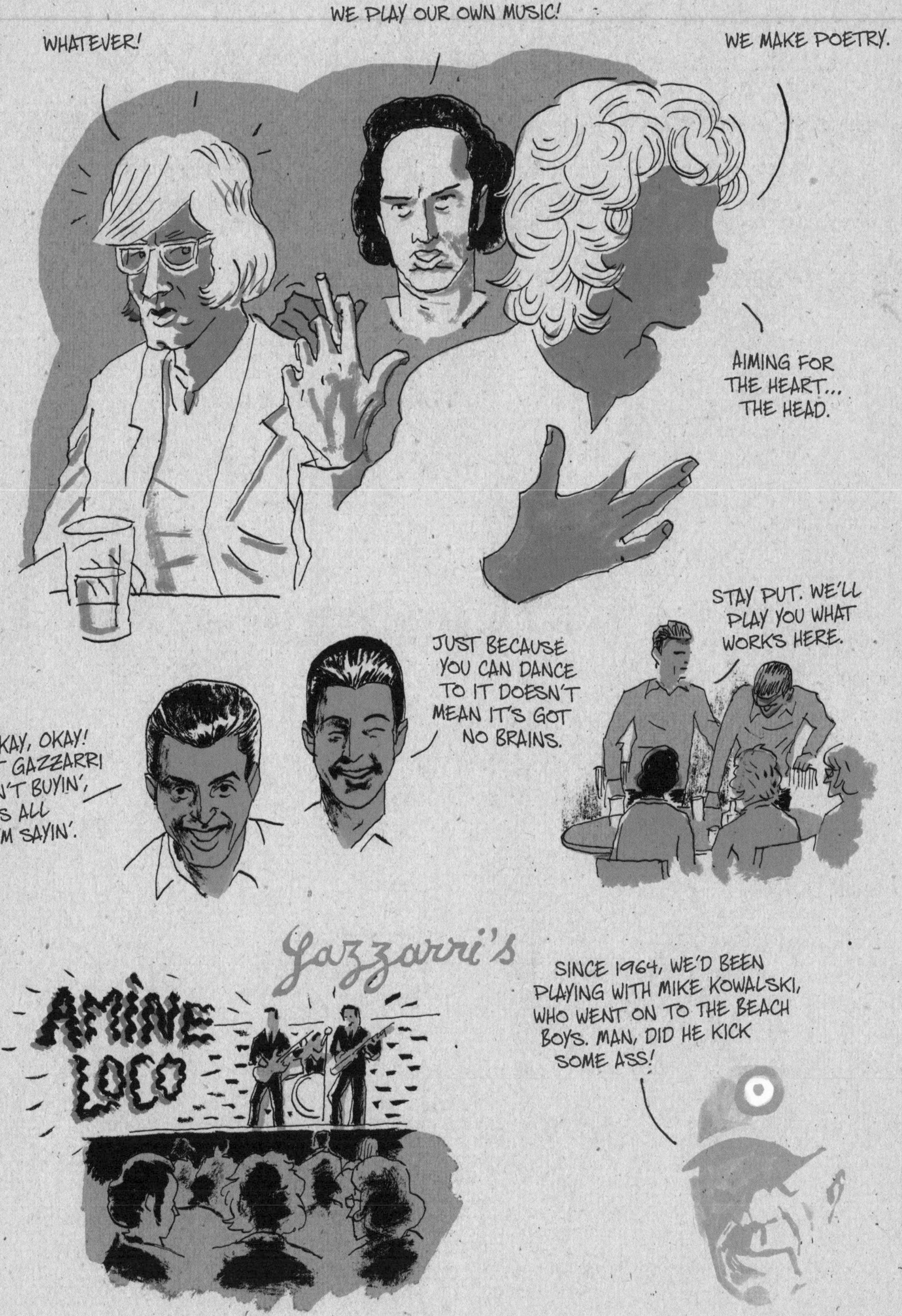
WHATEVER!
WE PLAY OUR OWN MUSIC!
WE MAKE POETRY.
AIMING FOR THE HEART... THE HEAD.
OKAY, OKAY! BUT GAZZARRI AIN'T BUYIN', IS ALL I'M SAYIN'.
JUST BECAUSE YOU CAN DANCE TO IT DOESN'T MEAN IT'S GOT NO BRAINS.
STAY PUT. WE'LL PLAY YOU WHAT WORKS HERE.
Gazzarri's
AMINE LOCO
SINCE 1964, WE'D BEEN PLAYING WITH MIKE KOWALSKI, WHO WENT ON TO THE BEACH BOYS. MAN, DID HE KICK SOME ASS!

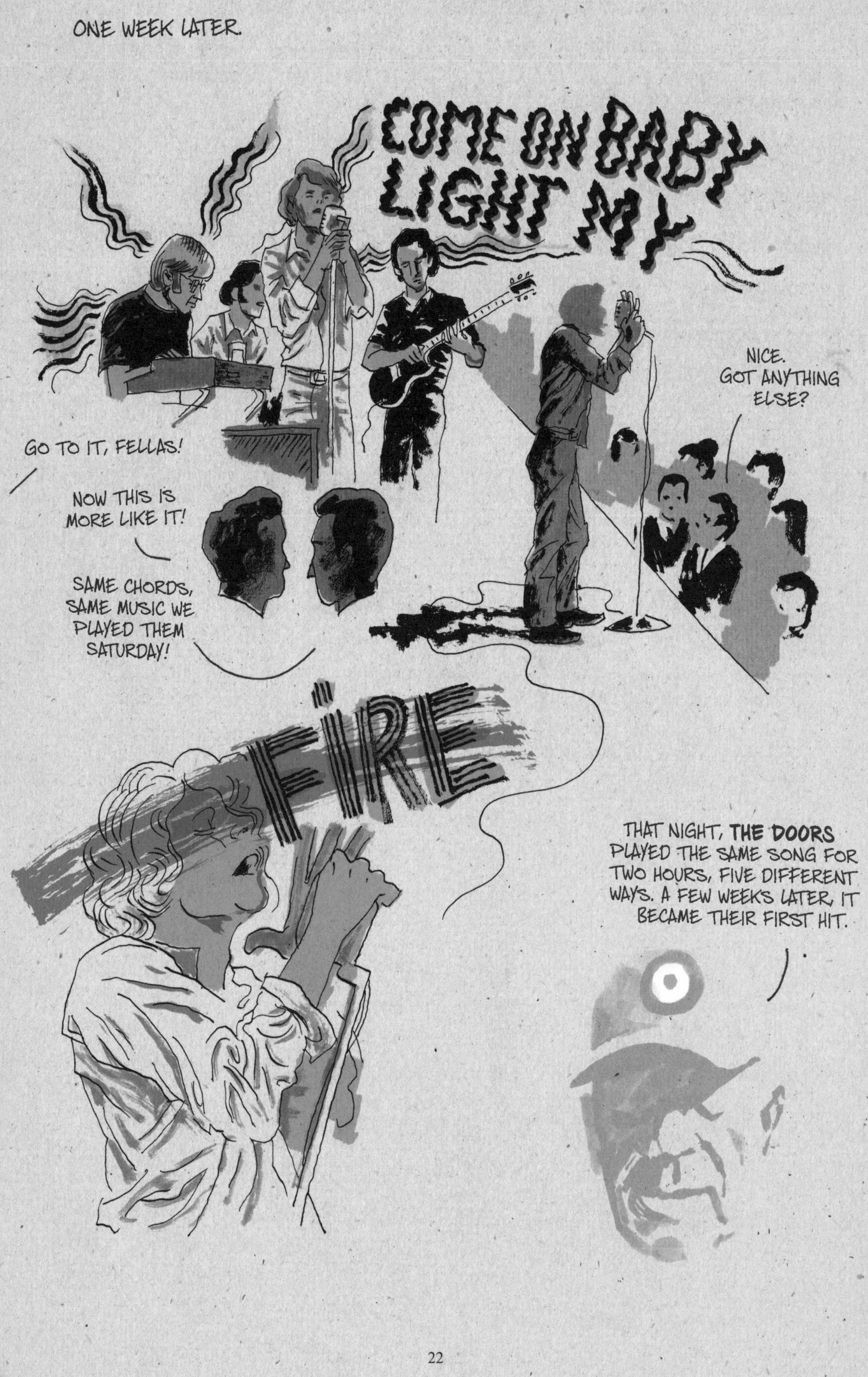
ONE WEEK LATER.
COME ON BABY LIGHT MY
NICE. GOT ANYTHING ELSE?
GO TO IT, FELLAS!
NOW THIS IS MORE LIKE IT!
SAME CHORDS, SAME MUSIC WE PLAYED THEM SATURDAY!
FIRE
THAT NIGHT, THE DOORS PLAYED THE SAME SONG FOR TWO HOURS, FIVE DIFFERENT WAYS. A FEW WEEKS LATER, IT BECAME THEIR FIRST HIT.

LOS ANGELES, THE HAUNTED HOUSE CLUB, 1966

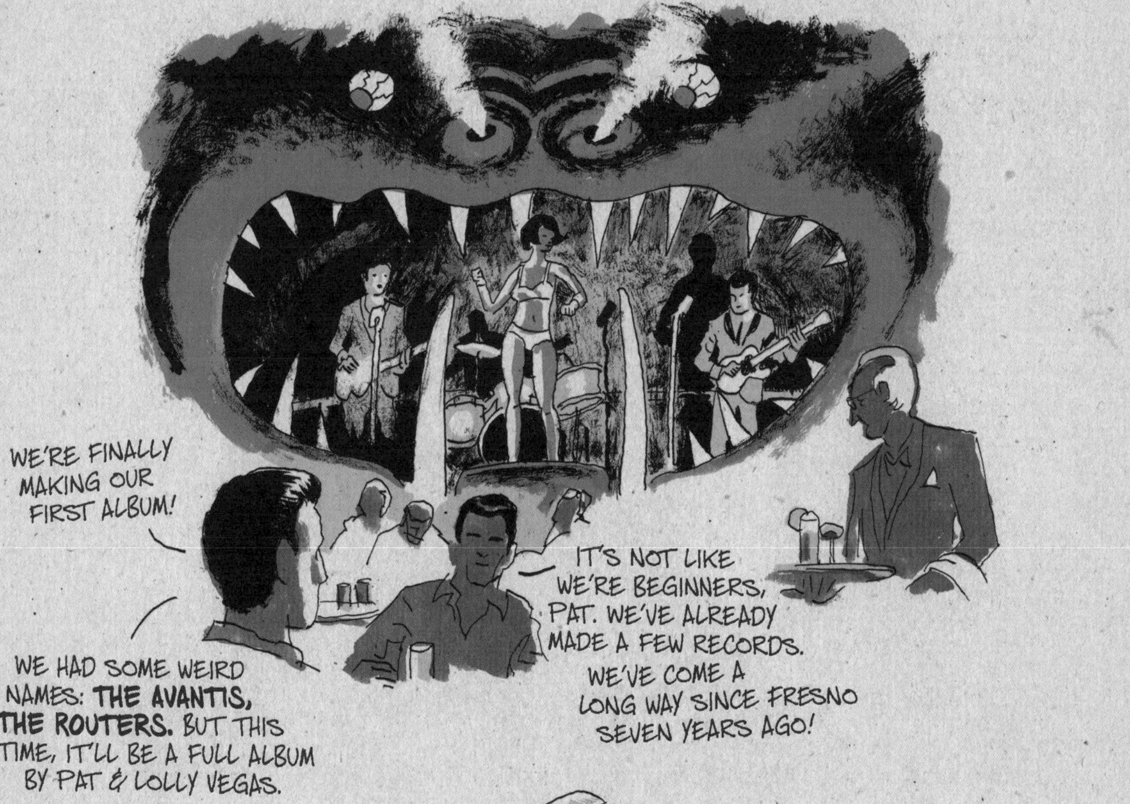

WE'RE FINALLY MAKING OUR FIRST ALBUM!
WE HAD SOME WEIRD NAMES: **THE AVANTIS, THE ROUTERS.** BUT THIS TIME, IT'LL BE A FULL ALBUM BY PAT & LOLLY VEGAS.
IT'S NOT LIKE WE'RE BEGINNERS, PAT. WE'VE ALREADY MADE A FEW RECORDS.
WE'VE COME A LONG WAY SINCE FRESNO SEVEN YEARS AGO!

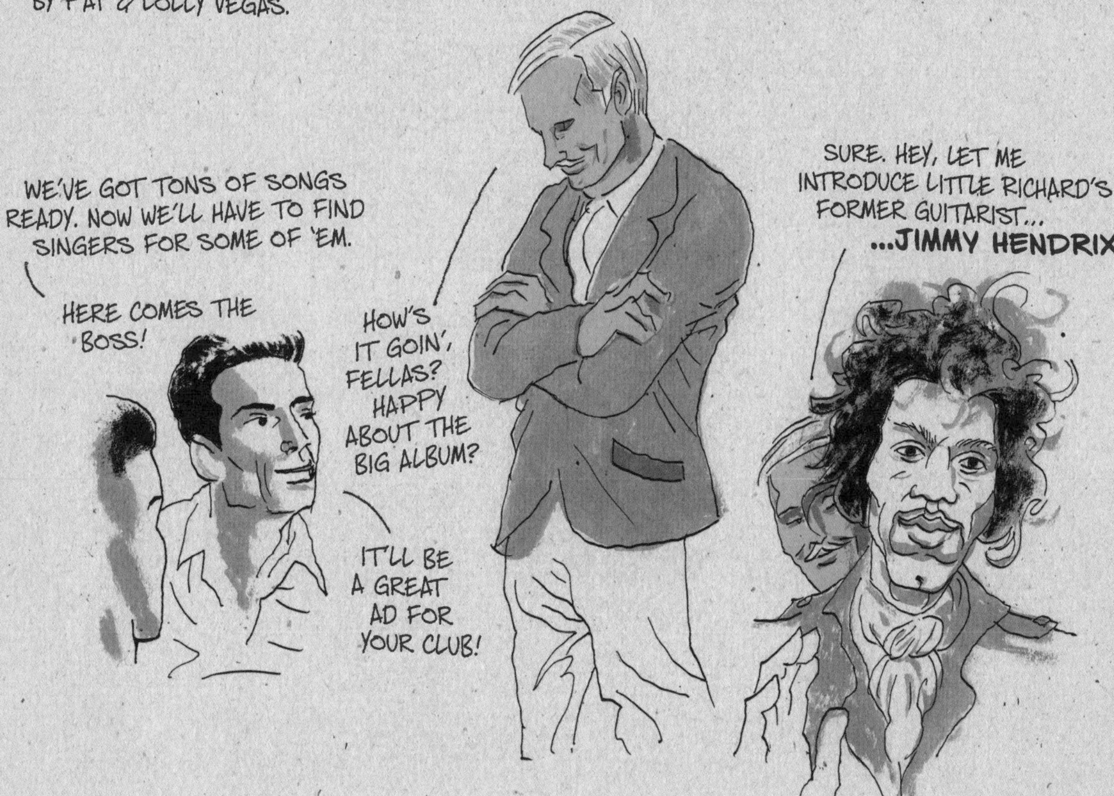

WE'VE GOT TONS OF SONGS READY. NOW WE'LL HAVE TO FIND SINGERS FOR SOME OF 'EM.
HERE COMES THE BOSS!
HOW'S IT GOIN', FELLAS? HAPPY ABOUT THE BIG ALBUM?
IT'LL BE A GREAT AD FOR YOUR CLUB!
SURE. HEY, LET ME INTRODUCE LITTLE RICHARD'S FORMER GUITARIST...
...JIMMY HENDRIX.

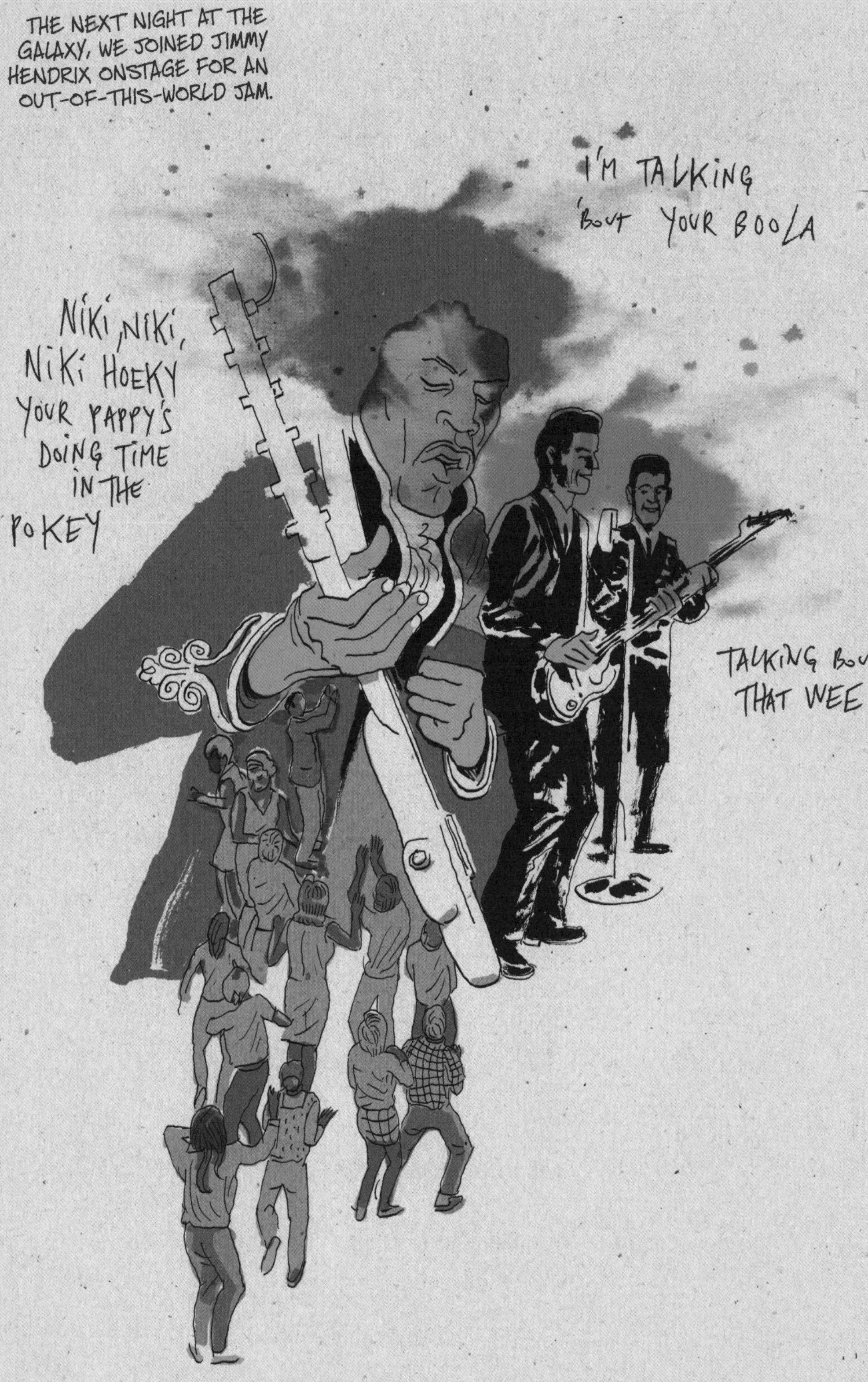
THE NEXT NIGHT AT THE GALAXY, WE JOINED JIMMY HENDRIX ONSTAGE FOR AN OUT-OF-THIS-WORLD JAM.
I'M TALKING 'BOUT YOUR BOOLA
NIKI, NIKI, NIKI HOEKY YOUR PAPPY'S DOING TIME IN THE POKEY
TALKING BOUT THAT WEE

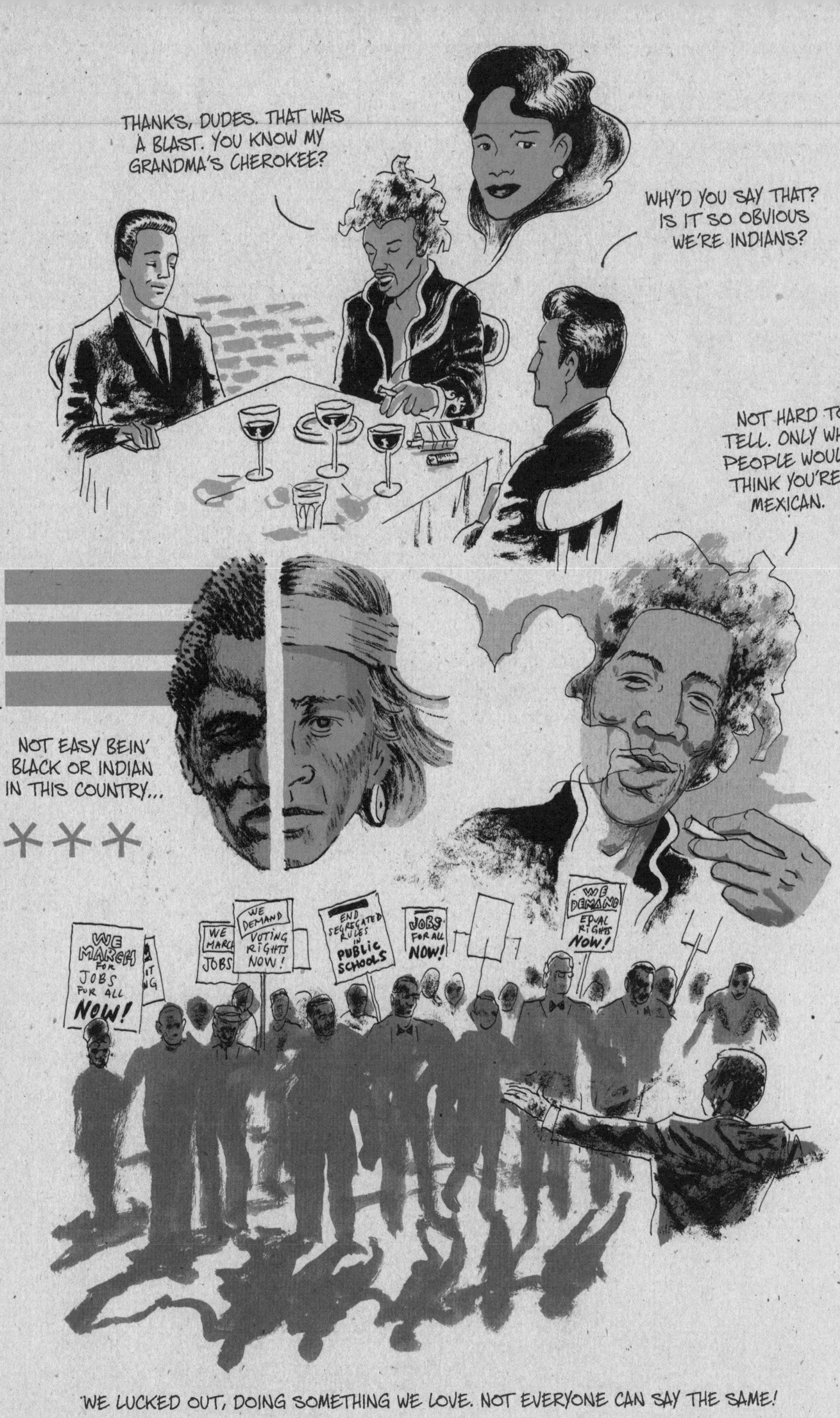
THANKS, DUDES. THAT WAS A BLAST. YOU KNOW MY GRANDMA'S CHEROKEE?
WHY'D YOU SAY THAT? IS IT SO OBVIOUS WE'RE INDIANS?
NOT HARD TO TELL. ONLY WHITE PEOPLE WOULD THINK YOU'RE MEXICAN.
NOT EASY BEIN' BLACK OR INDIAN IN THIS COUNTRY...
WE MARCH FOR JOBS FOR ALL NOW!
WE MARCH JOBS
WE DEMAND VOTING RIGHTS NOW!
END SEGREGATED RULES IN PUBLIC SCHOOLS
JOBS FOR ALL NOW!
WE DEMAND EQUAL RIGHTS NOW!
WE LUCKED OUT, DOING SOMETHING WE LOVE. NOT EVERYONE CAN SAY THE SAME!

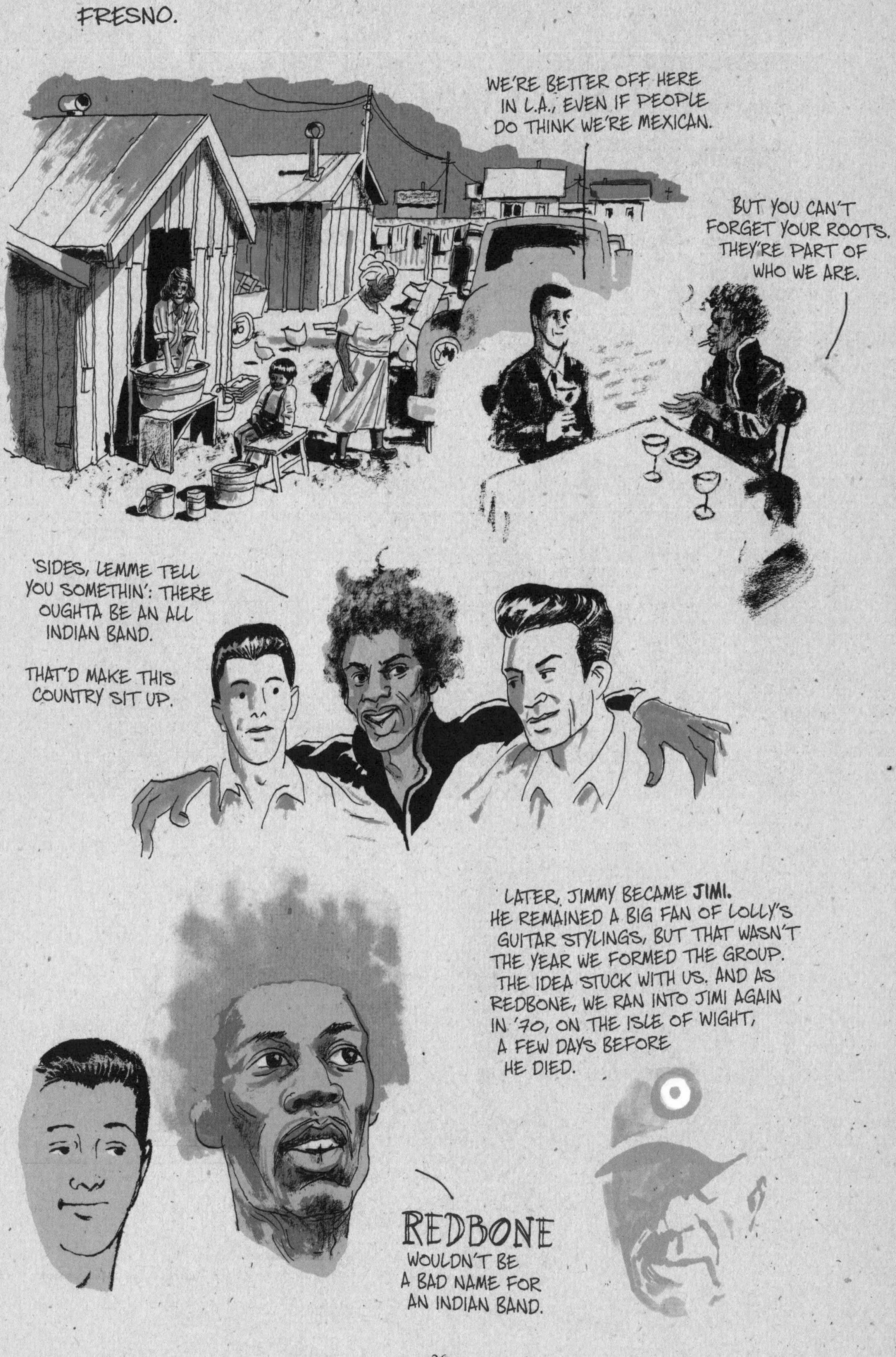
FRESNO.
WE'RE BETTER OFF HERE IN L.A., EVEN IF PEOPLE DO THINK WE'RE MEXICAN.
BUT YOU CAN'T FORGET YOUR ROOTS. THEY'RE PART OF WHO WE ARE.
'SIDES, LEMME TELL YOU SOMETHIN': THERE OUGHTA BE AN ALL INDIAN BAND.
THAT'D MAKE THIS COUNTRY SIT UP.
LATER, JIMMY BECAME JIMI. HE REMAINED A BIG FAN OF LOLLY'S GUITAR STYLINGS, BUT THAT WASN'T THE YEAR WE FORMED THE GROUP. THE IDEA STUCK WITH US. AND AS REDBONE, WE RAN INTO JIMI AGAIN IN '70, ON THE ISLE OF WIGHT, A FEW DAYS BEFORE HE DIED.
REDBONE WOULDN'T BE A BAD NAME FOR AN INDIAN BAND.

II
TONY BELLAMY
(1968)

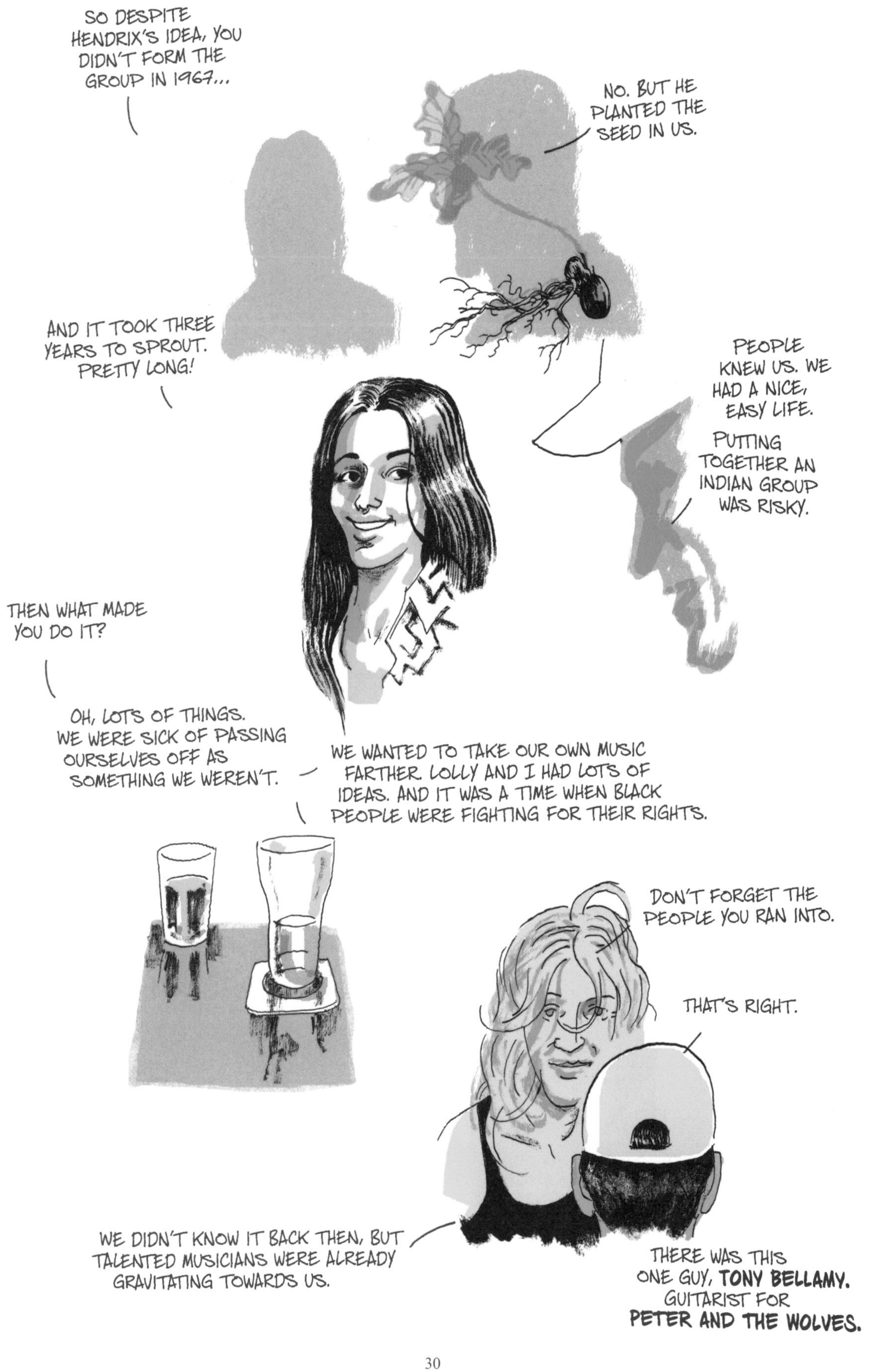
SO DESPITE HENDRIX'S IDEA, YOU DIDN'T FORM THE GROUP IN 1967...
NO. BUT HE PLANTED THE SEED IN US.
AND IT TOOK THREE YEARS TO SPROUT. PRETTY LONG!
PEOPLE KNEW US. WE HAD A NICE, EASY LIFE.
PUTTING TOGETHER AN INDIAN GROUP WAS RISKY.
THEN WHAT MADE YOU DO IT?
OH, LOTS OF THINGS. WE WERE SICK OF PASSING OURSELVES OFF AS SOMETHING WE WEREN'T.
WE WANTED TO TAKE OUR OWN MUSIC FARTHER. LOLLY AND I HAD LOTS OF IDEAS. AND IT WAS A TIME WHEN BLACK PEOPLE WERE FIGHTING FOR THEIR RIGHTS.
DON'T FORGET THE PEOPLE YOU RAN INTO.
THAT'S RIGHT.
WE DIDN'T KNOW IT BACK THEN, BUT TALENTED MUSICIANS WERE ALREADY GRAVITATING TOWARDS US.
THERE WAS THIS ONE GUY, **TONY BELLAMY.** GUITARIST FOR **PETER AND THE WOLVES.**

TONY HUNG OUT AT GAZZARRI'S A LOT. ONE DAY, HE ASKED IF HE COULD JAM WITH US. ME, I TOOK A SHINE TO HIM RIGHT AWAY. HE HAD THIS CHARISMA LIKE CHUCK BERRY'S.

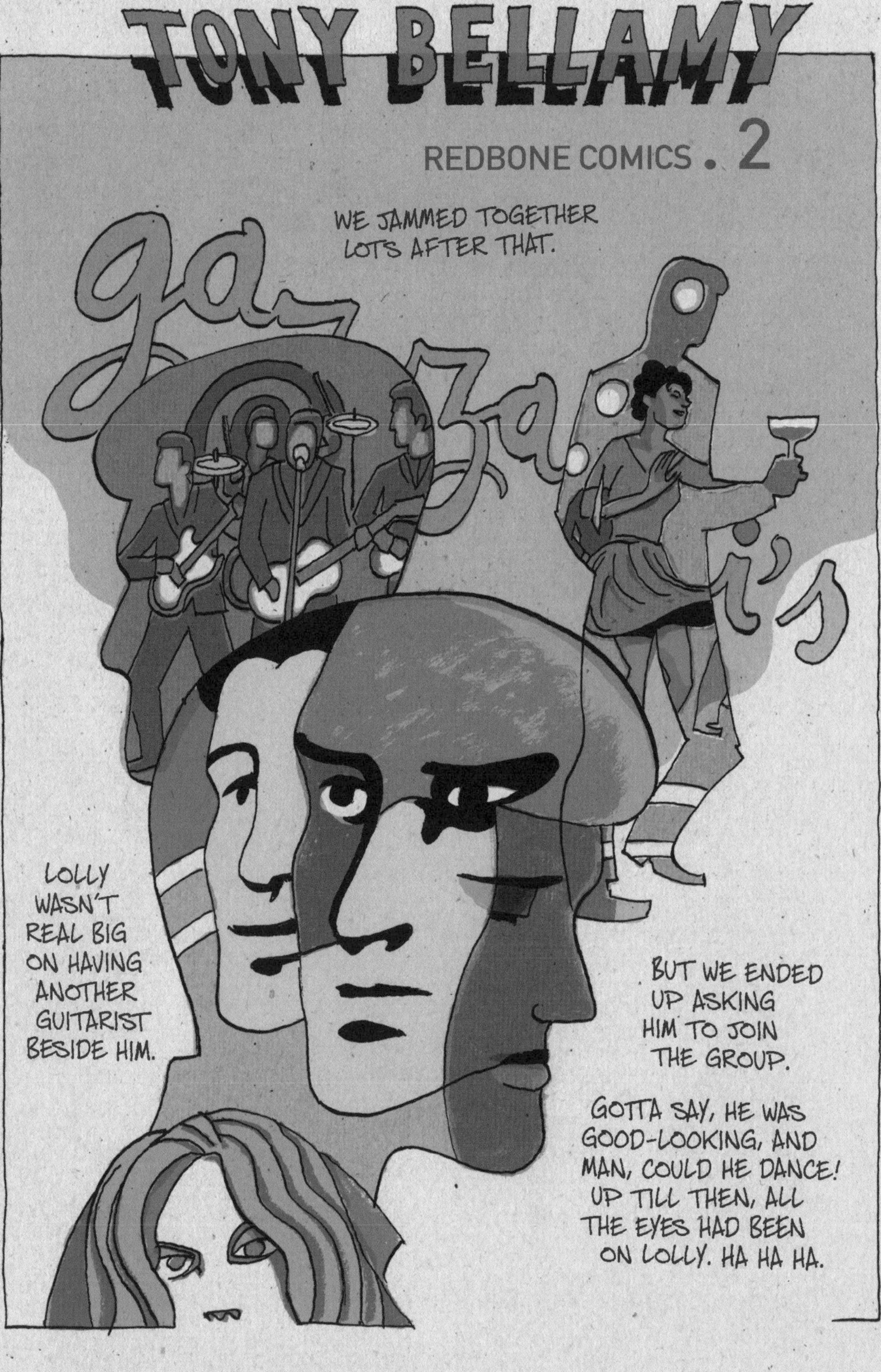
TONY BELLAMY
REDBONE COMICS . 2
WE JAMMED TOGETHER LOTS AFTER THAT.
LOLLY WASN'T REAL BIG ON HAVING ANOTHER GUITARIST BESIDE HIM.
BUT WE ENDED UP ASKING HIM TO JOIN THE GROUP.
GOTTA SAY, HE WAS GOOD-LOOKING, AND MAN, COULD HE DANCE! UP TILL THEN, ALL THE EYES HAD BEEN ON LOLLY. HA HA HA.

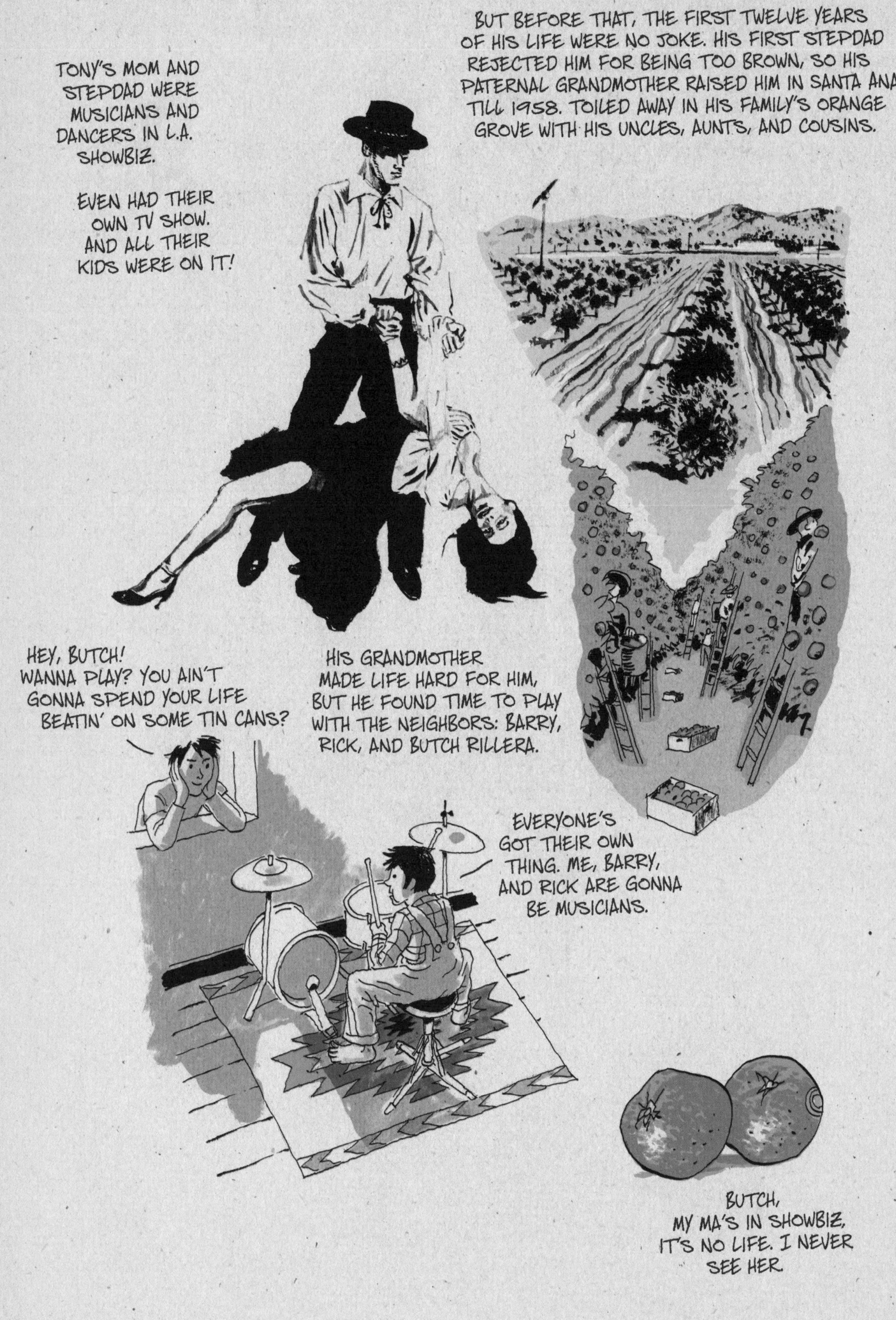
TONY'S MOM AND STEPDAD WERE MUSICIANS AND DANCERS IN L.A. SHOWBIZ.
EVEN HAD THEIR OWN TV SHOW. AND ALL THEIR KIDS WERE ON IT!
BUT BEFORE THAT, THE FIRST TWELVE YEARS OF HIS LIFE WERE NO JOKE. HIS FIRST STEPDAD REJECTED HIM FOR BEING TOO BROWN, SO HIS PATERNAL GRANDMOTHER RAISED HIM IN SANTA ANA TILL 1958. TOILED AWAY IN HIS FAMILY'S ORANGE GROVE WITH HIS UNCLES, AUNTS, AND COUSINS.
HIS GRANDMOTHER MADE LIFE HARD FOR HIM, BUT HE FOUND TIME TO PLAY WITH THE NEIGHBORS: BARRY, RICK, AND BUTCH RILLERA.
HEY, BUTCH! WANNA PLAY? YOU AIN'T GONNA SPEND YOUR LIFE BEATIN' ON SOME TIN CANS?
EVERYONE'S GOT THEIR OWN THING. ME, BARRY, AND RICK ARE GONNA BE MUSICIANS.
BUTCH, MY MA'S IN SHOWBIZ. IT'S NO LIFE. I NEVER SEE HER.

HIS MOM GOT MARRIED A THIRD TIME, TO **JAMES BELLAMY,** WHO DECIDED TO GET THE FAMILY BACK TOGETHER. SO IN 1958, TONY JOINED HIS FIVE BROTHERS AND SISTERS IN HOLLYWOOD.

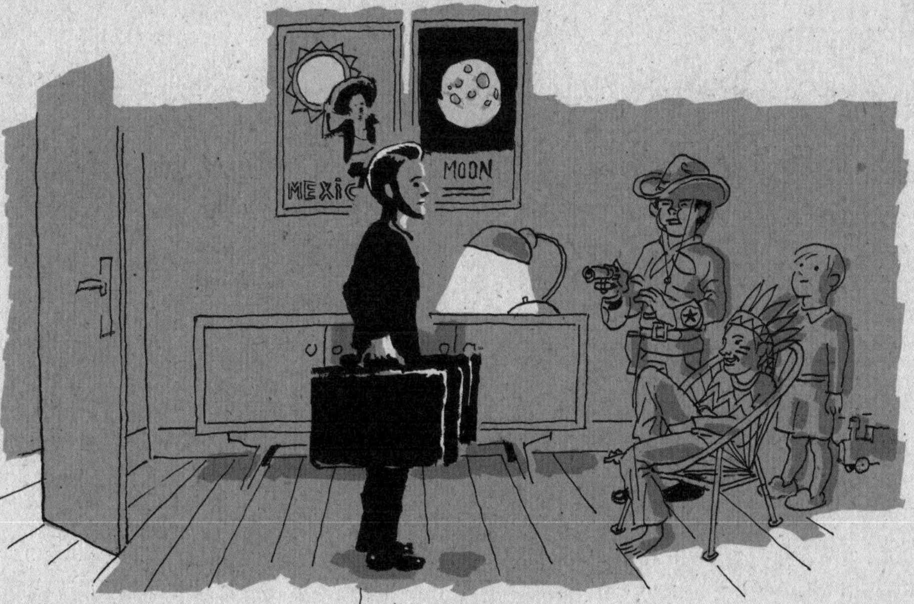
MEXIC
MOON

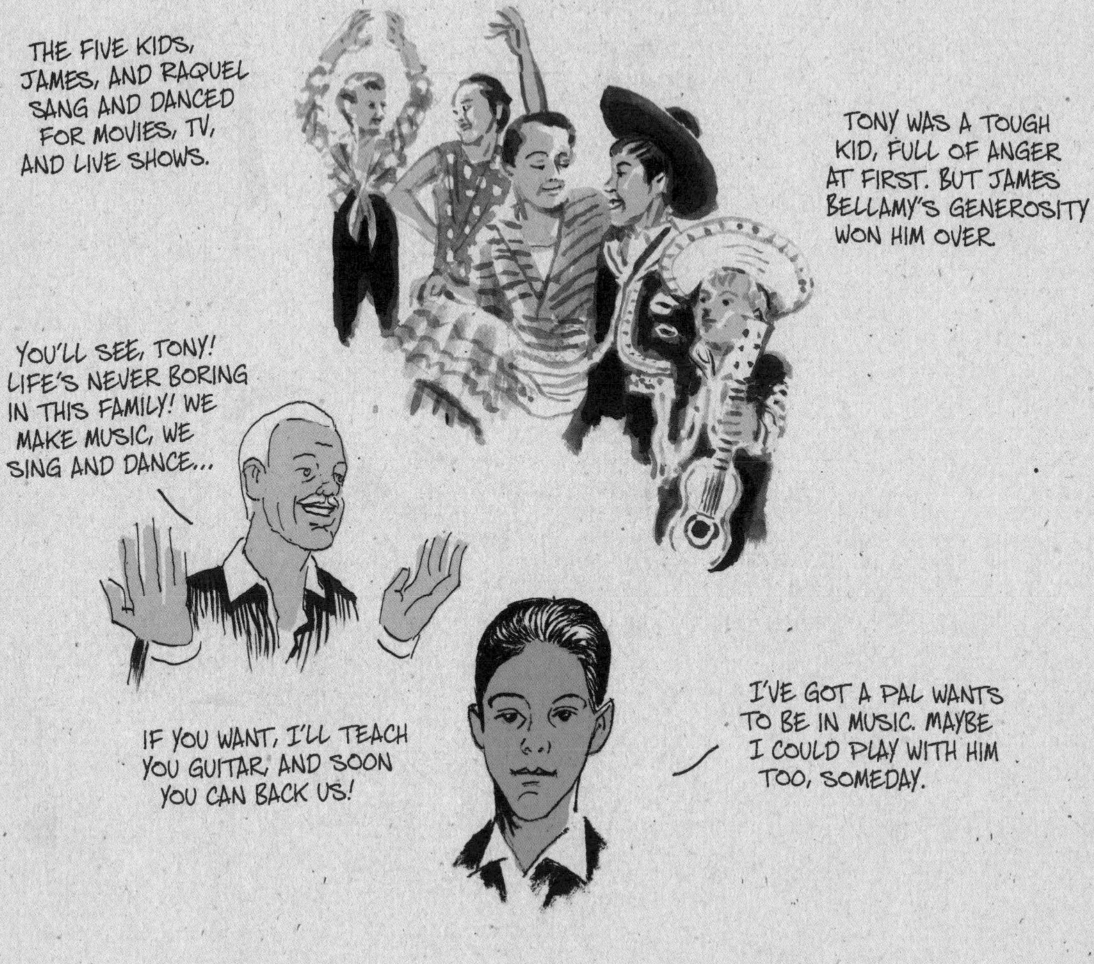
THE FIVE KIDS, JAMES, AND RAQUEL SANG AND DANCED FOR MOVIES, TV, AND LIVE SHOWS.
TONY WAS A TOUGH KID, FULL OF ANGER AT FIRST. BUT JAMES BELLAMY'S GENEROSITY WON HIM OVER.
YOU'LL SEE, TONY! LIFE'S NEVER BORING IN THIS FAMILY! WE MAKE MUSIC, WE SING AND DANCE...
IF YOU WANT, I'LL TEACH YOU GUITAR, AND SOON YOU CAN BACK US!
I'VE GOT A PAL WANTS TO BE IN MUSIC. MAYBE I COULD PLAY WITH HIM TOO, SOMEDAY.

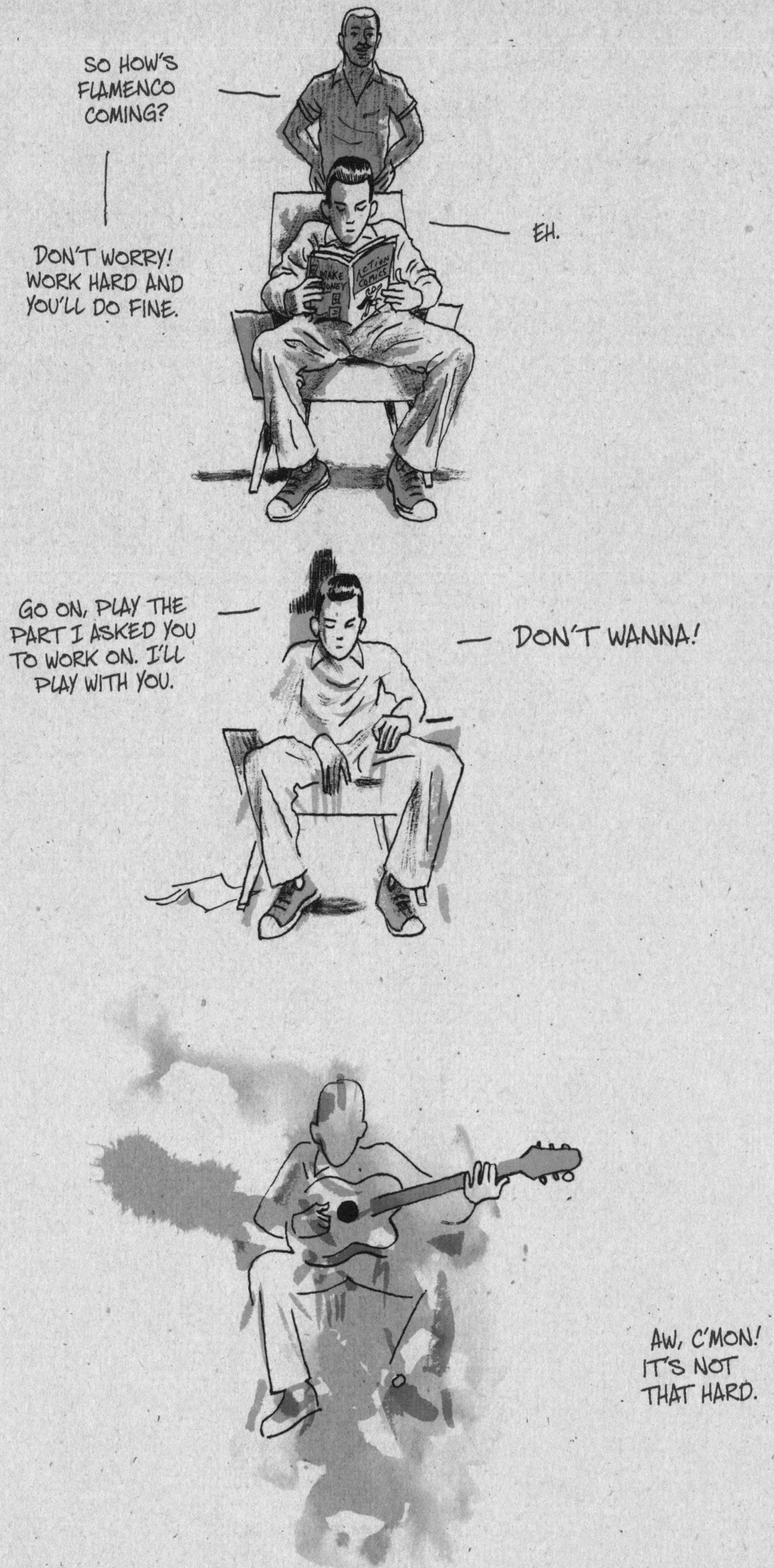
SO HOW'S FLAMENCO COMING?
EH.
DON'T WORRY! WORK HARD AND YOU'LL DO FINE.
GO ON, PLAY THE PART I ASKED YOU TO WORK ON. I'LL PLAY WITH YOU.
DON'T WANNA!
AW, C'MON! IT'S NOT THAT HARD.

AND HE LEARNED. FAST. FLAMENCO,
THEN ALL THE REST. ONE DAY, HE
SHOWED ME OLD PHOTOS OF HIS
WHOLE FAMILY MAKING MUSIC.

TONY OFTEN ACCOMPANIED
HIS PARENTS AND SIBLINGS,
ESPECIALLY IN THE RESTAURANT
THE BELLAMYS OWNED IN
SANTA ANA.

IT MUST'VE BEEN A HAPPY TIME
FOR HIM. IN THE END, HE TOOK
BELLAMY'S NAME INSTEAD OF HIS
YAQUI FATHER'S, AVILA, EVEN
THOUGH HE LIKED THE MAN A LOT.
THE BELLAMYS WERE A TIGHT CLAN.
THEY ALMOST ALL WENT ON TO
CAREERS IN MUSIC.

AROUND 1964, TONY LEFT THE
BOSOM OF HIS FAMILY TO BACK
DOBIE GRAY, A SUCCESSFUL BLACK
SINGER BACK THEN. TONY BECAME
A BIG NAME IN THE GUITAR WORLD,
BLENDING FLAMENCO, BLUES, AND
ROCK. AND LIKE MANY EXCELLENT
MUSICIANS, HE SAT IN ON A LOT
OF SESSIONS.

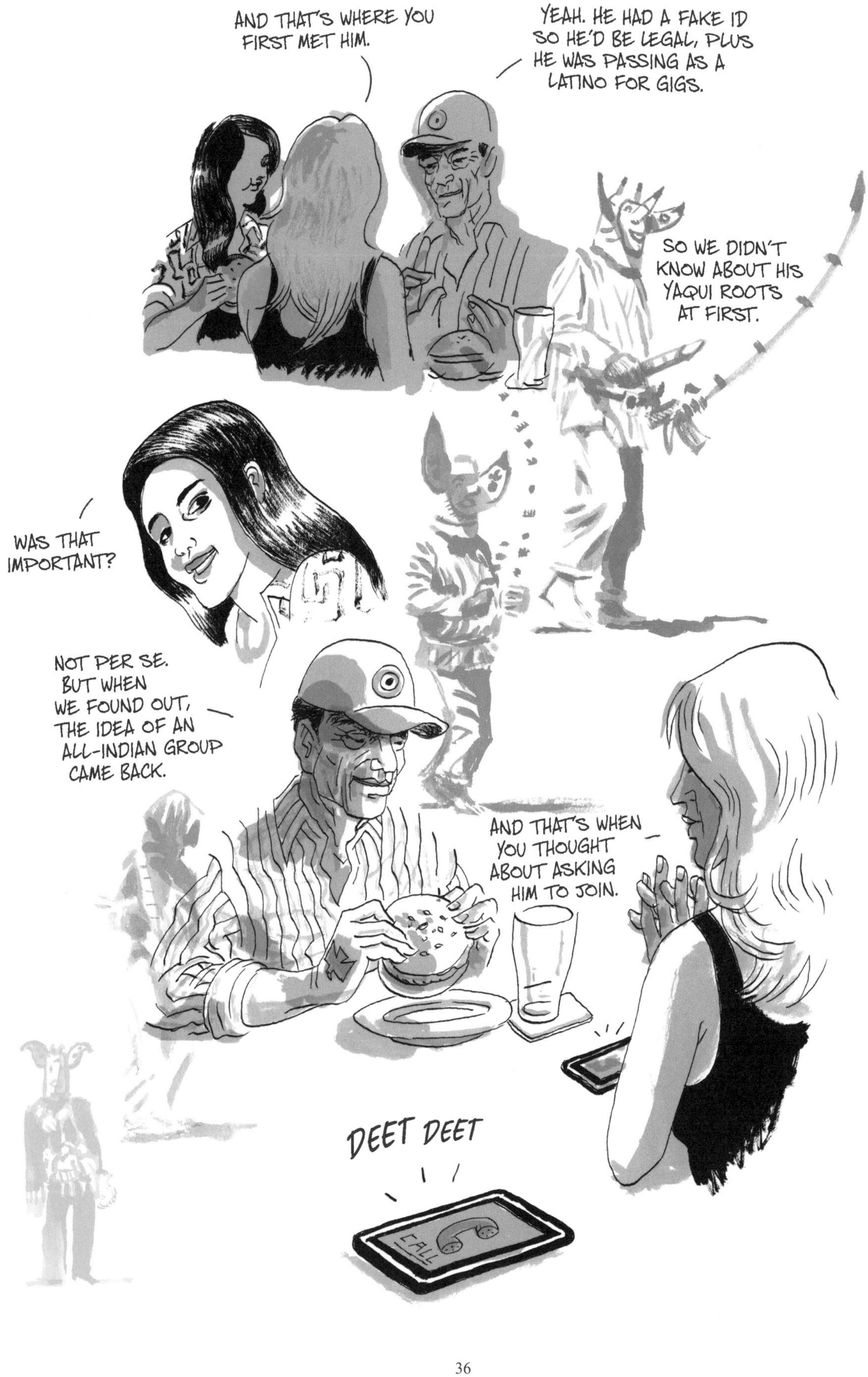
AND THAT'S WHERE YOU FIRST MET HIM.
YEAH. HE HAD A FAKE ID SO HE'D BE LEGAL, PLUS HE WAS PASSING AS A LATINO FOR GIGS.
SO WE DIDN'T KNOW ABOUT HIS YAQUI ROOTS AT FIRST.
WAS THAT IMPORTANT?
NOT PER SE. BUT WHEN WE FOUND OUT, THE IDEA OF AN ALL-INDIAN GROUP CAME BACK.
AND THAT'S WHEN YOU THOUGHT ABOUT ASKING HIM TO JOIN.
DEET DEET
CALL

III
PETE DEPOE
(1969)

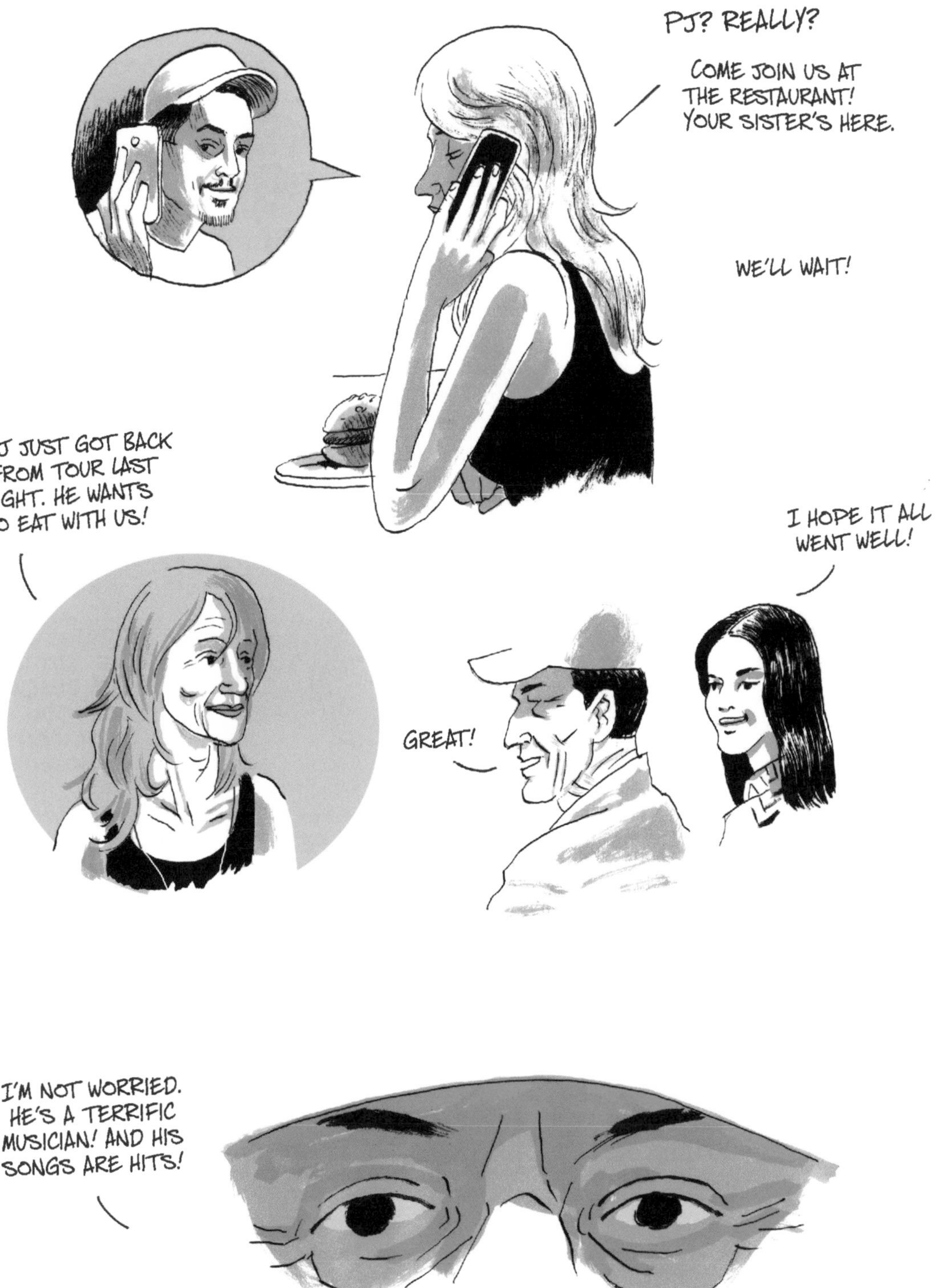
PJ? REALLY?
COME JOIN US AT THE RESTAURANT! YOUR SISTER'S HERE.
WE'LL WAIT!
PJ JUST GOT BACK FROM TOUR LAST NIGHT. HE WANTS TO EAT WITH US!
I HOPE IT ALL WENT WELL!
GREAT!
I'M NOT WORRIED. HE'S A TERRIFIC MUSICIAN! AND HIS SONGS ARE HITS!

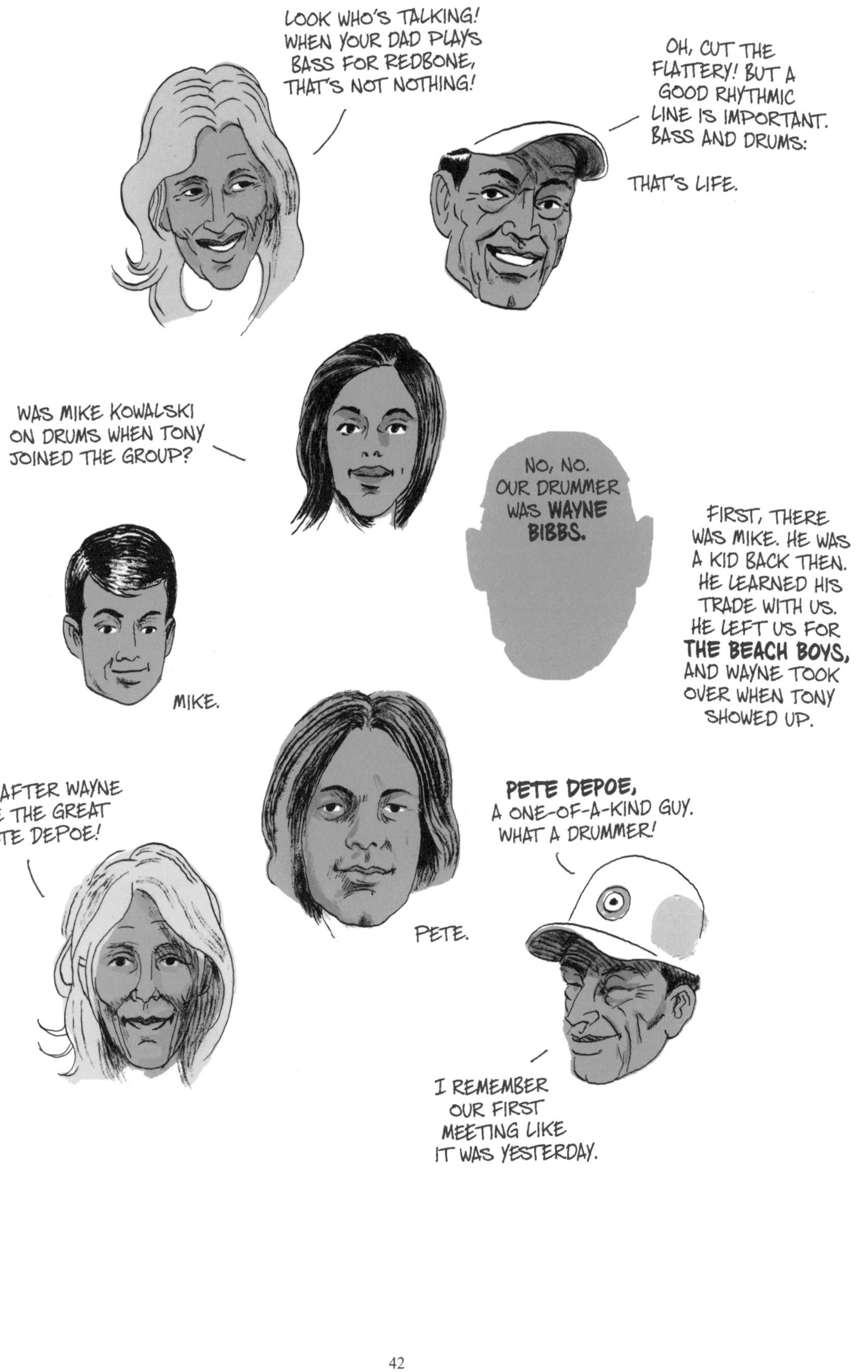
LOOK WHO'S TALKING! WHEN YOUR DAD PLAYS BASS FOR REDBONE, THAT'S NOT NOTHING!
OH, CUT THE FLATTERY! BUT A GOOD RHYTHMIC LINE IS IMPORTANT. BASS AND DRUMS:
THAT'S LIFE.
WAS MIKE KOWALSKI ON DRUMS WHEN TONY JOINED THE GROUP?
NO, NO. OUR DRUMMER WAS **WAYNE BIBBS.**
FIRST, THERE WAS MIKE. HE WAS A KID BACK THEN. HE LEARNED HIS TRADE WITH US. HE LEFT US FOR **THE BEACH BOYS,** AND WAYNE TOOK OVER WHEN TONY SHOWED UP.
MIKE.
AND AFTER WAYNE CAME THE GREAT PETE DEPOE!
PETE DEPOE, A ONE-OF-A-KIND GUY. WHAT A DRUMMER!
PETE.
I REMEMBER OUR FIRST MEETING LIKE IT WAS YESTERDAY.

BOBBY WOMACK, WHO WROTE FOR **THE STONES** AND **JOPLIN**, CALLED US TO SAY HE HAD A DRUMMER, AN INDIAN. WANTED TO TRADE US FOR OUR NEW DRUMMER WAYNE BIBBS.

Pete DePoe

REDBONE COMICS . 3

I WAS LATE TO THE MEETING WOMACK SET UP.

MULLHOLAND

THEY BEEN AT IT AN HOUR NOW!

THAT'S YOUR DRUMMER?

HE'S THE MAN WE NEED!

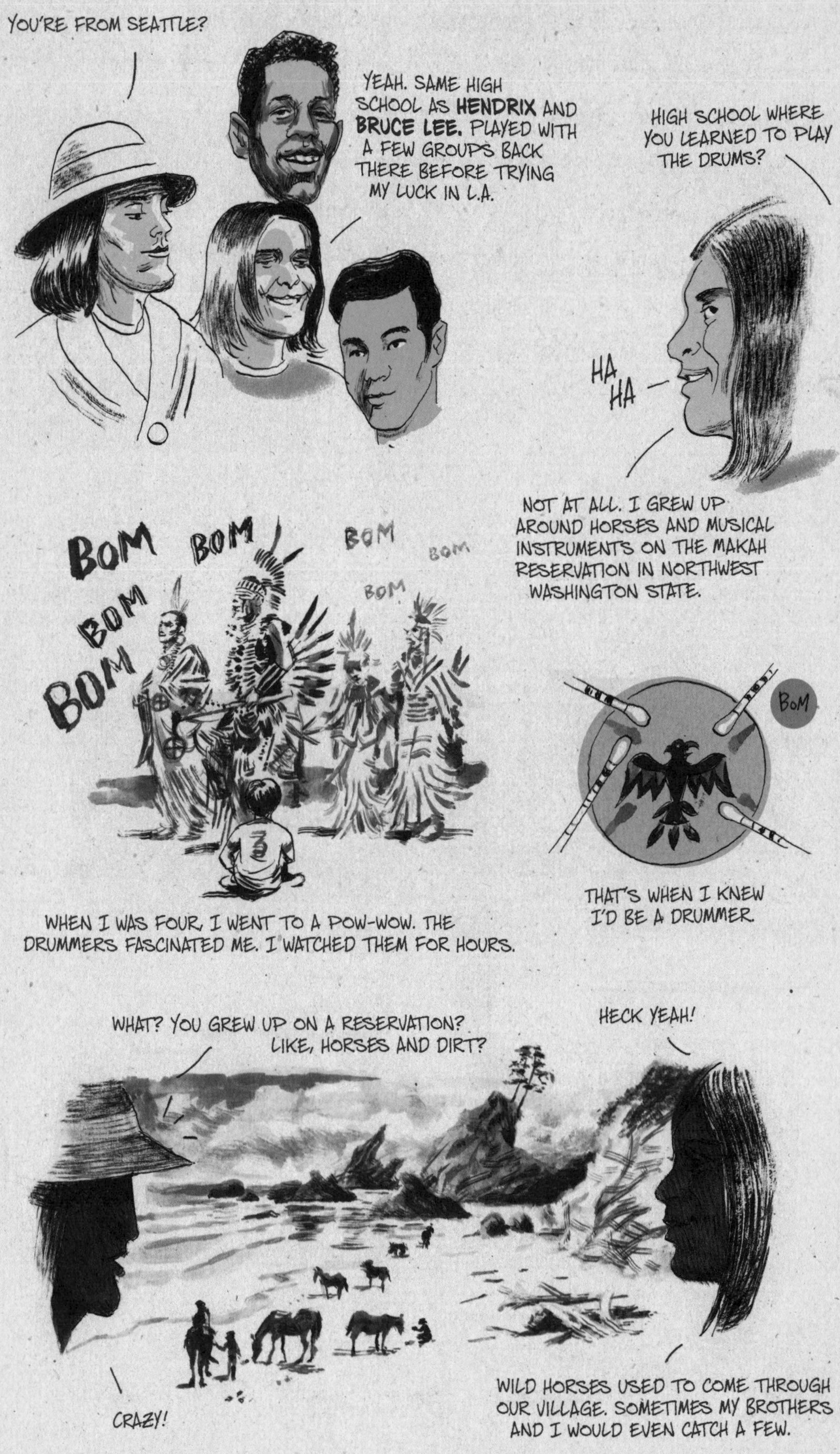

YOU'RE FROM SEATTLE?
YEAH. SAME HIGH SCHOOL AS **HENDRIX** AND **BRUCE LEE.** PLAYED WITH A FEW GROUPS BACK THERE BEFORE TRYING MY LUCK IN L.A.
HIGH SCHOOL WHERE YOU LEARNED TO PLAY THE DRUMS?
HA HA
NOT AT ALL. I GREW UP AROUND HORSES AND MUSICAL INSTRUMENTS ON THE MAKAH RESERVATION IN NORTHWEST WASHINGTON STATE.
BOM BOM BOM BOM BOM BOM BOM BOM
WHEN I WAS FOUR, I WENT TO A POW-WOW. THE DRUMMERS FASCINATED ME. I WATCHED THEM FOR HOURS.
BOM
THAT'S WHEN I KNEW I'D BE A DRUMMER.
WHAT? YOU GREW UP ON A RESERVATION? LIKE, HORSES AND DIRT?
HECK YEAH!
CRAZY!
WILD HORSES USED TO COME THROUGH OUR VILLAGE. SOMETIMES MY BROTHERS AND I WOULD EVEN CATCH A FEW.

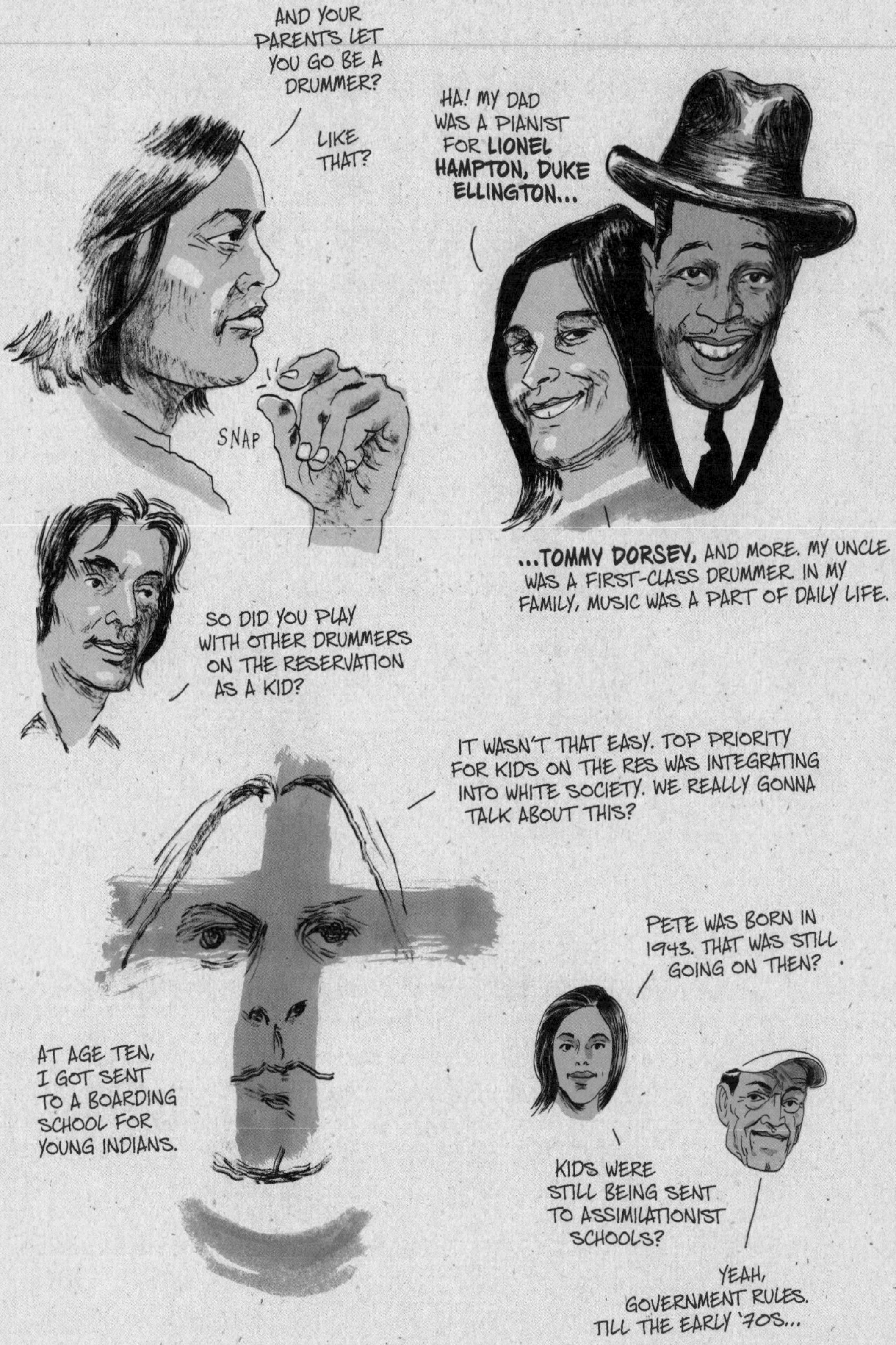
AND YOUR PARENTS LET YOU GO BE A DRUMMER?
LIKE THAT?
SNAP
HA! MY DAD WAS A PIANIST FOR **LIONEL HAMPTON, DUKE ELLINGTON...**
...TOMMY DORSEY, AND MORE. MY UNCLE WAS A FIRST-CLASS DRUMMER. IN MY FAMILY, MUSIC WAS A PART OF DAILY LIFE.
SO DID YOU PLAY WITH OTHER DRUMMERS ON THE RESERVATION AS A KID?
IT WASN'T THAT EASY. TOP PRIORITY FOR KIDS ON THE RES WAS INTEGRATING INTO WHITE SOCIETY. WE REALLY GONNA TALK ABOUT THIS?
AT AGE TEN, I GOT SENT TO A BOARDING SCHOOL FOR YOUNG INDIANS.
PETE WAS BORN IN 1943. THAT WAS STILL GOING ON THEN?
KIDS WERE STILL BEING SENT TO ASSIMILATIONIST SCHOOLS?
YEAH, GOVERNMENT RULES. TILL THE EARLY '70S...

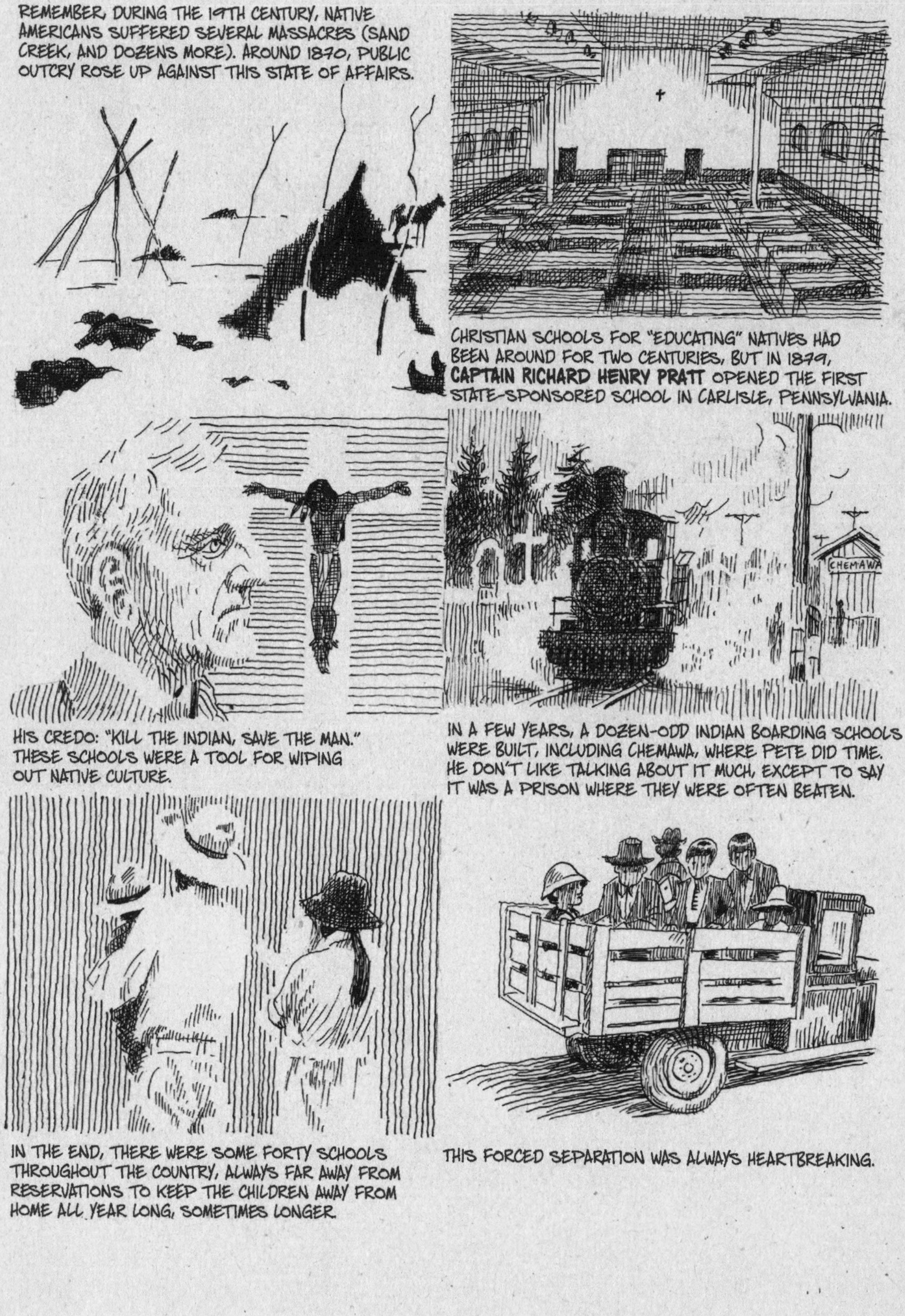
REMEMBER, DURING THE 19TH CENTURY, NATIVE AMERICANS SUFFERED SEVERAL MASSACRES (SAND CREEK, AND DOZENS MORE). AROUND 1870, PUBLIC OUTCRY ROSE UP AGAINST THIS STATE OF AFFAIRS.
CHRISTIAN SCHOOLS FOR "EDUCATING" NATIVES HAD BEEN AROUND FOR TWO CENTURIES, BUT IN 1879, **CAPTAIN RICHARD HENRY PRATT** OPENED THE FIRST STATE-SPONSORED SCHOOL IN CARLISLE, PENNSYLVANIA.
HIS CREDO: "KILL THE INDIAN, SAVE THE MAN." THESE SCHOOLS WERE A TOOL FOR WIPING OUT NATIVE CULTURE.
CHEMAWA
IN A FEW YEARS, A DOZEN-ODD INDIAN BOARDING SCHOOLS WERE BUILT, INCLUDING CHEMAWA, WHERE PETE DID TIME. HE DON'T LIKE TALKING ABOUT IT MUCH, EXCEPT TO SAY IT WAS A PRISON WHERE THEY WERE OFTEN BEATEN.
IN THE END, THERE WERE SOME FORTY SCHOOLS THROUGHOUT THE COUNTRY, ALWAYS FAR AWAY FROM RESERVATIONS TO KEEP THE CHILDREN AWAY FROM HOME ALL YEAR LONG, SOMETIMES LONGER.
THIS FORCED SEPARATION WAS ALWAYS HEARTBREAKING.

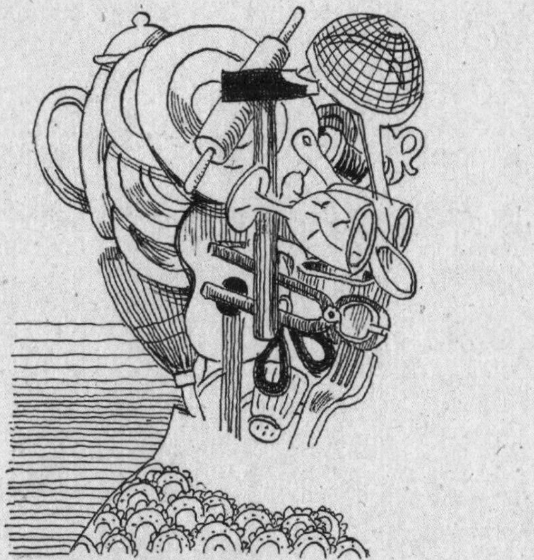

IN THEORY, THE SCHOOLS WERE MEANT TO HELP YOUNG NATIVE AMERICANS INTEGRATE INTO WHITE SOCIETY. **ESTELLE REEL** WAS THE SUPERINTENDENT OF THE INDIAN SCHOOLS FROM 1898 TO 1910.

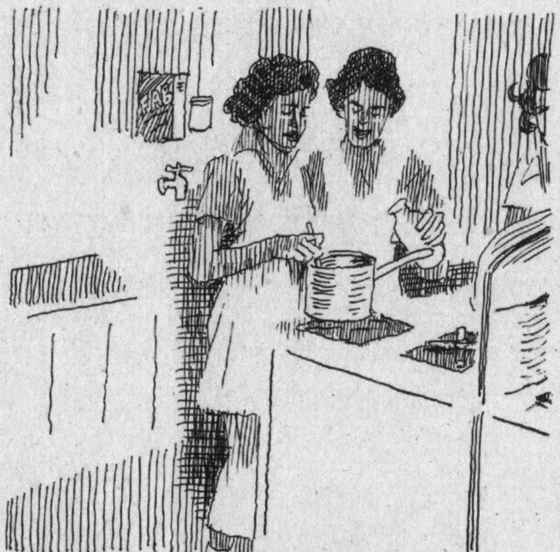

HER VISION OF INDIANS AS AN "INFERIOR RACE" DROVE HER TO TEACH ONLY SIMPLE MANUAL TRADES: FARM AND FIELD WORK AND CARPENTRY FOR THE BOYS, COOKING, SEWING, AND HOUSEKEEPING FOR THE GIRLS.

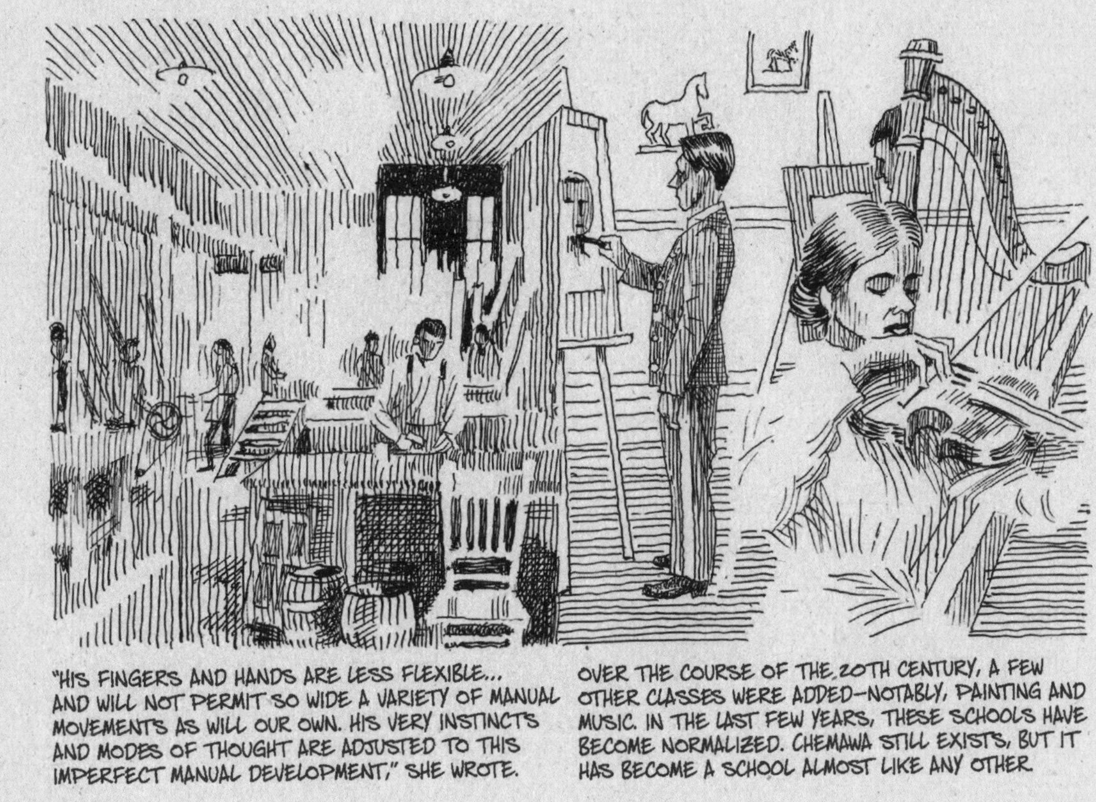

"HIS FINGERS AND HANDS ARE LESS FLEXIBLE... AND WILL NOT PERMIT SO WIDE A VARIETY OF MANUAL MOVEMENTS AS WILL OUR OWN. HIS VERY INSTINCTS AND MODES OF THOUGHT ARE ADJUSTED TO THIS IMPERFECT MANUAL DEVELOPMENT," SHE WROTE.

OVER THE COURSE OF THE 20TH CENTURY, A FEW OTHER CLASSES WERE ADDED—NOTABLY, PAINTING AND MUSIC. IN THE LAST FEW YEARS, THESE SCHOOLS HAVE BECOME NORMALIZED. CHEMAWA STILL EXISTS, BUT IT HAS BECOME A SCHOOL ALMOST LIKE ANY OTHER.

CARLISLE INDIAN SCHOOL. 1879-1918

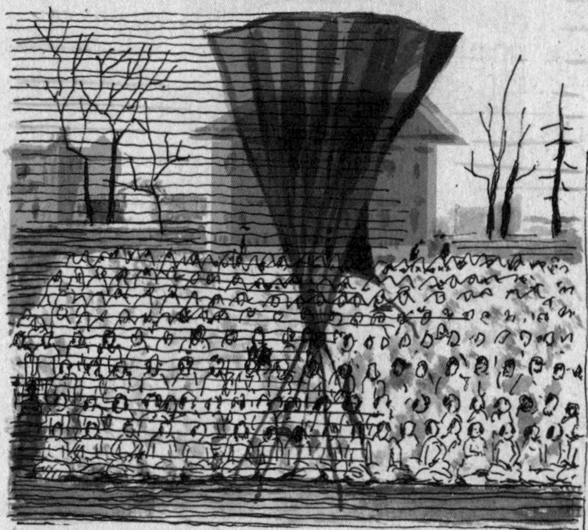

GIVEN THE WAY THESE SCHOOLS WORKED UNTIL 1970, "GENOCIDE" REALLY IS THE RIGHT WORD. ENTIRE PEOPLES WERE DELIBERATELY EFFACED THROUGH THE SUPPRESSION OF THEIR LANGUAGES, BELIEFS, AND CULTURES, BY SHATTERING THE BONDS BETWEEN GENERATIONS.

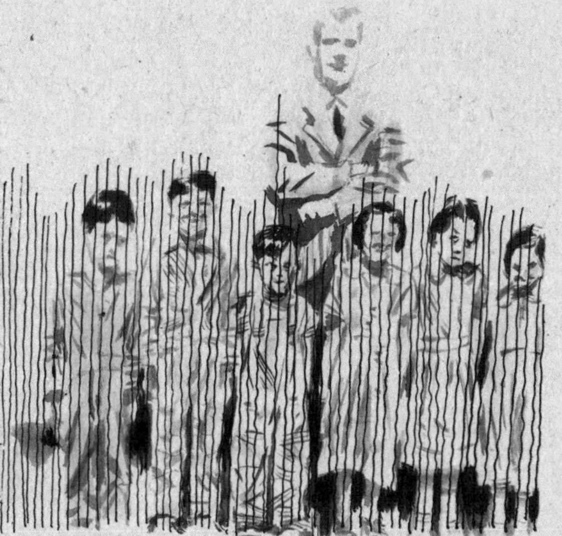

EVERYTHING CONNECTING THE CHILDREN TO THEIR LIVES BEFORE SCHOOL WAS FORBIDDEN. THE CLOTHES THEY CAME IN? FORBIDDEN, REPLACED WITH SCRATCHY, UNCOMFORTABLE UNIFORMS UPON ARRIVAL.

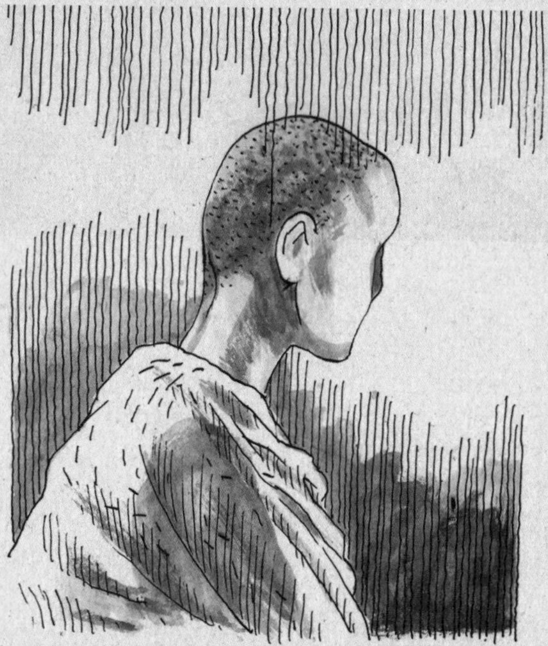

HAIRSTYLES FROM HOME? FORBIDDEN. BOYS' HEADS WERE SHAVED AND GIRLS GIVEN WESTERN HAIRDOS. NATIVE LANGUAGES? FORBIDDEN. ONLY ENGLISH WAS PERMITTED.

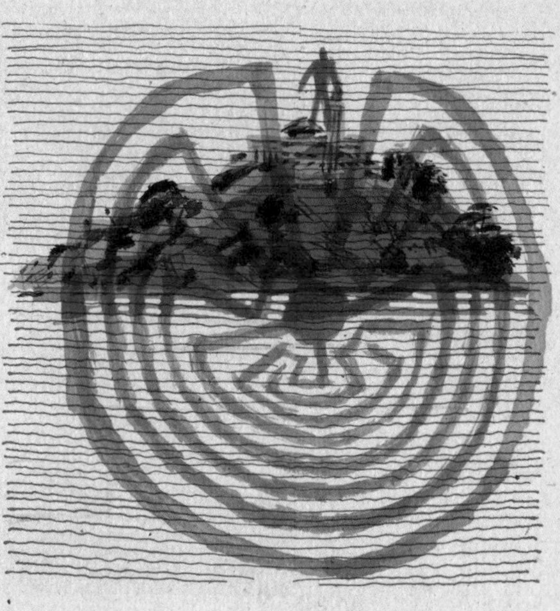

YOU MIGHT WONDER WHY THEIR PARENTS LET THEM GO. THEY HAD NO CHOICE. THOSE WHO RESISTED WERE LOCKED UP, AS HAPPENED TO SOME TWENTY HOPI MEN, SENT TO ALCATRAZ IN 1894.

ON TOP OF ALL THESE ENFORCED CHANGES, CHILDREN WERE SUBJECTED TO PUNISHMENTS, HUMILIATION, AND ABUSE THAT WENT SO FAR AS MALNUTRITION, SEXUAL VIOLENCE, AND RAPE.

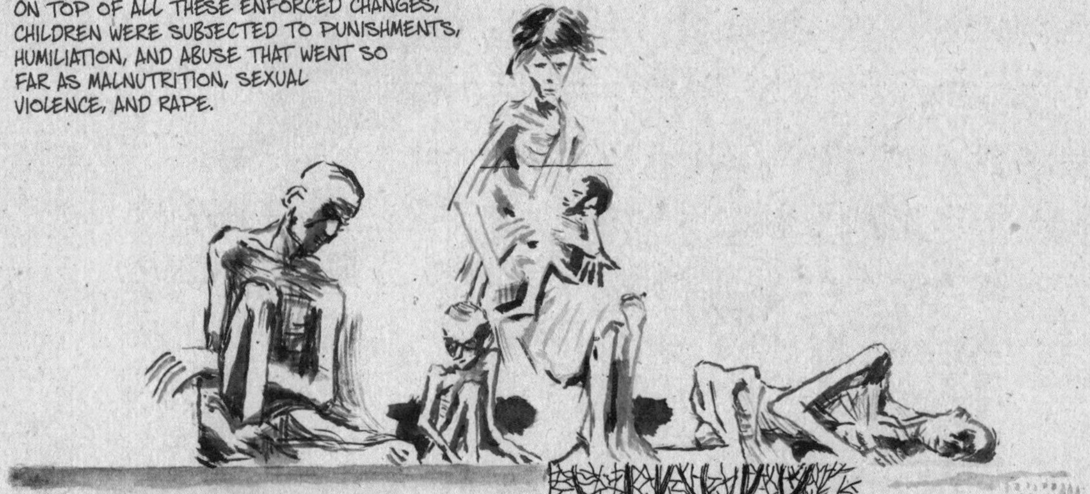

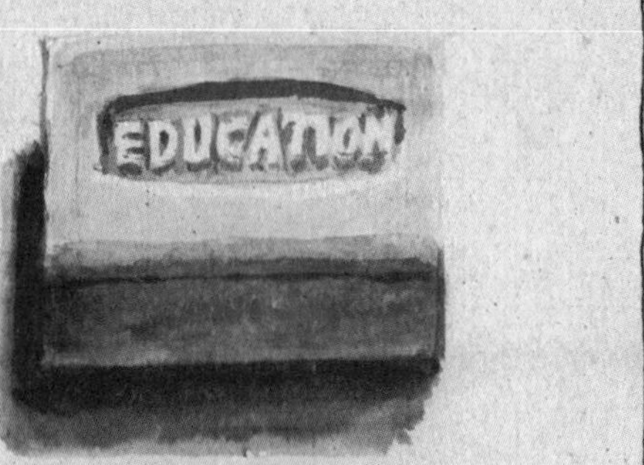
EDUCATION

THE MOST COMMON PUNISHMENT WAS WASHING THEIR MOUTHS OUT WITH SOAP WHEN THEY DARED SPEAK THEIR NATIVE LANGUAGES.

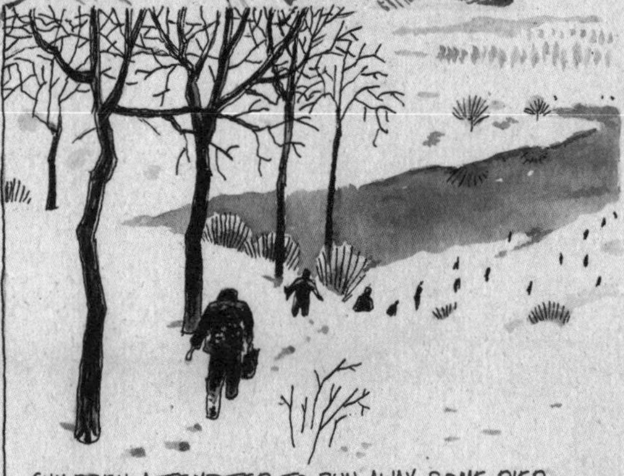

CHILDREN ATTEMPTED TO RUN AWAY. SOME DIED TRYING. THOSE CAUGHT WERE SEVERELY DISCIPLINED, LOCKED UP, OR BEATEN.

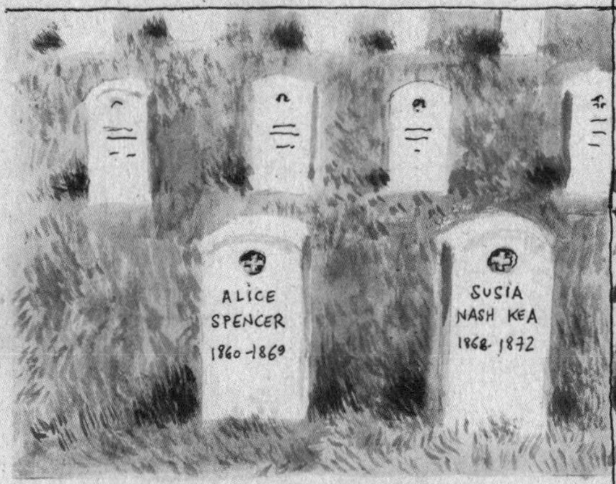
ALICE SPENCER 1860-1869
SUSIA NASH KEA 1868-1872

THEIR CHILDHOODS WERE HELLISH, WITH LITTLE MEDICAL ATTENTION. CHILDREN OFTEN SUCCUMBED TO DISEASE OR EPIDEMICS (FLU, TUBERCULOSIS). RECENTLY, DOZENS OF CHILD GRAVES WERE DISCOVERED NEAR CHEMAWA.

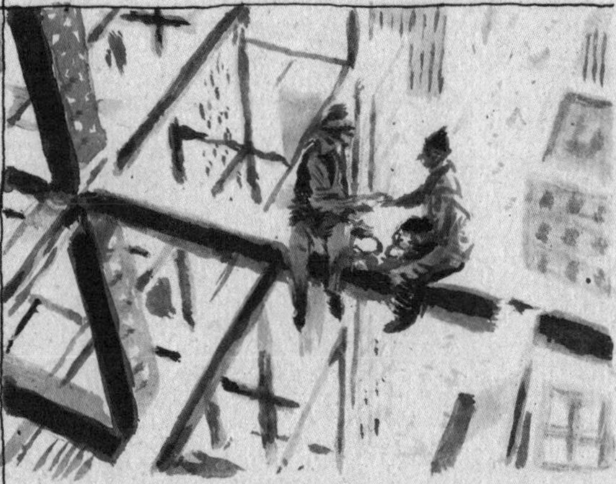

NATIVE AMERICANS WERE TREATED LIKE SLAVES AND THEN SENT OFF TO SERVE WHITES. AS ONE FRIEND PUT IT: "THE CHRISTIANS HAD THE BIBLE, AND WE HAD THE LAND. NOW WE HAVE THE BIBLE, AND THEY HAVE ALL THE LAND." THAT ABOUT SUMS IT UP.

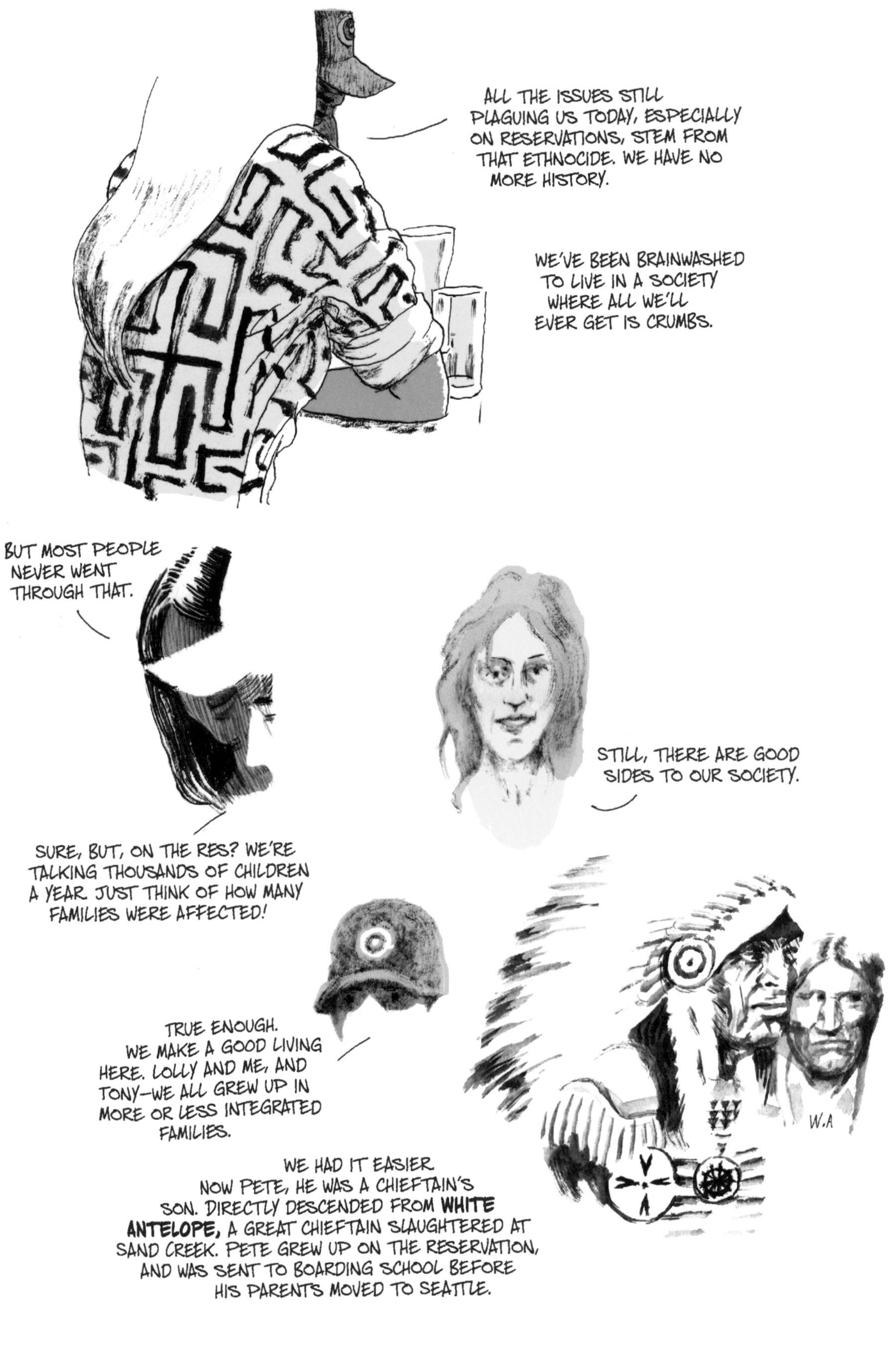
ALL THE ISSUES STILL PLAGUING US TODAY, ESPECIALLY ON RESERVATIONS, STEM FROM THAT ETHNOCIDE. WE HAVE NO MORE HISTORY.
WE'VE BEEN BRAINWASHED TO LIVE IN A SOCIETY WHERE ALL WE'LL EVER GET IS CRUMBS.
BUT MOST PEOPLE NEVER WENT THROUGH THAT.
STILL, THERE ARE GOOD SIDES TO OUR SOCIETY.
SURE, BUT, ON THE RES? WE'RE TALKING THOUSANDS OF CHILDREN A YEAR. JUST THINK OF HOW MANY FAMILIES WERE AFFECTED!
TRUE ENOUGH. WE MAKE A GOOD LIVING HERE. LOLLY AND ME, AND TONY—WE ALL GREW UP IN MORE OR LESS INTEGRATED FAMILIES.
W.A
WE HAD IT EASIER NOW PETE, HE WAS A CHIEFTAIN'S SON. DIRECTLY DESCENDED FROM **WHITE ANTELOPE,** A GREAT CHIEFTAIN SLAUGHTERED AT SAND CREEK. PETE GREW UP ON THE RESERVATION, AND WAS SENT TO BOARDING SCHOOL BEFORE HIS PARENTS MOVED TO SEATTLE.

IV
REDBONE
(1969)

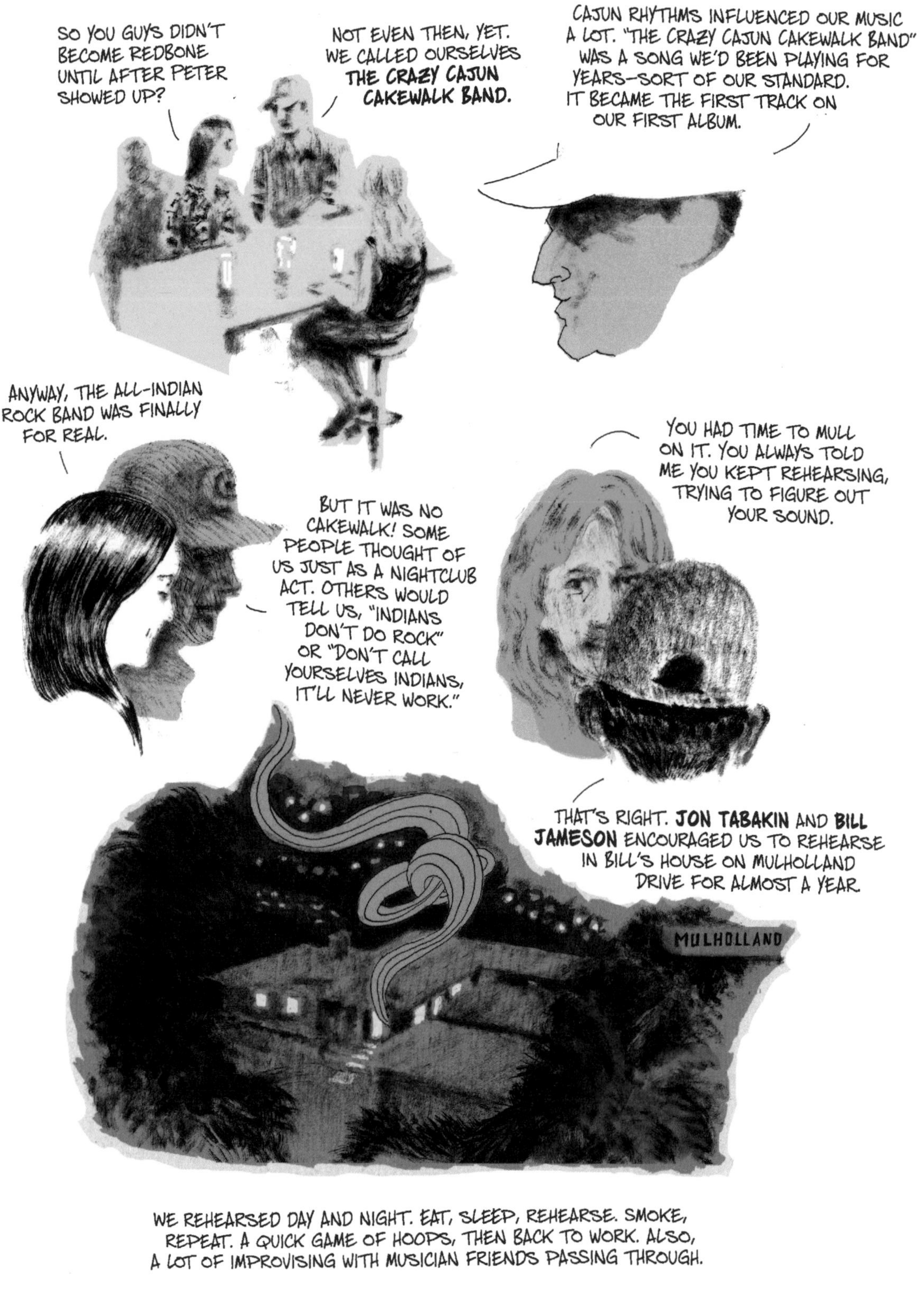
SO YOU GUYS DIDN'T BECOME REDBONE UNTIL AFTER PETER SHOWED UP?
NOT EVEN THEN, YET. WE CALLED OURSELVES **THE CRAZY CAJUN CAKEWALK BAND.**
CAJUN RHYTHMS INFLUENCED OUR MUSIC A LOT. "THE CRAZY CAJUN CAKEWALK BAND" WAS A SONG WE'D BEEN PLAYING FOR YEARS—SORT OF OUR STANDARD. IT BECAME THE FIRST TRACK ON OUR FIRST ALBUM.
ANYWAY, THE ALL-INDIAN ROCK BAND WAS FINALLY FOR REAL.
BUT IT WAS NO CAKEWALK! SOME PEOPLE THOUGHT OF US JUST AS A NIGHTCLUB ACT. OTHERS WOULD TELL US, "INDIANS DON'T DO ROCK" OR "DON'T CALL YOURSELVES INDIANS, IT'LL NEVER WORK."
YOU HAD TIME TO MULL ON IT. YOU ALWAYS TOLD ME YOU KEPT REHEARSING, TRYING TO FIGURE OUT YOUR SOUND.
THAT'S RIGHT. **JON TABAKIN** AND **BILL JAMESON** ENCOURAGED US TO REHEARSE IN BILL'S HOUSE ON MULHOLLAND DRIVE FOR ALMOST A YEAR.
MULHOLLAND
WE REHEARSED DAY AND NIGHT. EAT, SLEEP, REHEARSE. SMOKE, REPEAT. A QUICK GAME OF HOOPS, THEN BACK TO WORK. ALSO, A LOT OF IMPROVISING WITH MUSICIAN FRIENDS PASSING THROUGH.

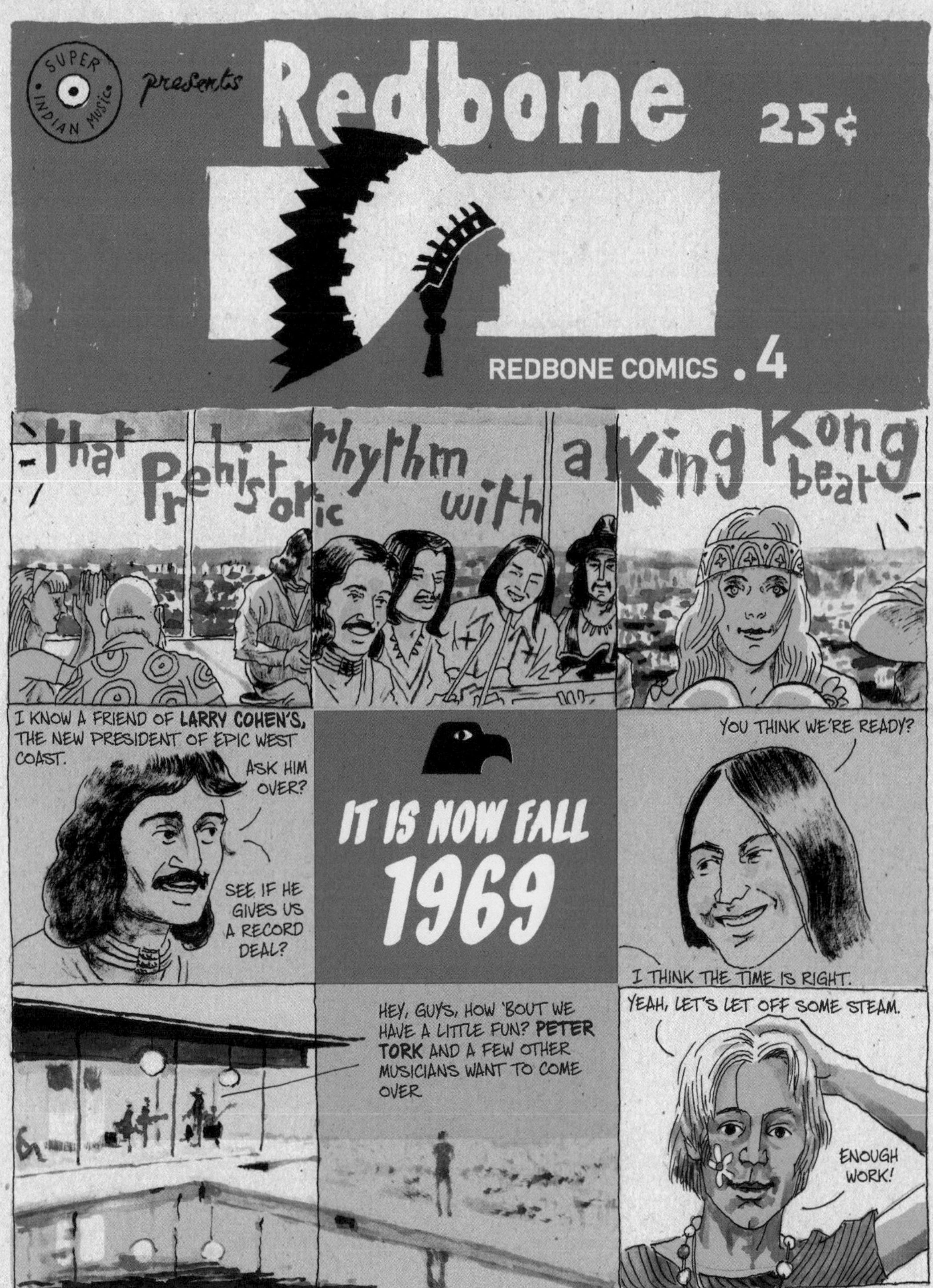
SUPER INDIAN MUSIC
presents
Redbone
25¢
REDBONE COMICS .4
that Prehistoric rhythm with a King Kong beat
I KNOW A FRIEND OF LARRY COHEN'S, THE NEW PRESIDENT OF EPIC WEST COAST.
ASK HIM OVER?
SEE IF HE GIVES US A RECORD DEAL?
IT IS NOW FALL 1969
YOU THINK WE'RE READY?
I THINK THE TIME IS RIGHT.
HEY, GUYS, HOW 'BOUT WE HAVE A LITTLE FUN? PETER TORK AND A FEW OTHER MUSICIANS WANT TO COME OVER
YEAH, LET'S LET OFF SOME STEAM.
ENOUGH WORK!

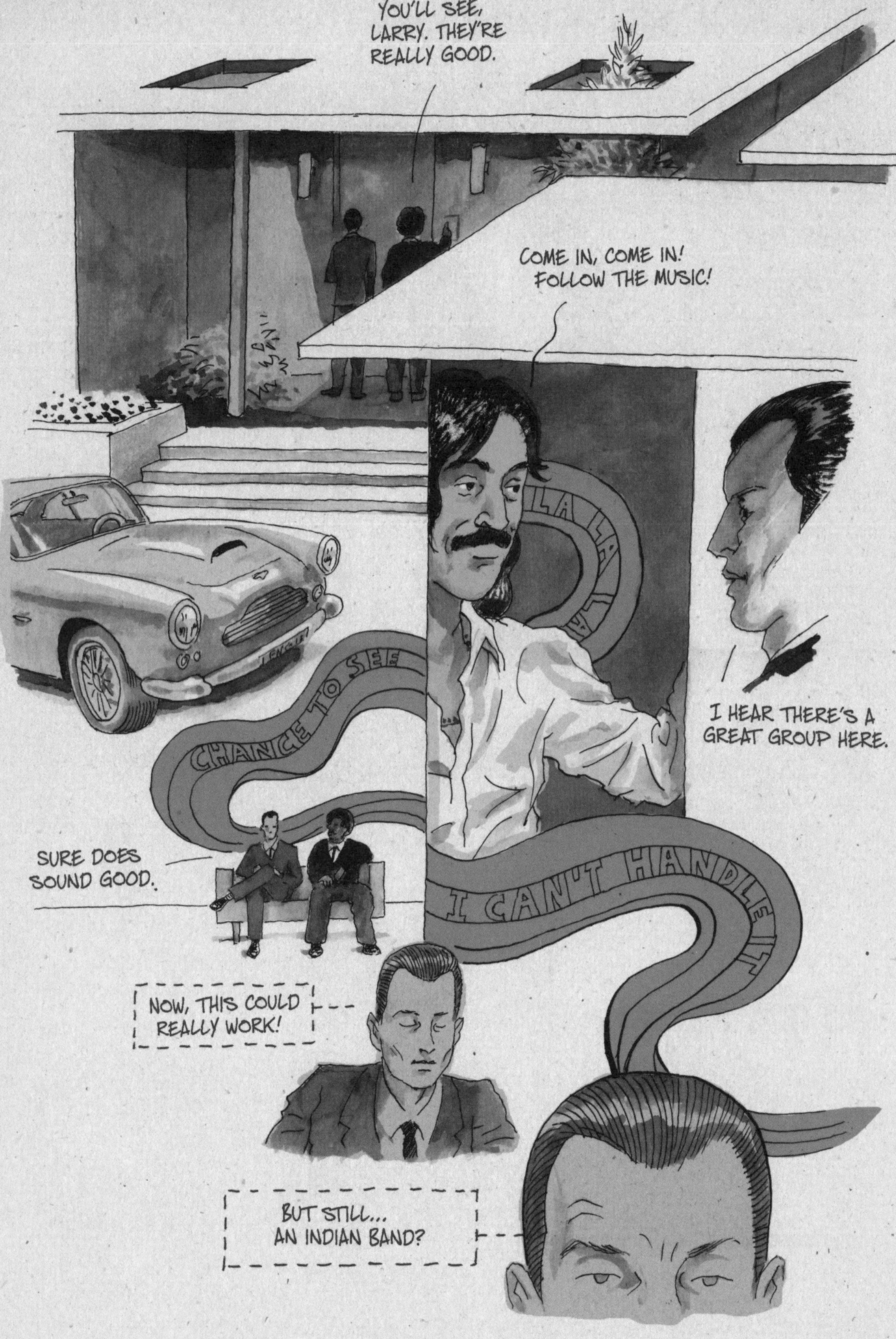
YOU'LL SEE, LARRY. THEY'RE REALLY GOOD.
COME IN, COME IN! FOLLOW THE MUSIC!
LA LA
CHANCE TO SEE
I HEAR THERE'S A GREAT GROUP HERE.
SURE DOES SOUND GOOD.
I CAN'T HANDLE IT
NOW, THIS COULD REALLY WORK!
BUT STILL... AN INDIAN BAND?

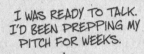

I WAS READY TO TALK. I'D BEEN PREPPING MY PITCH FOR WEEKS.

LARRY, THIS IS PETE, LOLLY, AND TONY. FIRST, I WANTED TO—

MEET ME AT EPIC TOMORROW MORNING AT TEN O'CLOCK.

YES!

YOU'RE ALL TERRIFIC MUSICIANS, AND THE SONGS ARE INTERESTING, BUT WHY PUSH YOUR INDIAN IDENTITY?

WE'VE BEEN PASSING AS LATINO FOR TEN YEARS. COMES A TIME...

Epic

WE'RE NOT JUST A GROUP, LARRY. WE'RE A MOVEMENT!

YOU SURE ARE OPTIMISTIC, BUT... LET'S GO FOR IT. HOW'S $10,000 SOUND?

EACH?

NATURALLY!

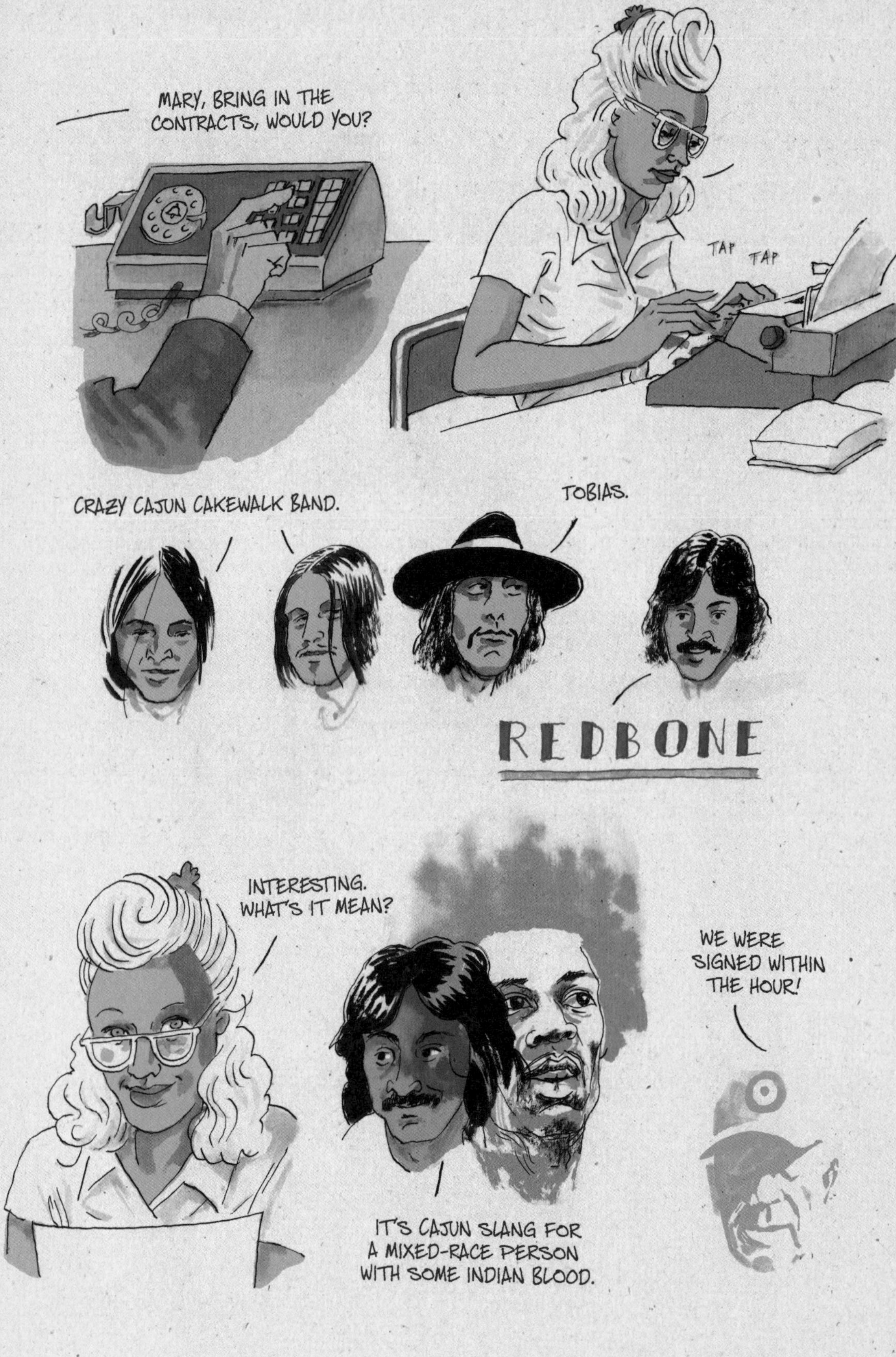
MARY, BRING IN THE CONTRACTS, WOULD YOU?
TAP TAP
CRAZY CAJUN CAKEWALK BAND.
TOBIAS.
REDBONE
INTERESTING. WHAT'S IT MEAN?
IT'S CAJUN SLANG FOR A MIXED-RACE PERSON WITH SOME INDIAN BLOOD.
WE WERE SIGNED WITHIN THE HOUR!

WE REHEARSED ON MULHOLLAND DRIVE FOR ANOTHER FEW WEEKS TO FINE-TUNE OUR SONGS. THEN WE WENT TO THE STUDIO.

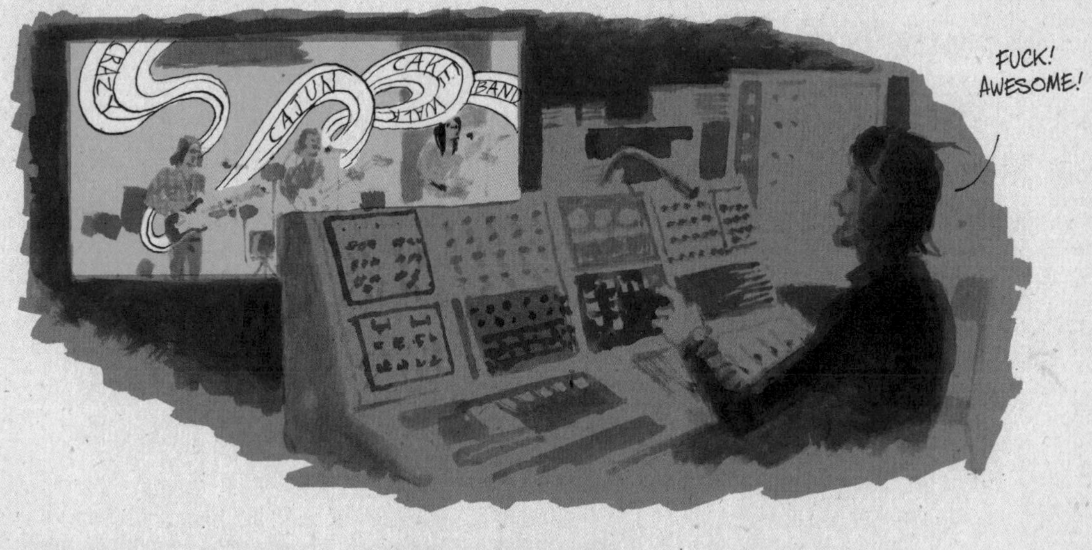
CRAZY CAJUN CAKE WALK BAND
FUCK! AWESOME!

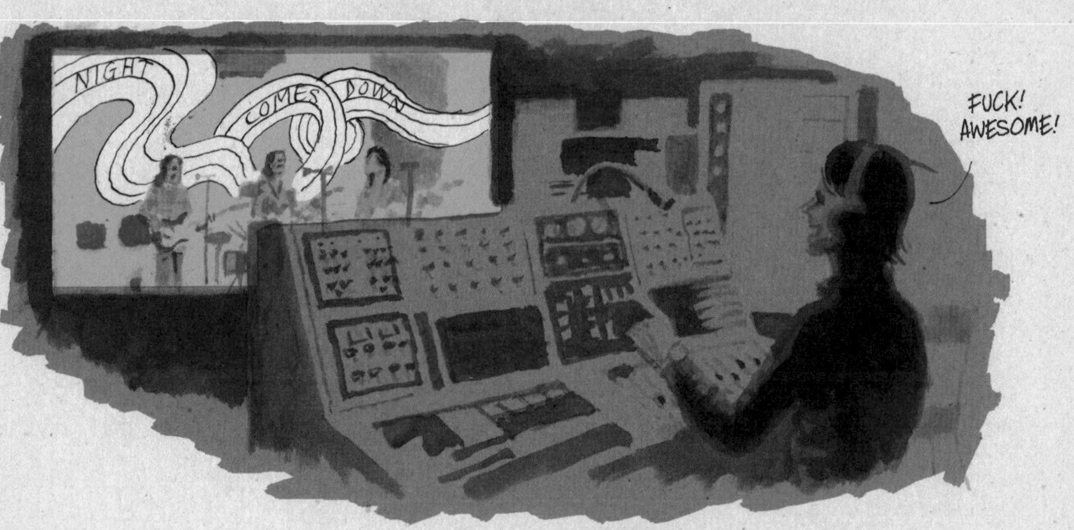
NIGHT COMES DOWN
FUCK! AWESOME!

THREE WEEKS LATER...

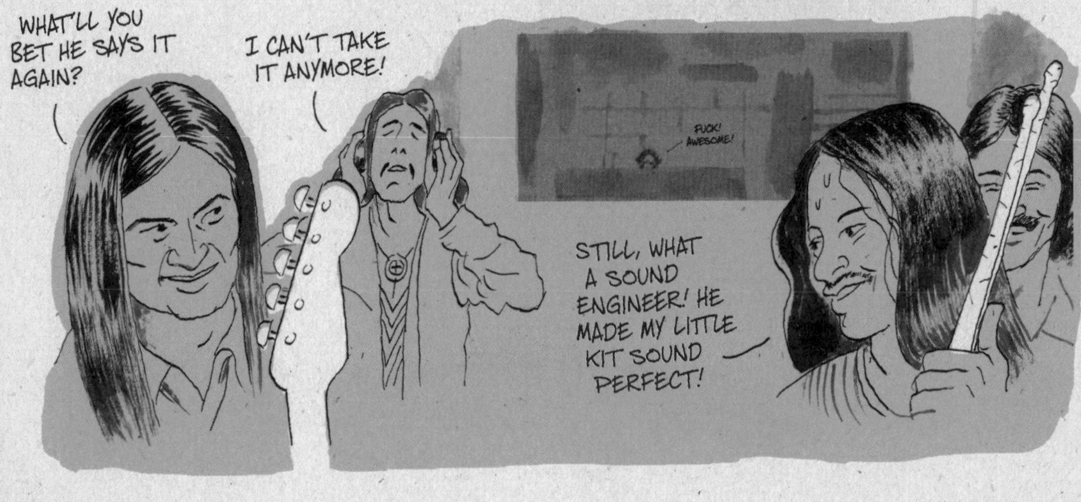
WHAT'LL YOU BET HE SAYS IT AGAIN?
I CAN'T TAKE IT ANYMORE!
FUCK! AWESOME!
STILL, WHAT A SOUND ENGINEER! HE MADE MY LITTLE KIT SOUND PERFECT!

WE LAID DOWN THIRTY TRACKS IN THREE WEEKS. IT TOOK THREE MONTHS TO MIX IT ALL AND FINALIZE IT. WE KEPT SEVENTEEN, INCLUDING THREE INSTRUMENTALS EACH EIGHT MINUTES LONG. THEN WE PUT OUT A DOUBLE ALBUM, WHICH WAS UNUSUAL BACK THEN, AND DEFINITELY UNHEARD OF FOR A DEBUT. EPIC BELIEVED IN US!

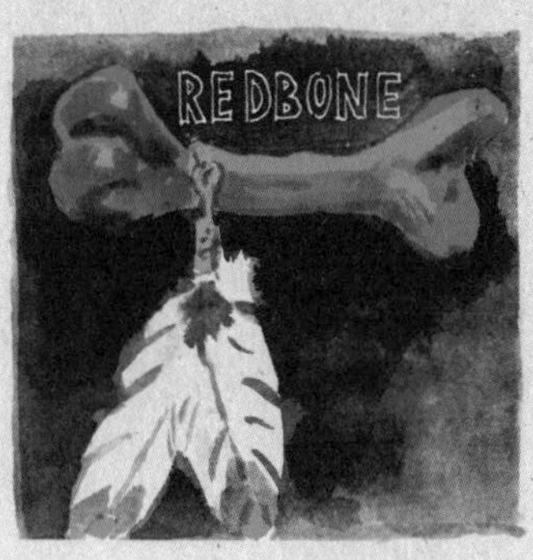
REDBONE

DATES FOR THE UPCOMING WEEKS...

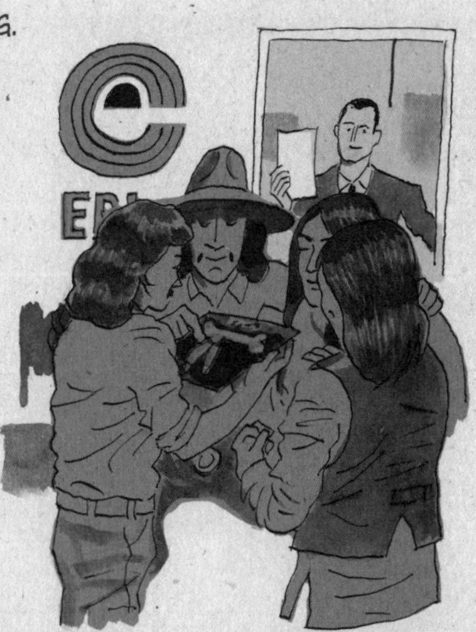

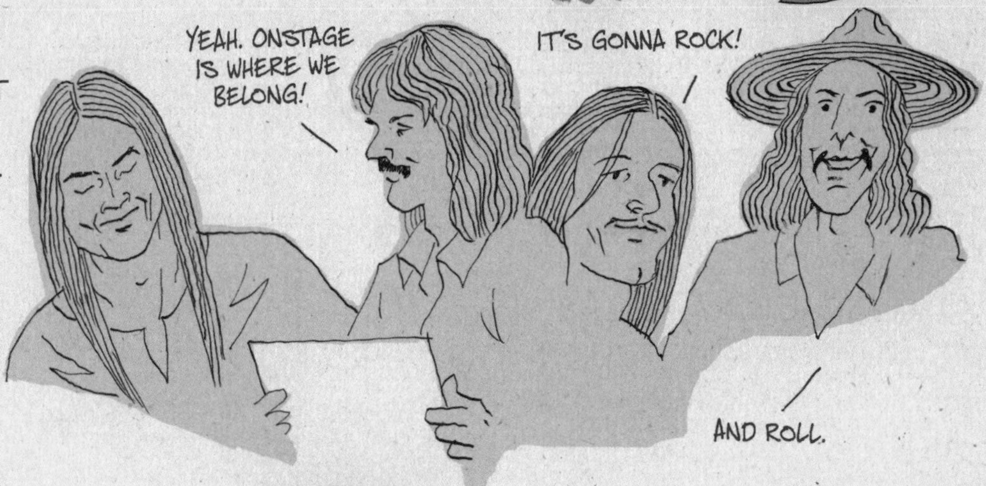
HA! ABOUT TIME!
YEAH. ONSTAGE IS WHERE WE BELONG!
IT'S GONNA ROCK!
AND ROLL.

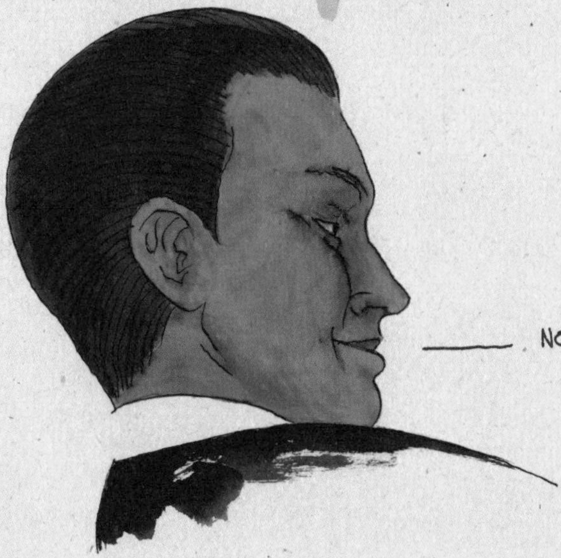
NO MORE MESSING AROUND!

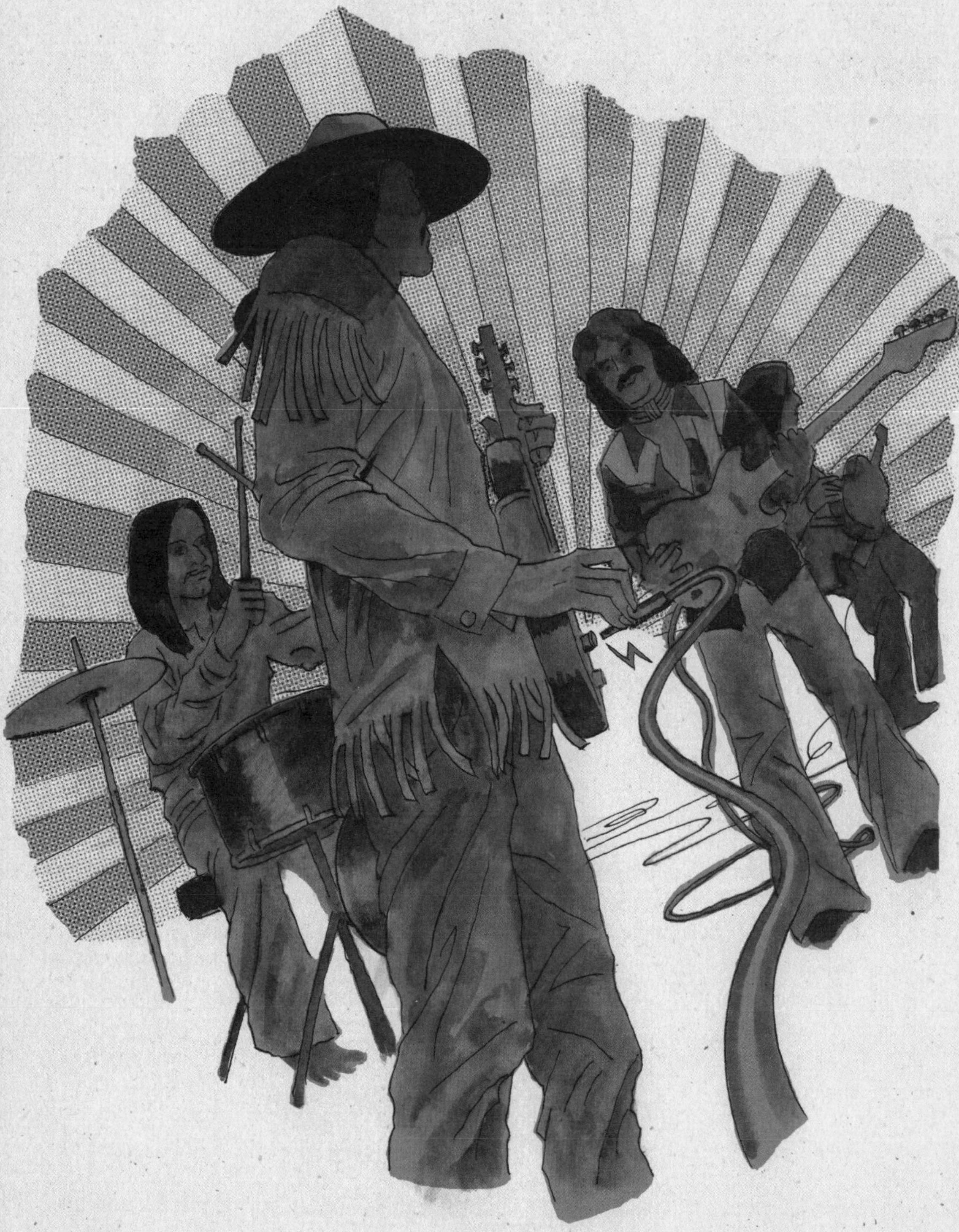

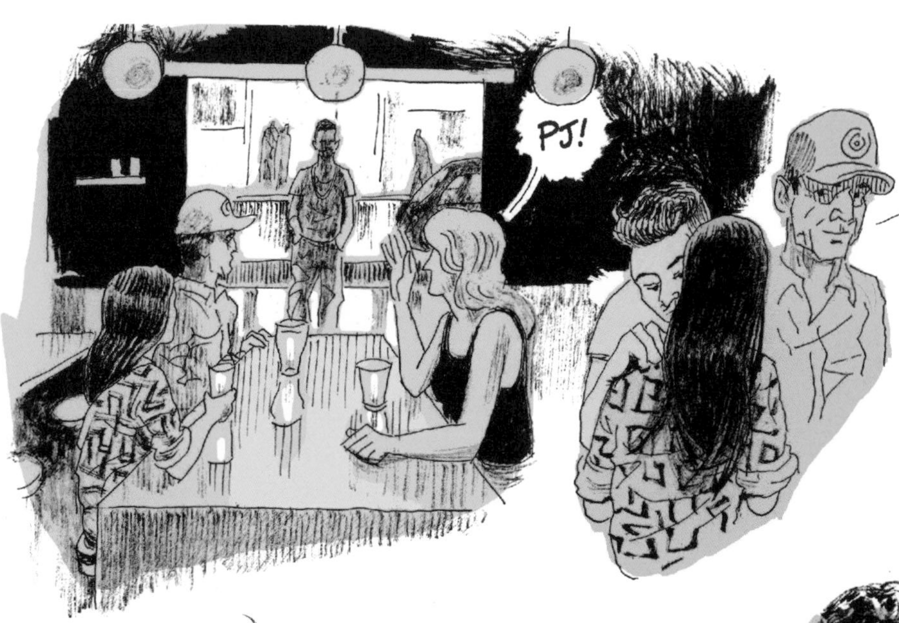
PJ!
HEY, HOW'S IT GOING, SON?

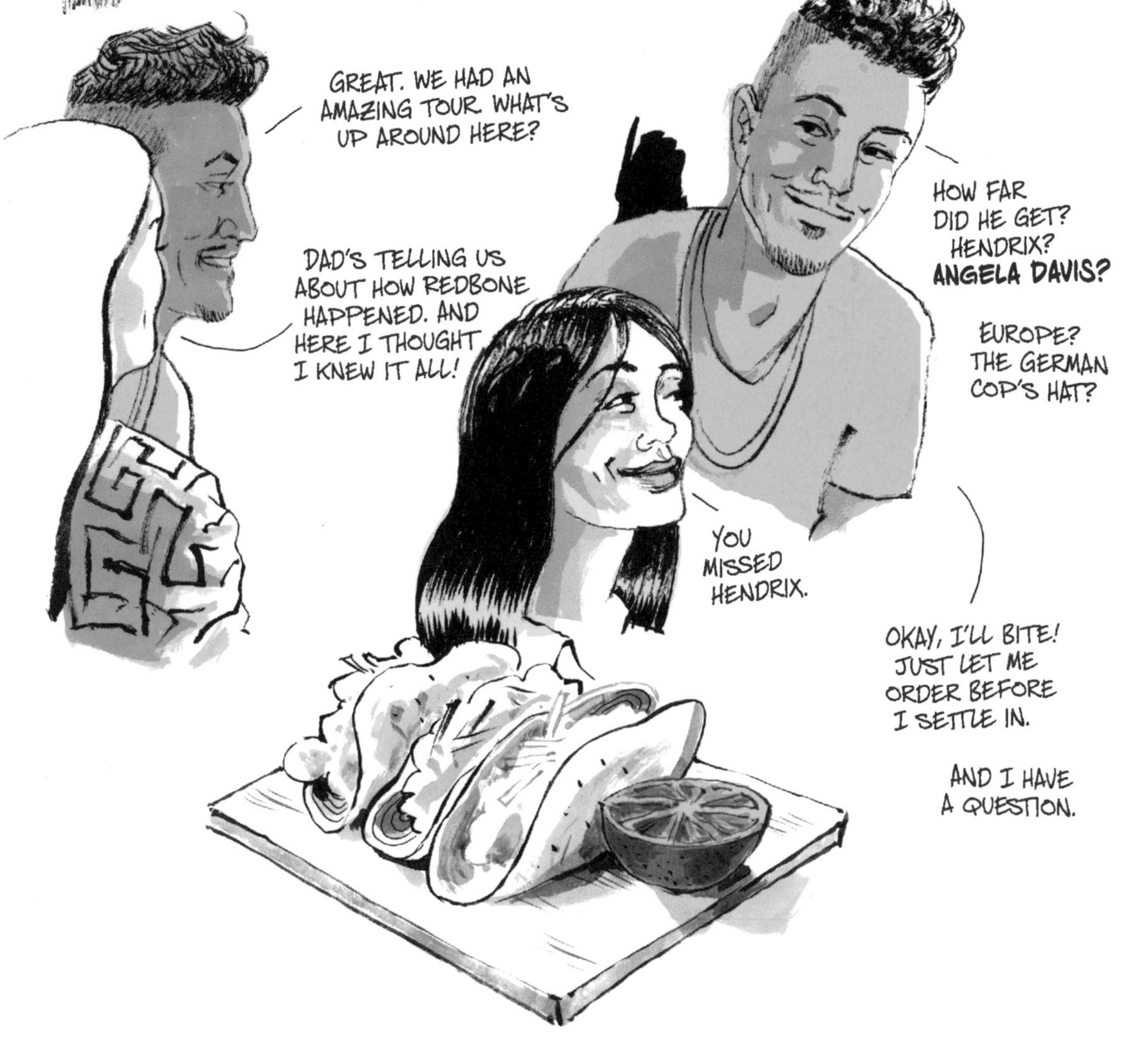
GREAT. WE HAD AN AMAZING TOUR. WHAT'S UP AROUND HERE?
DAD'S TELLING US ABOUT HOW REDBONE HAPPENED. AND HERE I THOUGHT I KNEW IT ALL!
HOW FAR DID HE GET? HENDRIX? **ANGELA DAVIS?**
EUROPE? THE GERMAN COP'S HAT?
YOU MISSED HENDRIX.
OKAY, I'LL BITE! JUST LET ME ORDER BEFORE I SETTLE IN.
AND I HAVE A QUESTION.

V

AIM
(1970)

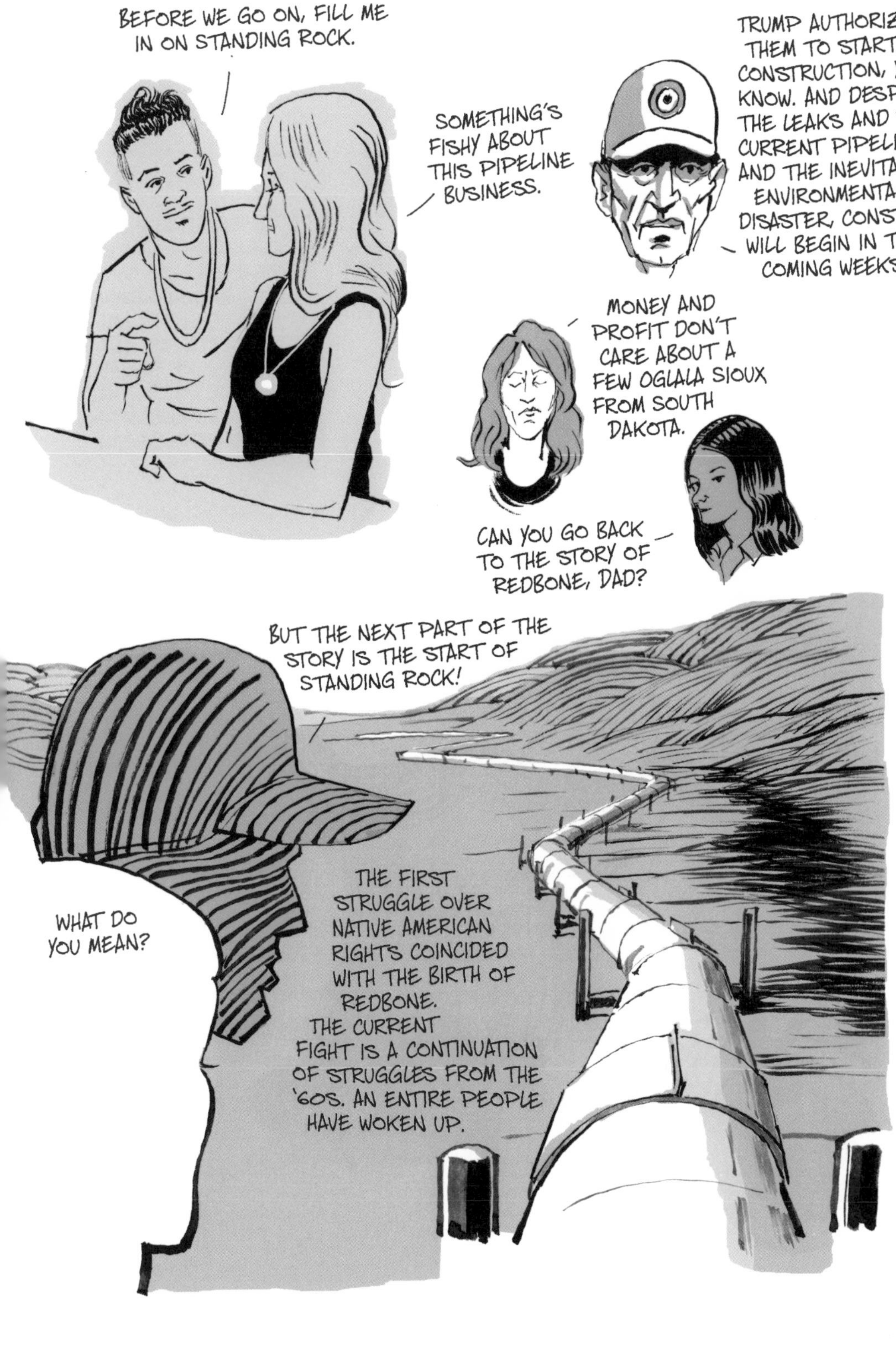
BEFORE WE GO ON, FILL ME IN ON STANDING ROCK.
SOMETHING'S FISHY ABOUT THIS PIPELINE BUSINESS.
TRUMP AUTHORIZED THEM TO START CONSTRUCTION, YOU KNOW. AND DESPITE THE LEAKS AND THE CURRENT PIPELINE AND THE INEVITABLE ENVIRONMENTAL DISASTER, CONSTRUCTION WILL BEGIN IN THE COMING WEEKS.
MONEY AND PROFIT DON'T CARE ABOUT A FEW OGLALA SIOUX FROM SOUTH DAKOTA.
CAN YOU GO BACK TO THE STORY OF REDBONE, DAD?
BUT THE NEXT PART OF THE STORY IS THE START OF STANDING ROCK!
WHAT DO YOU MEAN?
THE FIRST STRUGGLE OVER NATIVE AMERICAN RIGHTS COINCIDED WITH THE BIRTH OF REDBONE. THE CURRENT FIGHT IS A CONTINUATION OF STRUGGLES FROM THE '60S. AN ENTIRE PEOPLE HAVE WOKEN UP.

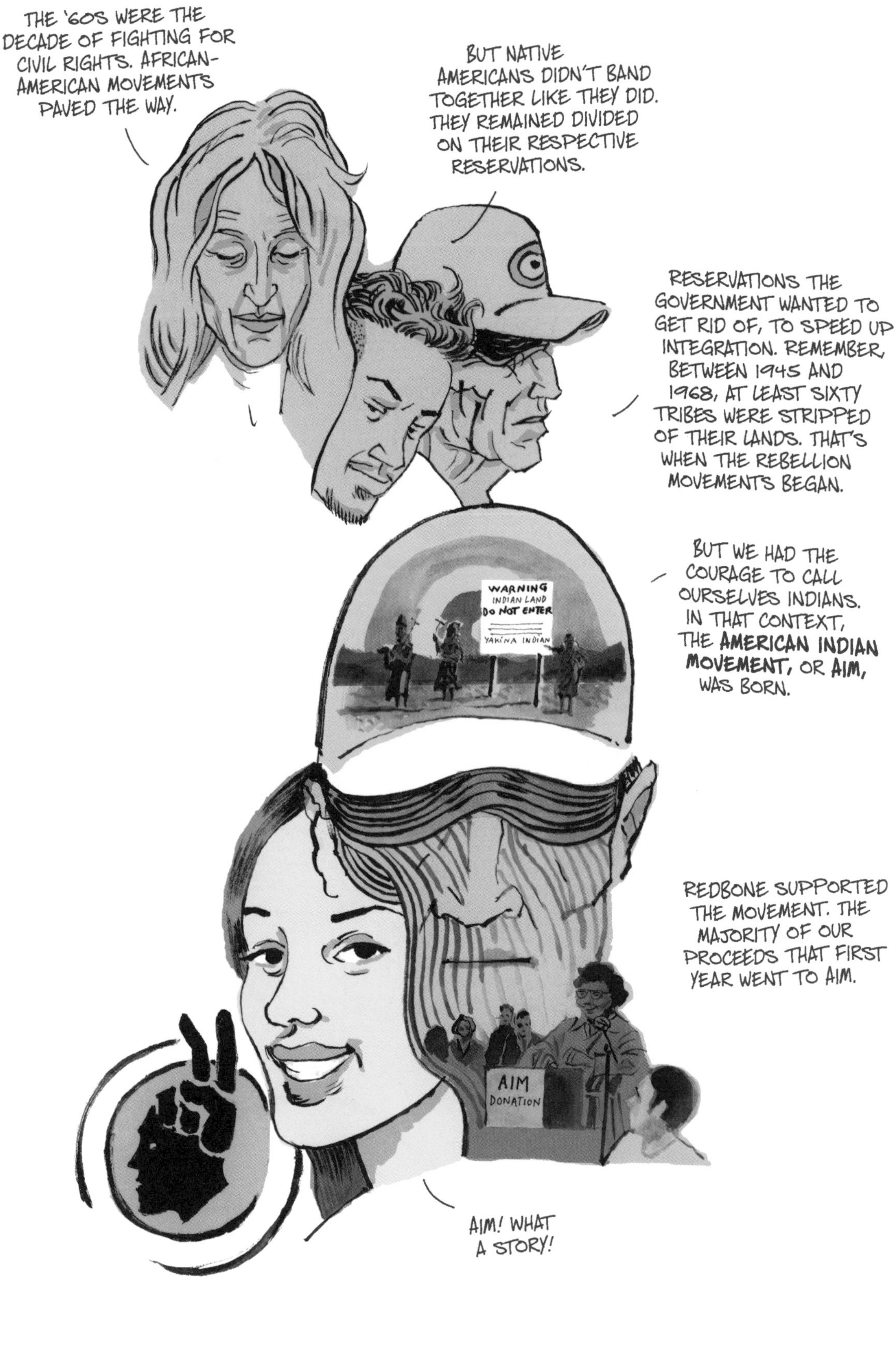
THE '60S WERE THE DECADE OF FIGHTING FOR CIVIL RIGHTS. AFRICAN-AMERICAN MOVEMENTS PAVED THE WAY.
BUT NATIVE AMERICANS DIDN'T BAND TOGETHER LIKE THEY DID. THEY REMAINED DIVIDED ON THEIR RESPECTIVE RESERVATIONS.
RESERVATIONS THE GOVERNMENT WANTED TO GET RID OF, TO SPEED UP INTEGRATION. REMEMBER, BETWEEN 1945 AND 1968, AT LEAST SIXTY TRIBES WERE STRIPPED OF THEIR LANDS. THAT'S WHEN THE REBELLION MOVEMENTS BEGAN.
WARNING
INDIAN LAND
DO NOT ENTER
YAKINA INDIAN
BUT WE HAD THE COURAGE TO CALL OURSELVES INDIANS. IN THAT CONTEXT, THE **AMERICAN INDIAN MOVEMENT**, OR **AIM**, WAS BORN.
REDBONE SUPPORTED THE MOVEMENT. THE MAJORITY OF OUR PROCEEDS THAT FIRST YEAR WENT TO AIM.
AIM
DONATION
AIM! WHAT A STORY!

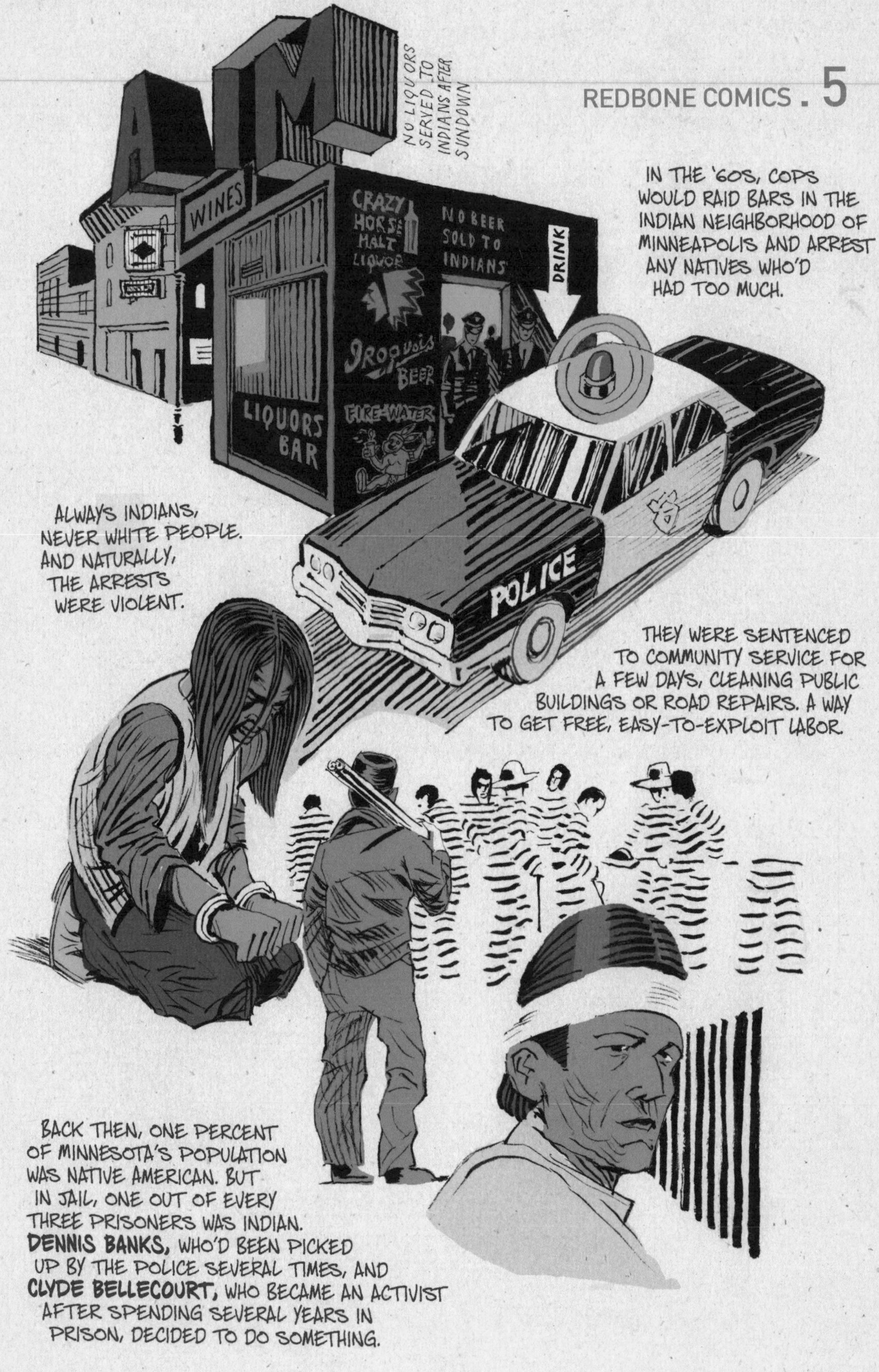
AIM
NO LIQUORS SERVED TO INDIANS AFTER SUNDOWN
WINES
CRAZY HORSE MALT LIQUOR
NO BEER SOLD TO INDIANS
DRINK
Iroquois BEER
FIRE-WATER
LIQUORS BAR
IN THE '60S, COPS WOULD RAID BARS IN THE INDIAN NEIGHBORHOOD OF MINNEAPOLIS AND ARREST ANY NATIVES WHO'D HAD TOO MUCH.
ALWAYS INDIANS, NEVER WHITE PEOPLE. AND NATURALLY, THE ARRESTS WERE VIOLENT.
POLICE
THEY WERE SENTENCED TO COMMUNITY SERVICE FOR A FEW DAYS, CLEANING PUBLIC BUILDINGS OR ROAD REPAIRS. A WAY TO GET FREE, EASY-TO-EXPLOIT LABOR.
BACK THEN, ONE PERCENT OF MINNESOTA'S POPULATION WAS NATIVE AMERICAN. BUT IN JAIL, ONE OUT OF EVERY THREE PRISONERS WAS INDIAN. **DENNIS BANKS,** WHO'D BEEN PICKED UP BY THE POLICE SEVERAL TIMES, AND **CLYDE BELLECOURT,** WHO BECAME AN ACTIVIST AFTER SPENDING SEVERAL YEARS IN PRISON, DECIDED TO DO SOMETHING.

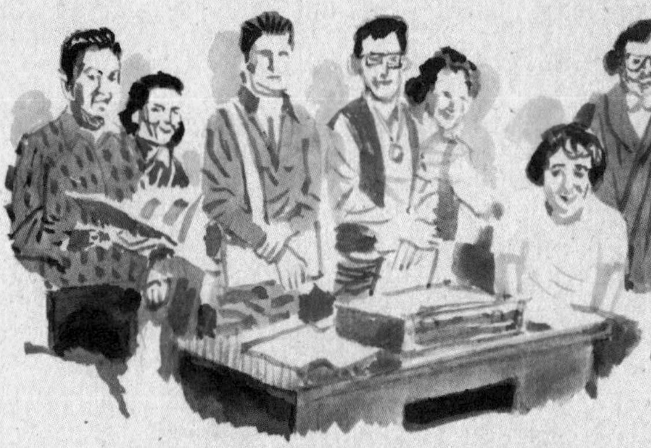

DENNIS AND CLYDE, ALONG WITH **VERNON BELLECOURT** AND **GEORGE MITCHELL,** ORGANIZED A MEETING IN MINNEAPOLIS ON JULY 28, 1968. THEY WEREN'T EXPECTING MUCH TURNOUT, BUT OVER TWO HUNDRED PEOPLE SHOWED UP, AND THAT NIGHT, THE **AMERICAN INDIAN MOVEMENVT** WAS BORN. THE NAME AIM WAS A REAL FIND*.

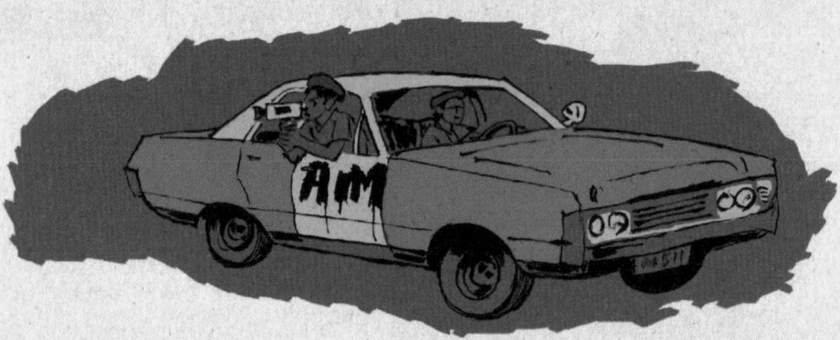
AIM

THE FIRST THING THEY DID WAS MOUNT A PATROL: THREE OLD COP CARS PAINTED RED, WITH RED BERETS SO THEIR OWN WOULD RECOGNIZE THEM. THEY'D HANG AROUND OUTSIDE BARS AND FILM POLICE ABUSES.

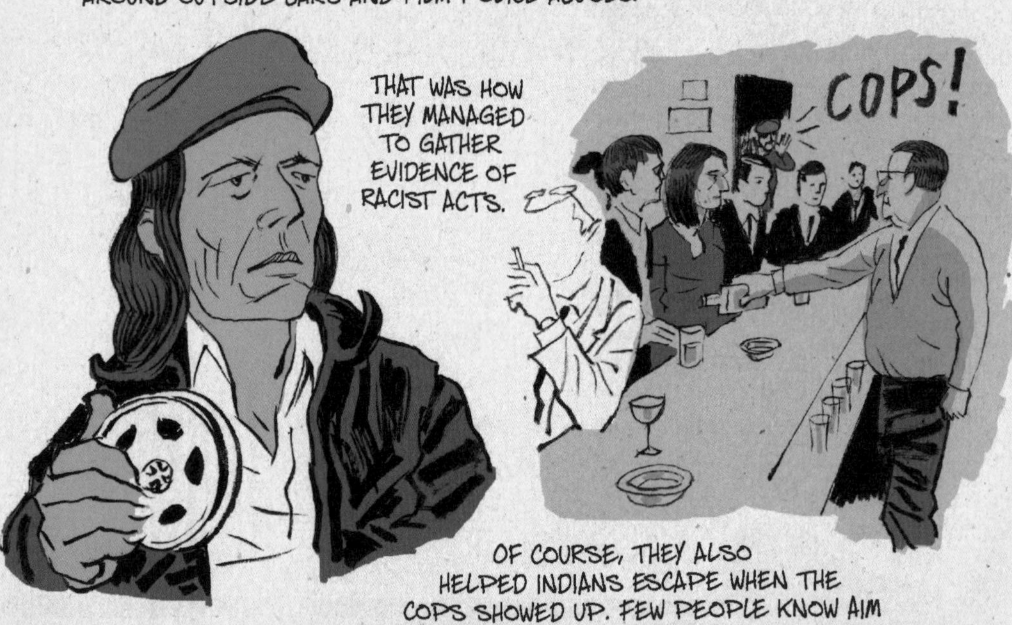
THAT WAS HOW THEY MANAGED TO GATHER EVIDENCE OF RACIST ACTS.
COPS!

OF COURSE, THEY ALSO HELPED INDIANS ESCAPE WHEN THE COPS SHOWED UP. FEW PEOPLE KNOW AIM WAS TRYING TO BE A NONVIOLENT MOVEMENT.

* ALBERTA DOWNWIND SUGGESTED THE NAME, AND INSISTED ON RECLAIMING THE WORD "INDIAN" FROM OUR WHITE OPPRESSORS.

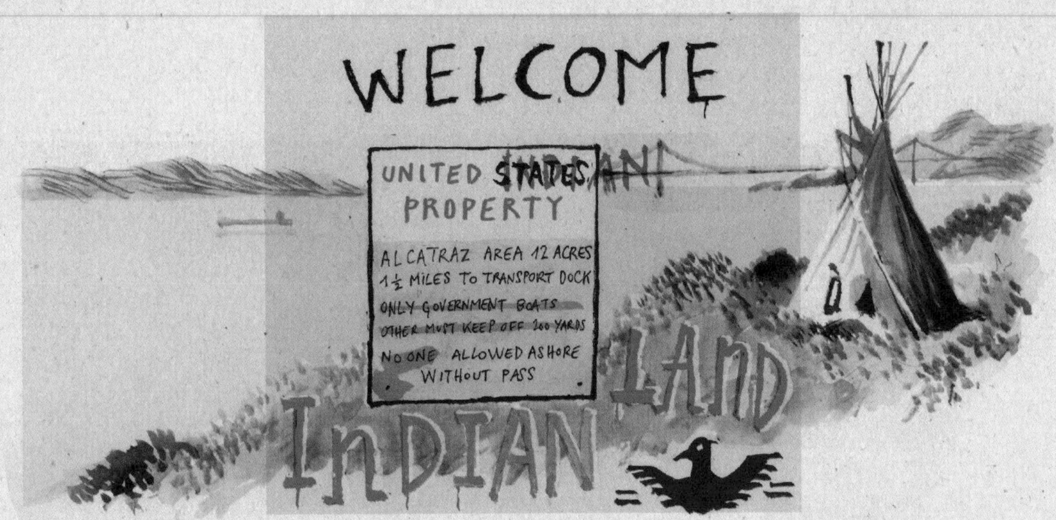
WELCOME
UNITED STATES
PROPERTY
ALCATRAZ AREA 12 ACRES
1½ MILES TO TRANSPORT DOCK
ONLY GOVERNMENT BOATS
OTHER MUST KEEP OFF 200 YARDS
NO ONE ALLOWED ASHORE
WITHOUT PASS
INDIAN LAND

AIM WAS SOON ON THE RISE THROUGHOUT THE COUNTRY. IN THAT SAME PERIOD, OTHER MOVEMENTS AND ASSOCIATIONS WERE FOUNDED, SUCH AS **UNITED INDIANS OF ALL TRIBES,** WHICH WENT ON TO OCCUPY ALCATRAZ FROM NOVEMBER 1969 TO JUNE 1971.

REDBONE'S FIRST PROTEST SONG, ON OUR SECOND ALBUM (1970), WAS DEDICATED TO THEM.

IN LATE 1969, AN AIM DELEGATION JOINED THE OCCUPIERS.

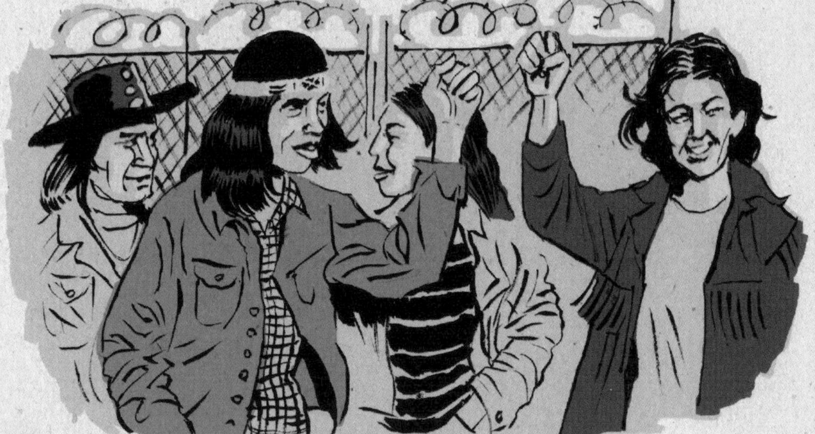

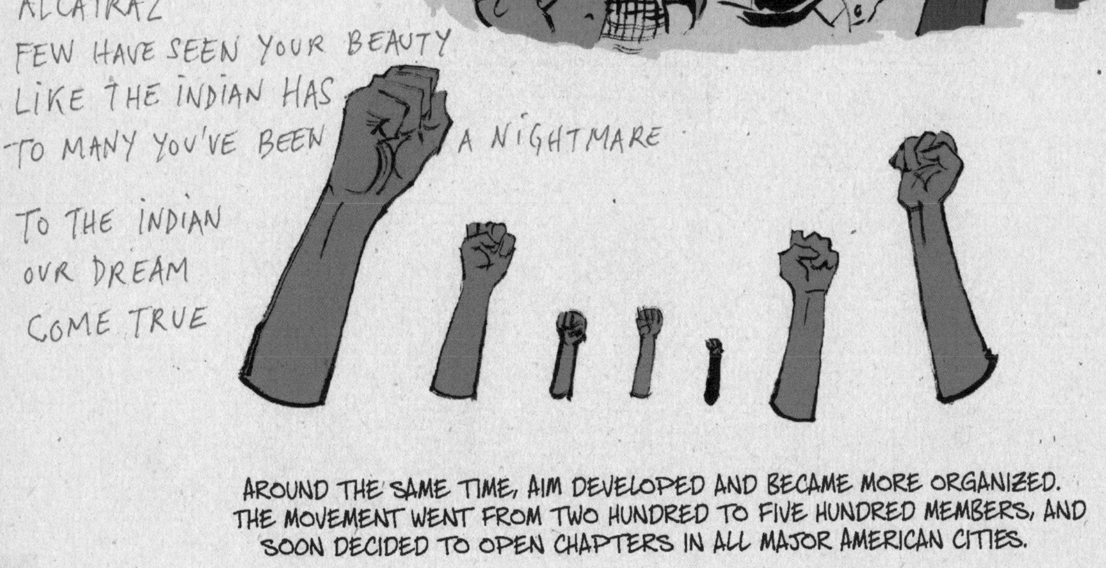
ALCATRAZ
FEW HAVE SEEN YOUR BEAUTY
LIKE THE INDIAN HAS
TO MANY YOU'VE BEEN A NIGHTMARE
TO THE INDIAN
OUR DREAM
COME TRUE

AROUND THE SAME TIME, AIM DEVELOPED AND BECAME MORE ORGANIZED. THE MOVEMENT WENT FROM TWO HUNDRED TO FIVE HUNDRED MEMBERS, AND SOON DECIDED TO OPEN CHAPTERS IN ALL MAJOR AMERICAN CITIES.

IN 1970, WITH THE HELP OF ATTORNEY **DOUG HALL,** AIM FOUNDED THE LEGAL RIGHTS CENTER IN MINNEAPOLIS, WHICH HAS REPRESENTED ALMOST NINETEEN THOUSAND INDIANS IN AMERICAN COURTS OVER THE LAST FEW DECADES.

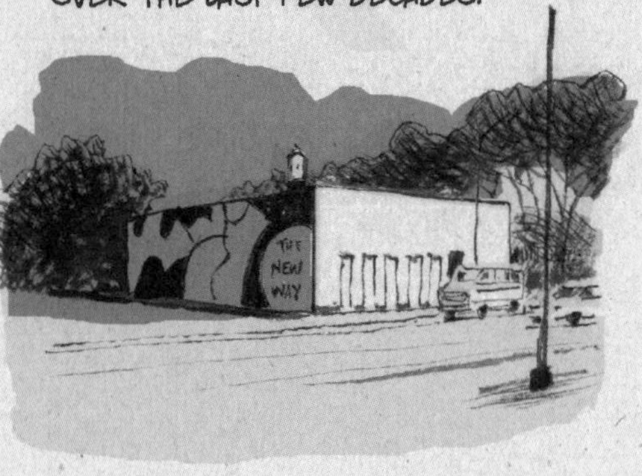
THE NEW WAY

AIM ALSO FOUNDED INSTITUTIONS, SUCH AS **THE HEART OF THE EARTH SURVIVAL SCHOOL,** TO KEEP NATIVE CULTURES ALIVE.

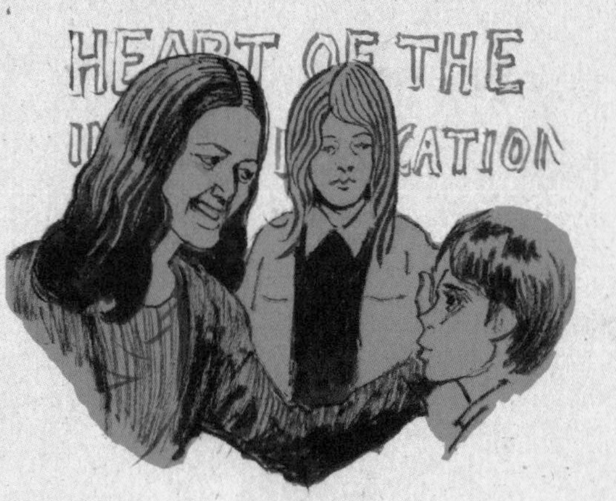
HEART OF THE
CATION

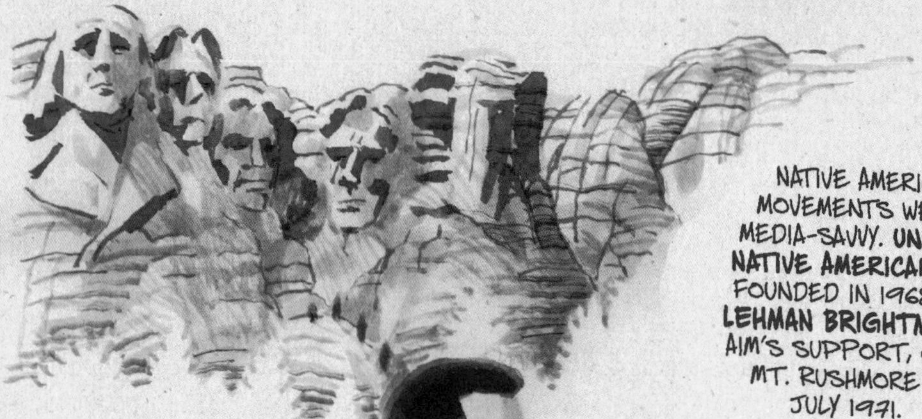

NATIVE AMERICAN MOVEMENTS WERE MEDIA-SAVVY. **UNITED NATIVE AMERICANS,** FOUNDED IN 1968 BY **LEHMAN BRIGHTMAN** WITH AIM'S SUPPORT, OCCUPIED MT. RUSHMORE IN JULY 1971.

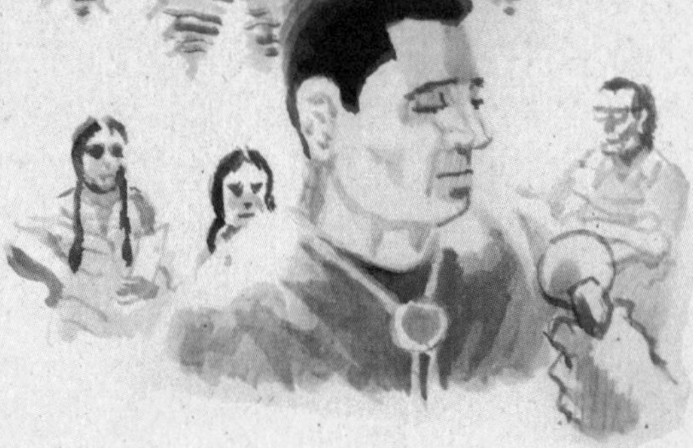

LOCATED IN THE SACRED LANDS OF THE BLACK HILLS, THE MONUMENT GLORIFYING AMERICAN PRESIDENTS HAD ALWAYS BEEN SEEN AS AN INSULT.

CERTAIN MEDIA OUTLETS AND CELEBRITIES SOON NOTICED AND TOOK UP AIM'S CAUSE. **MARLON BRANDO** WOULD ALWAYS BE A CLOSE SUPPORTER.

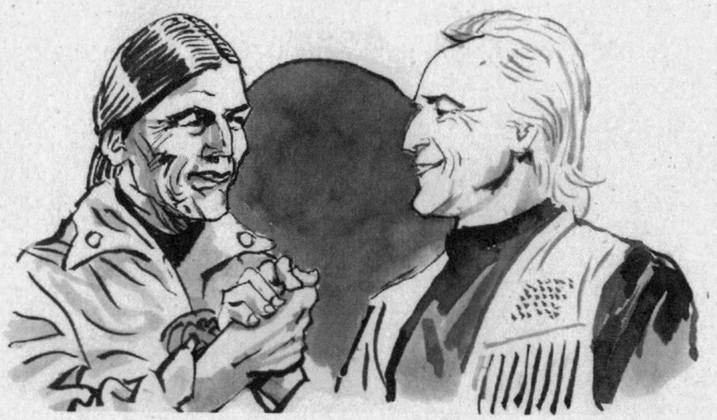

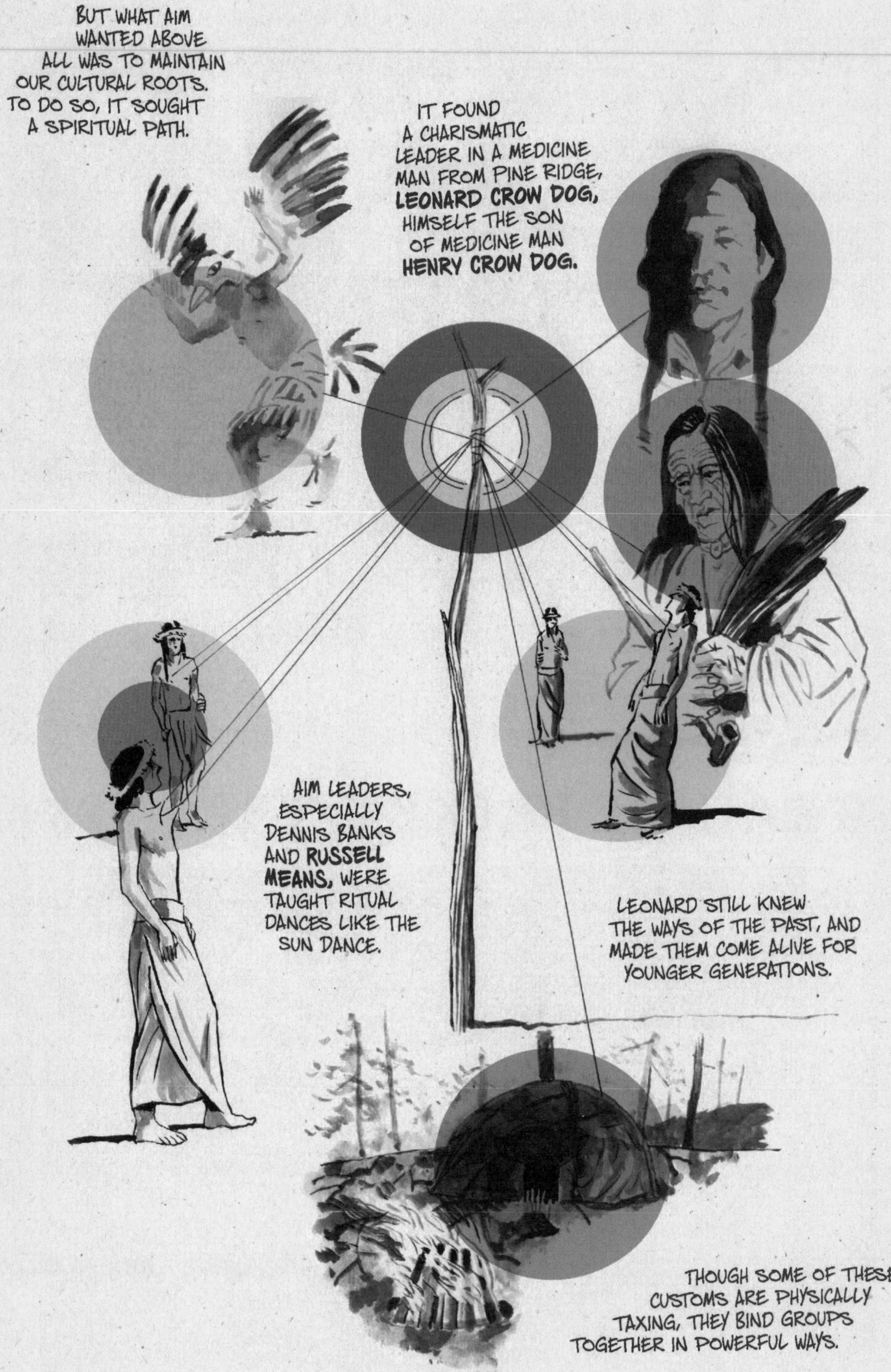
BUT WHAT AIM WANTED ABOVE ALL WAS TO MAINTAIN OUR CULTURAL ROOTS. TO DO SO, IT SOUGHT A SPIRITUAL PATH.
IT FOUND A CHARISMATIC LEADER IN A MEDICINE MAN FROM PINE RIDGE, LEONARD CROW DOG, HIMSELF THE SON OF MEDICINE MAN HENRY CROW DOG.
AIM LEADERS, ESPECIALLY DENNIS BANKS AND RUSSELL MEANS, WERE TAUGHT RITUAL DANCES LIKE THE SUN DANCE.
LEONARD STILL KNEW THE WAYS OF THE PAST, AND MADE THEM COME ALIVE FOR YOUNGER GENERATIONS.
THOUGH SOME OF THESE CUSTOMS ARE PHYSICALLY TAXING, THEY BIND GROUPS TOGETHER IN POWERFUL WAYS.

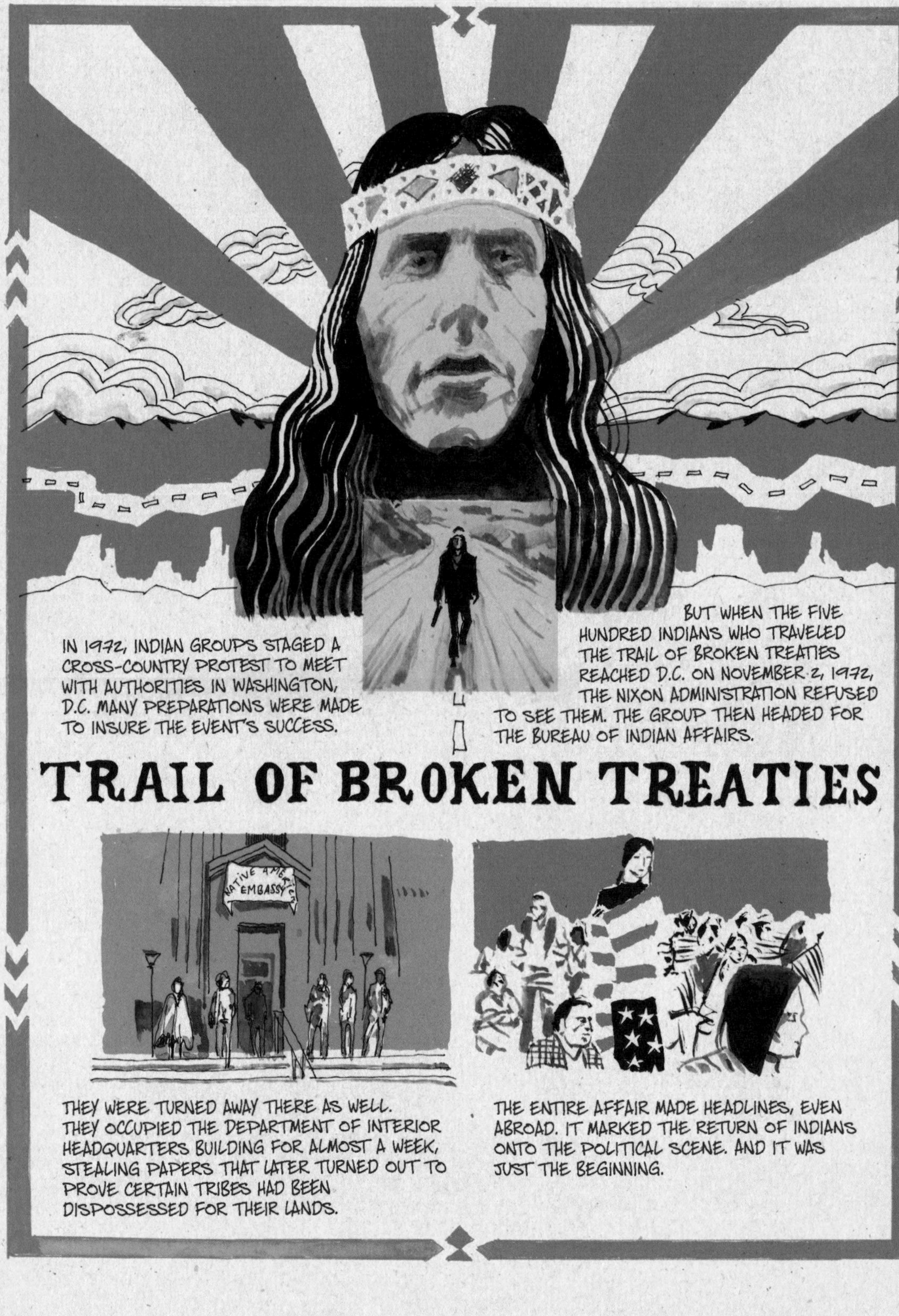
IN 1972, INDIAN GROUPS STAGED A CROSS-COUNTRY PROTEST TO MEET WITH AUTHORITIES IN WASHINGTON, D.C. MANY PREPARATIONS WERE MADE TO INSURE THE EVENT'S SUCCESS.
BUT WHEN THE FIVE HUNDRED INDIANS WHO TRAVELED THE TRAIL OF BROKEN TREATIES REACHED D.C. ON NOVEMBER 2, 1972, THE NIXON ADMINISTRATION REFUSED TO SEE THEM. THE GROUP THEN HEADED FOR THE BUREAU OF INDIAN AFFAIRS.
TRAIL OF BROKEN TREATIES
EMBASSY
THEY WERE TURNED AWAY THERE AS WELL. THEY OCCUPIED THE DEPARTMENT OF INTERIOR HEADQUARTERS BUILDING FOR ALMOST A WEEK, STEALING PAPERS THAT LATER TURNED OUT TO PROVE CERTAIN TRIBES HAD BEEN DISPOSSESSED FOR THEIR LANDS.
THE ENTIRE AFFAIR MADE HEADLINES, EVEN ABROAD. IT MARKED THE RETURN OF INDIANS ONTO THE POLITICAL SCENE. AND IT WAS JUST THE BEGINNING.

VI
SUCCESS
(1971)

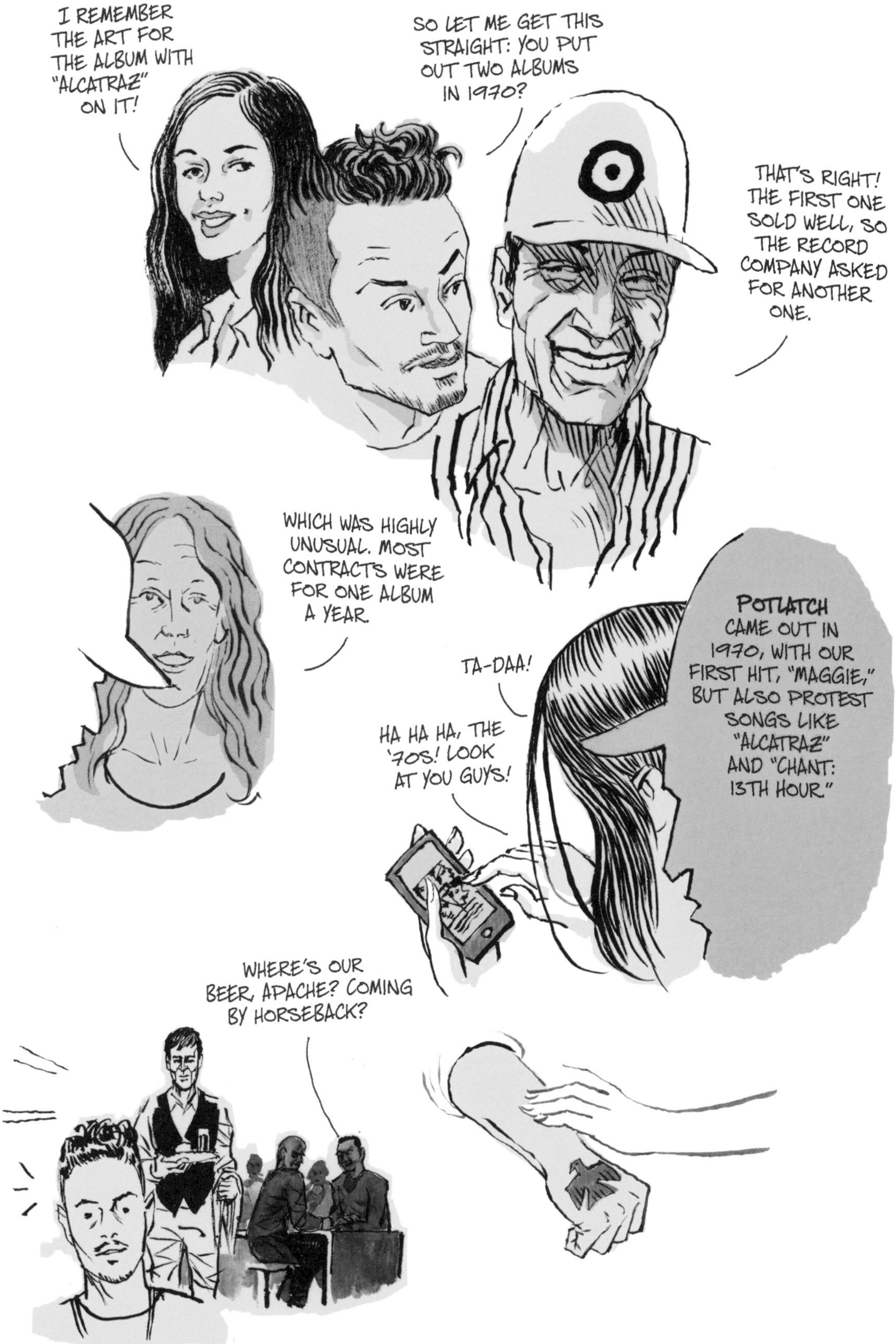
I REMEMBER THE ART FOR THE ALBUM WITH "ALCATRAZ" ON IT!
SO LET ME GET THIS STRAIGHT: YOU PUT OUT TWO ALBUMS IN 1970?
THAT'S RIGHT! THE FIRST ONE SOLD WELL, SO THE RECORD COMPANY ASKED FOR ANOTHER ONE.
WHICH WAS HIGHLY UNUSUAL. MOST CONTRACTS WERE FOR ONE ALBUM A YEAR.
POTLATCH CAME OUT IN 1970, WITH OUR FIRST HIT, "MAGGIE," BUT ALSO PROTEST SONGS LIKE "ALCATRAZ" AND "CHANT: 13TH HOUR."
TA-DAA!
HA HA HA, THE '70S! LOOK AT YOU GUYS!
WHERE'S OUR BEER, APACHE? COMING BY HORSEBACK?

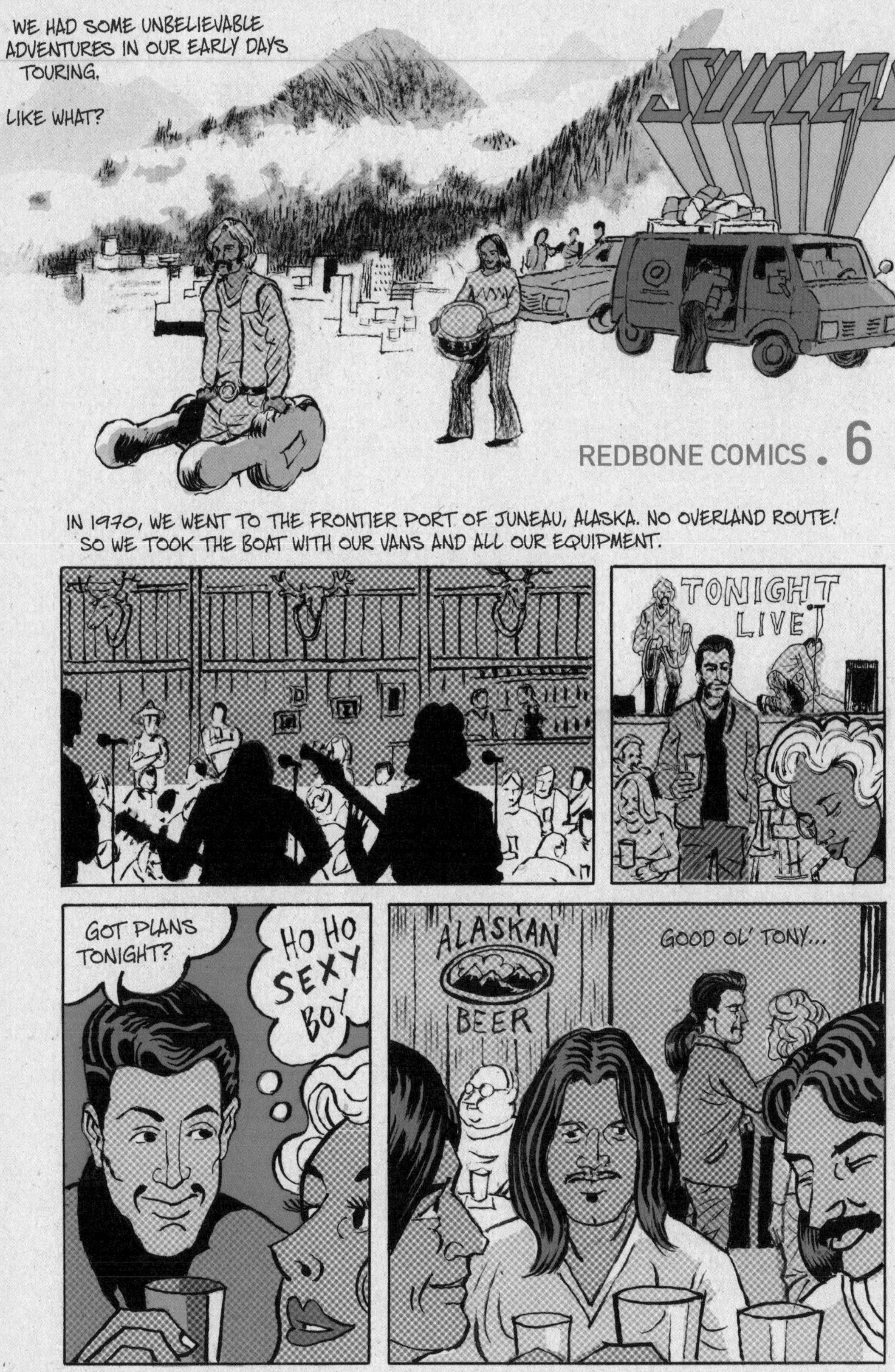
WE HAD SOME UNBELIEVABLE ADVENTURES IN OUR EARLY DAYS TOURING.
LIKE WHAT?
REDBONE COMICS . 6
IN 1970, WE WENT TO THE FRONTIER PORT OF JUNEAU, ALASKA. NO OVERLAND ROUTE! SO WE TOOK THE BOAT WITH OUR VANS AND ALL OUR EQUIPMENT.
TONIGHT LIVE
GOT PLANS TONIGHT?
HO HO SEXY BOY
ALASKAN BEER
GOOD OL' TONY...

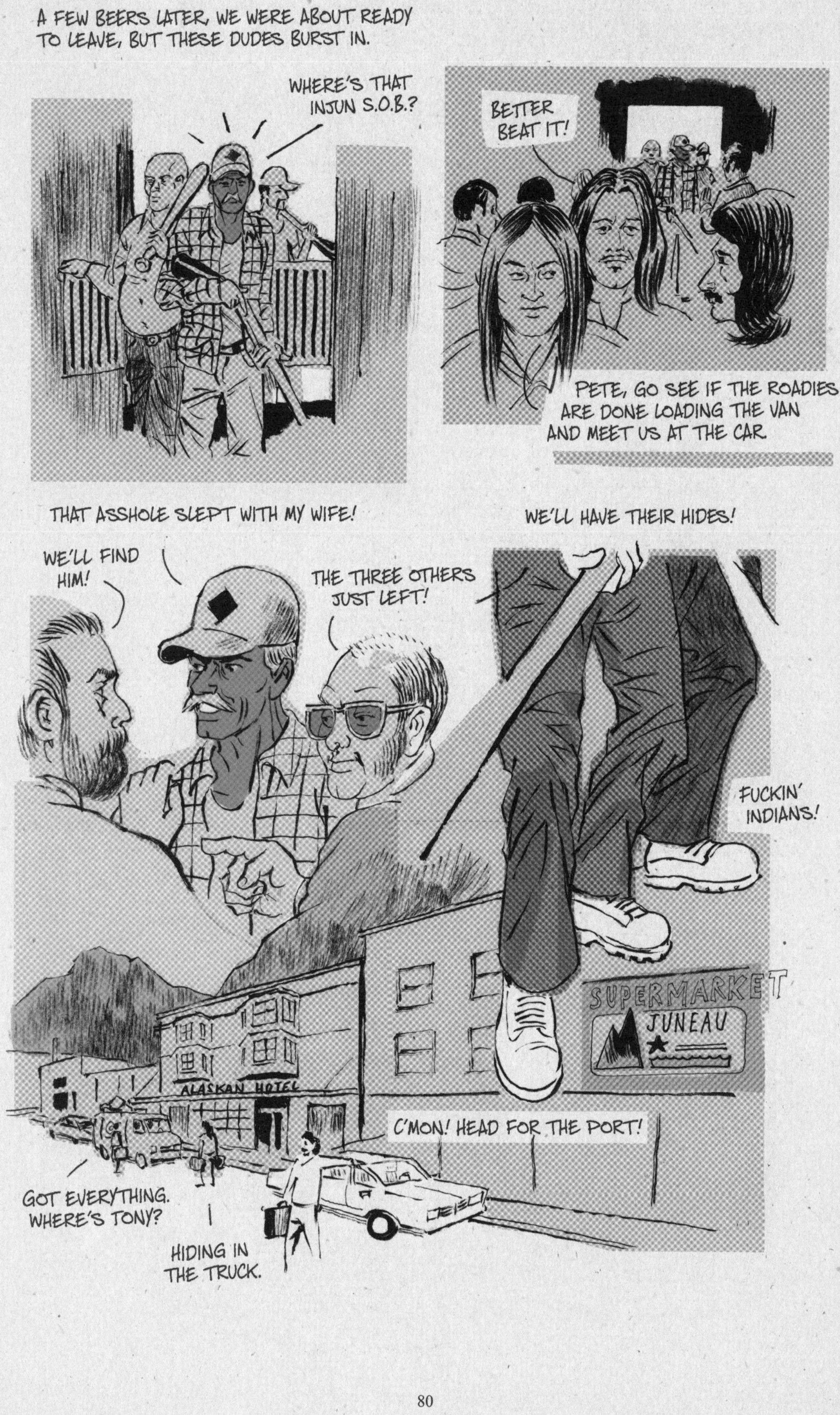
A FEW BEERS LATER, WE WERE ABOUT READY TO LEAVE, BUT THESE DUDES BURST IN.
WHERE'S THAT INJUN S.O.B.?
BETTER BEAT IT!
PETE, GO SEE IF THE ROADIES ARE DONE LOADING THE VAN AND MEET US AT THE CAR.
THAT ASSHOLE SLEPT WITH MY WIFE!
WE'LL HAVE THEIR HIDES!
WE'LL FIND HIM!
THE THREE OTHERS JUST LEFT!
FUCKIN' INDIANS!
SUPERMARKET
JUNEAU
ALASKAN HOTEL
C'MON! HEAD FOR THE PORT!
GOT EVERYTHING. WHERE'S TONY?
HIDING IN THE TRUCK.

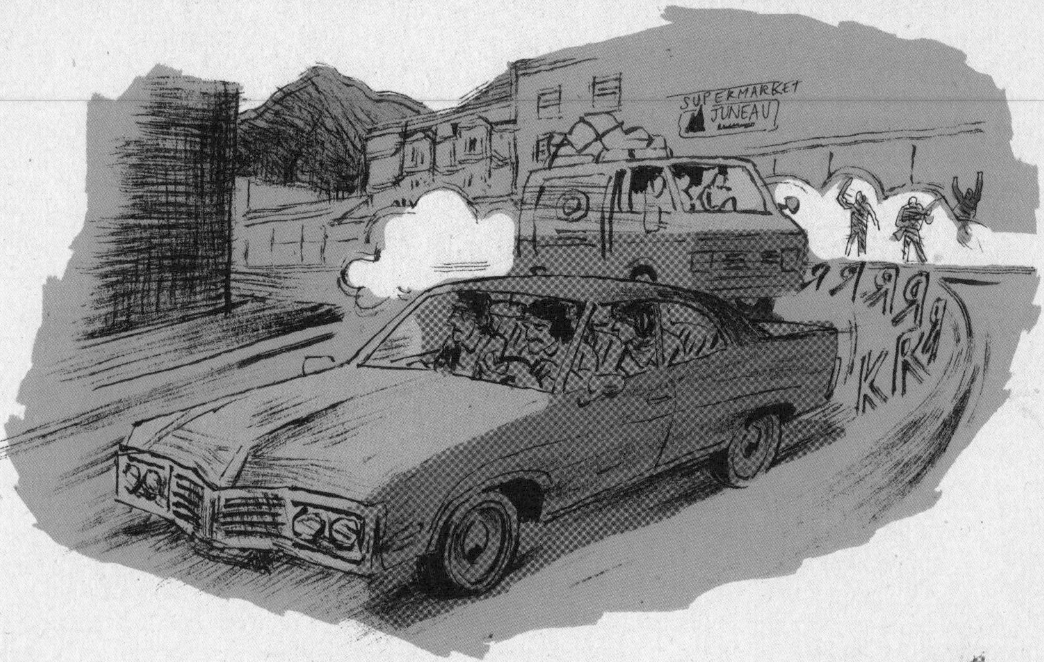
SUPERMARKET
JUNEAU

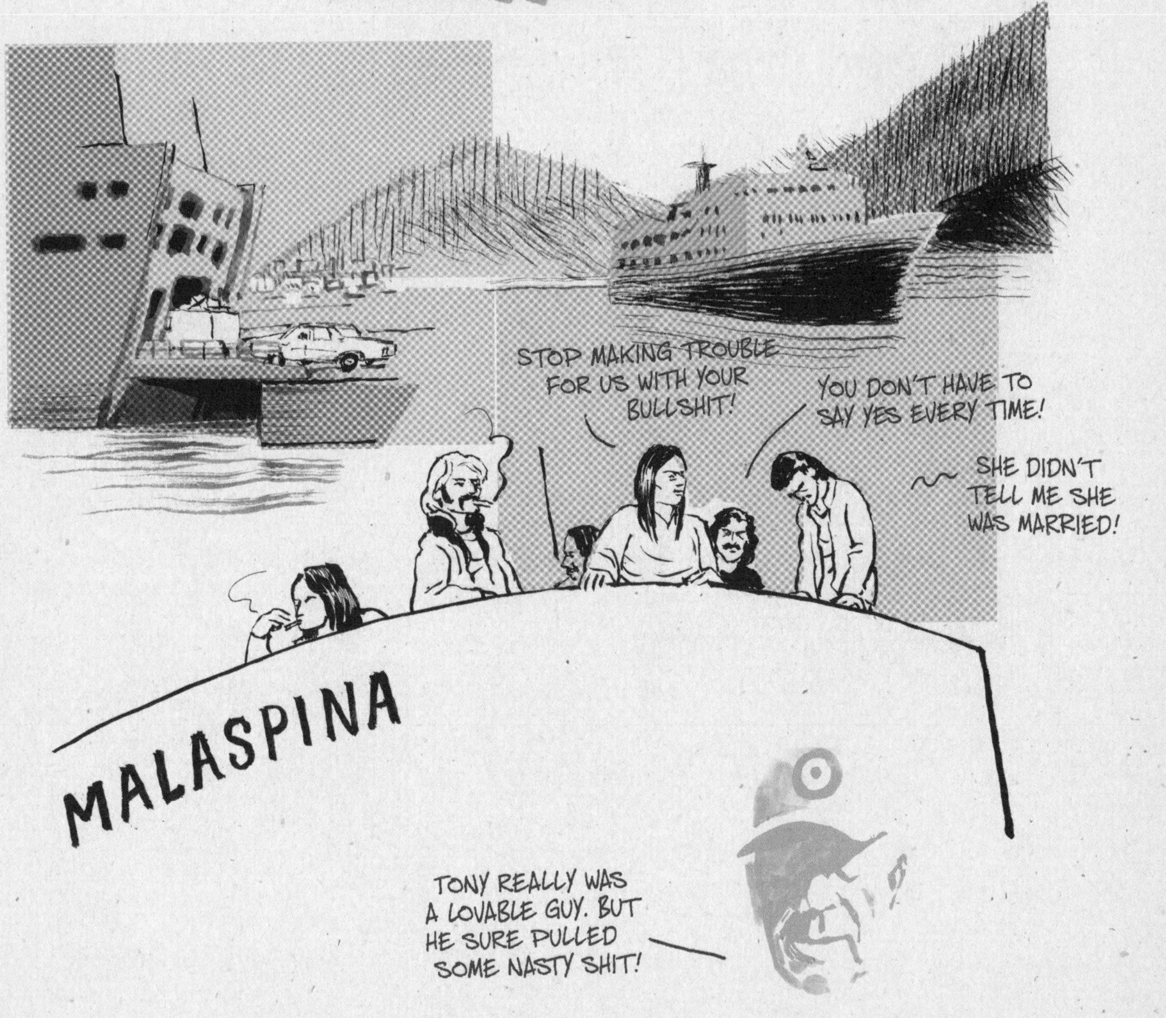
STOP MAKING TROUBLE FOR US WITH YOUR BULLSHIT!
YOU DON'T HAVE TO SAY YES EVERY TIME!
SHE DIDN'T TELL ME SHE WAS MARRIED!
MALASPINA
TONY REALLY WAS A LOVABLE GUY. BUT HE SURE PULLED SOME NASTY SHIT!

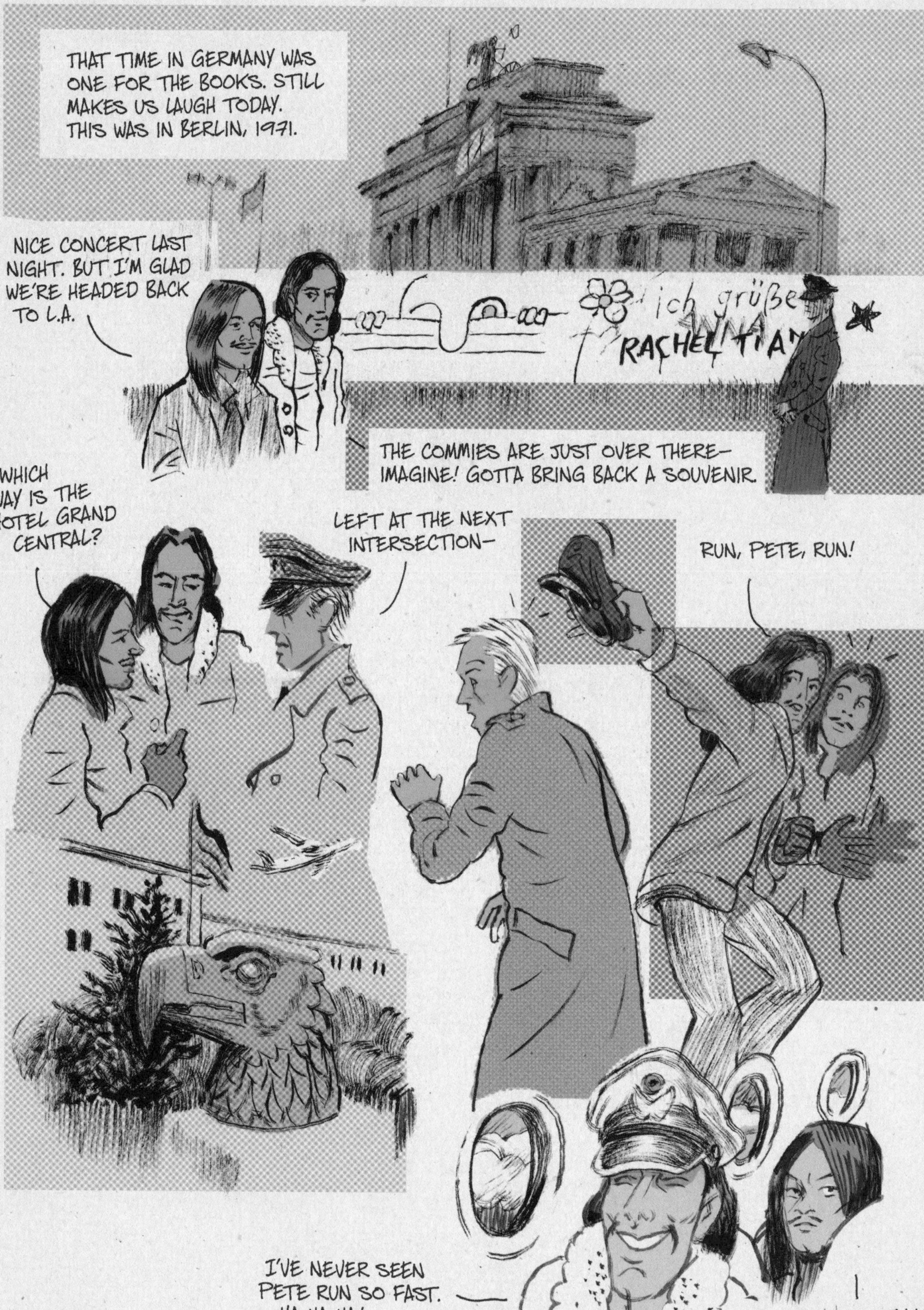
THAT TIME IN GERMANY WAS ONE FOR THE BOOKS. STILL MAKES US LAUGH TODAY. THIS WAS IN BERLIN, 1971.
NICE CONCERT LAST NIGHT. BUT I'M GLAD WE'RE HEADED BACK TO L.A.
ich grüße
THE COMMIES ARE JUST OVER THERE– IMAGINE! GOTTA BRING BACK A SOUVENIR.
WHICH WAY IS THE HOTEL GRAND CENTRAL?
LEFT AT THE NEXT INTERSECTION–
RUN, PETE, RUN!
I'VE NEVER SEEN PETE RUN SO FAST. HA HA HA!
YOU'RE TOTALLY PSYCHO. THEY COULDA JAILED US!

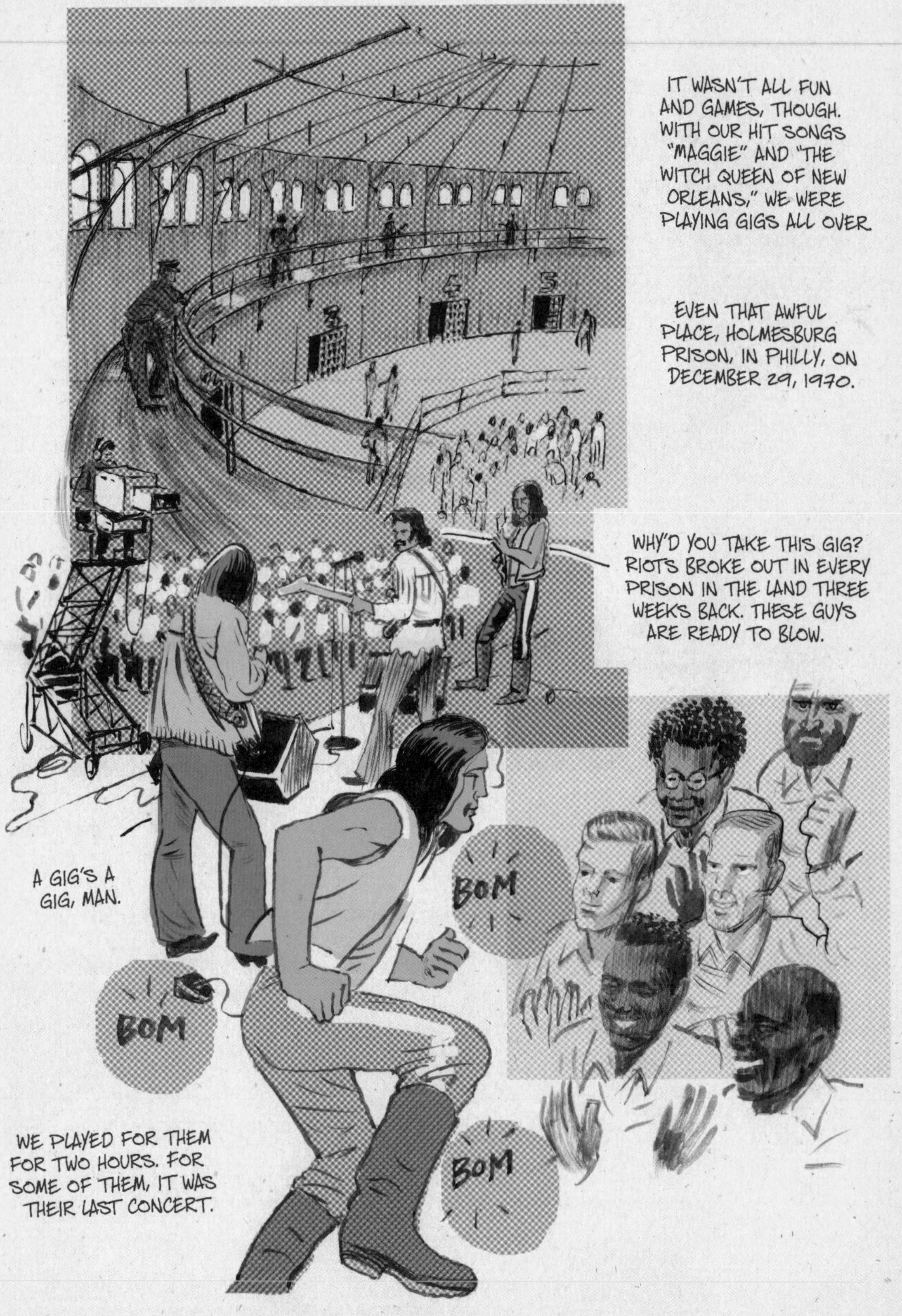
IT WASN'T ALL FUN AND GAMES, THOUGH. WITH OUR HIT SONGS "MAGGIE" AND "THE WITCH QUEEN OF NEW ORLEANS," WE WERE PLAYING GIGS ALL OVER.
EVEN THAT AWFUL PLACE, HOLMESBURG PRISON, IN PHILLY, ON DECEMBER 29, 1970.
WHY'D YOU TAKE THIS GIG? RIOTS BROKE OUT IN EVERY PRISON IN THE LAND THREE WEEKS BACK. THESE GUYS ARE READY TO BLOW.
A GIG'S A GIG, MAN.
BOM
BOM
BOM
WE PLAYED FOR THEM FOR TWO HOURS. FOR SOME OF THEM, IT WAS THEIR LAST CONCERT.

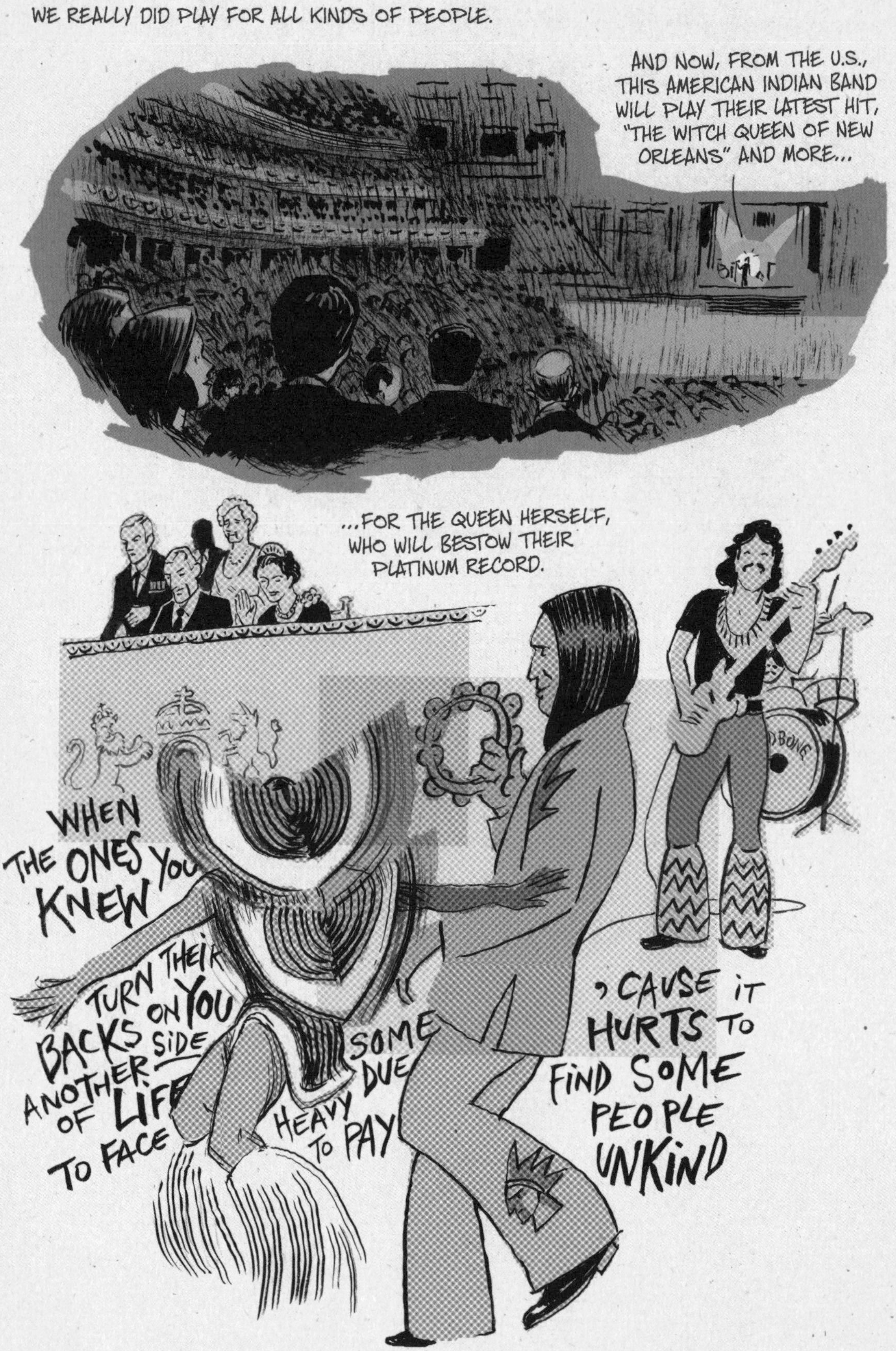
WE REALLY DID PLAY FOR ALL KINDS OF PEOPLE.
AND NOW, FROM THE U.S., THIS AMERICAN INDIAN BAND WILL PLAY THEIR LATEST HIT, "THE WITCH QUEEN OF NEW ORLEANS" AND MORE...
...FOR THE QUEEN HERSELF, WHO WILL BESTOW THEIR PLATINUM RECORD.
WHEN THE ONES YOU KNEW
TURN THEIR BACKS ON YOU
ANOTHER SIDE OF LIFE TO FACE
SOME HEAVY DUE TO PAY
'CAUSE IT HURTS TO FIND SOME PEOPLE UNKIND

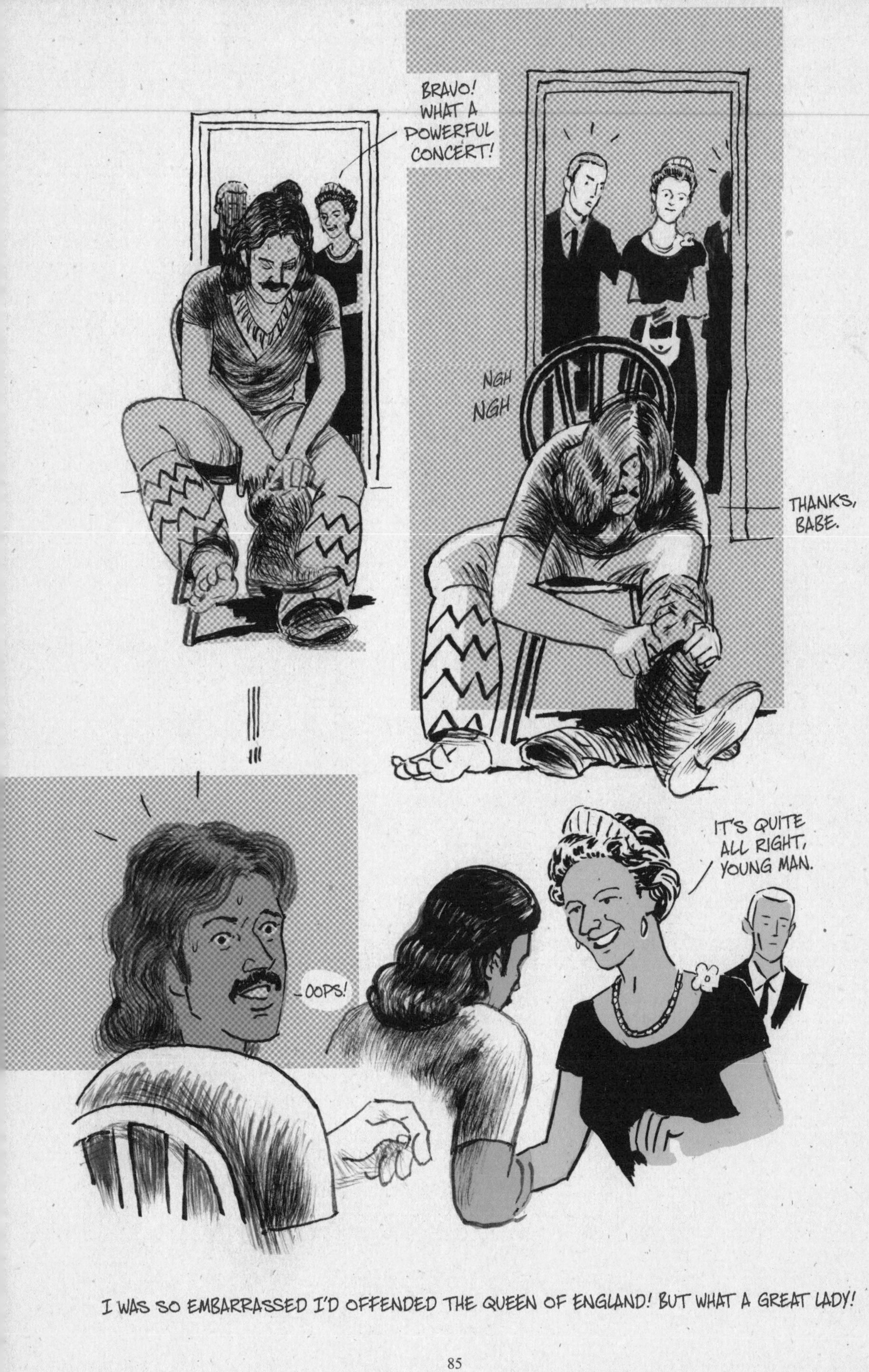
BRAVO! WHAT A POWERFUL CONCERT!
NGH NGH
THANKS, BABE.
!!!
-OOPS!
IT'S QUITE ALL RIGHT, YOUNG MAN.

I WAS SO EMBARRASSED I'D OFFENDED THE QUEEN OF ENGLAND! BUT WHAT A GREAT LADY!

WE'D PUT OUT FOUR ALBUMS IN THREE YEARS, WITH HIT AFTER HIT. IN EARLY 1973, WE HEADED BACK TO THE STUDIO FOR OUR FIFTH ALBUM: **WOVOKA.** PETE WAS AWAY LOOKING AFTER HIS AILING FATHER **ARTURO PEREZ** HAD PLAYED ON THE FOURTH ALBUM, **ALREADY HERE.** ON THE FIFTH, **BUTCH RILLERA** WOULD TAKE OVER ON DRUMS.

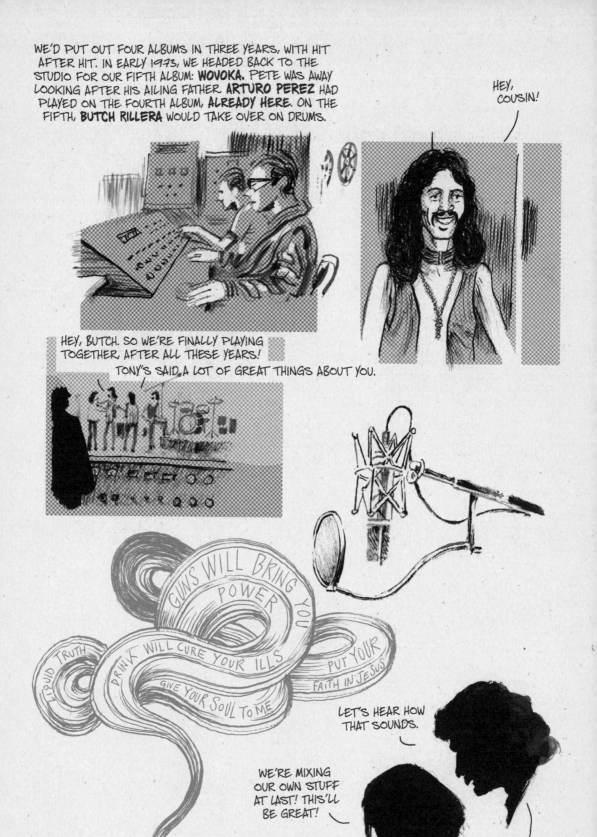

HEY, COUSIN!

HEY, BUTCH. SO WE'RE FINALLY PLAYING TOGETHER, AFTER ALL THESE YEARS! TONY'S SAID A LOT OF GREAT THINGS ABOUT YOU.

GUNS WILL BRING YOU POWER

DRINK WILL CURE YOUR ILLS

LIQUID TRUTH

GIVE YOUR SOUL TO ME

PUT YOUR FAITH IN JESUS

LET'S HEAR HOW THAT SOUNDS.

WE'RE MIXING OUR OWN STUFF AT LAST! THIS'LL BE GREAT!

SURE. BUT CONVINCING CBS TO GIVE US THE REINS WASN'T EASY.

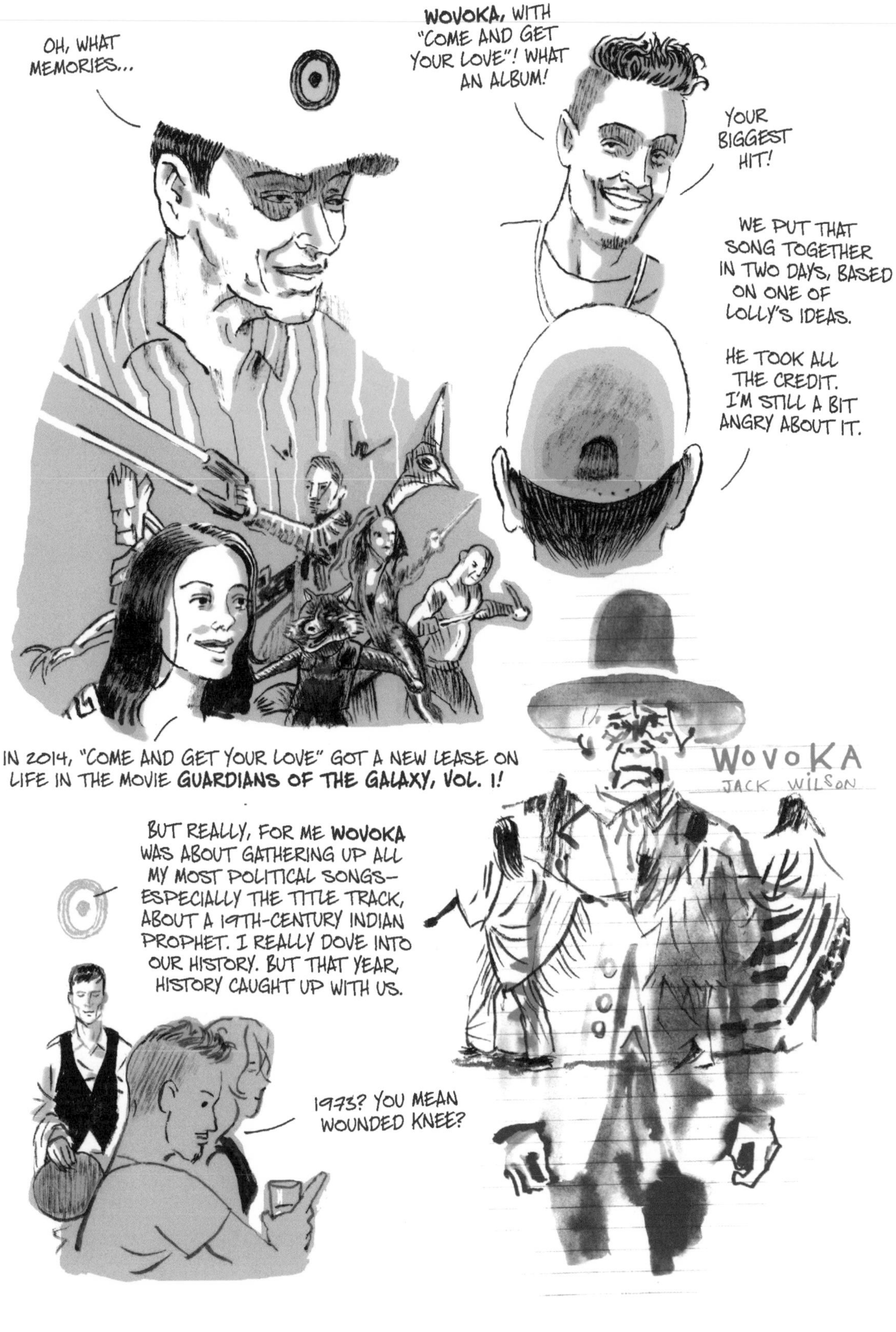

OH, WHAT MEMORIES...
WOVOKA, WITH "COME AND GET YOUR LOVE"! WHAT AN ALBUM!
YOUR BIGGEST HIT!
WE PUT THAT SONG TOGETHER IN TWO DAYS, BASED ON ONE OF LOLLY'S IDEAS.
HE TOOK ALL THE CREDIT. I'M STILL A BIT ANGRY ABOUT IT.
IN 2014, "COME AND GET YOUR LOVE" GOT A NEW LEASE ON LIFE IN THE MOVIE GUARDIANS OF THE GALAXY, VOL. 1!
WOVOKA
JACK WILSON
BUT REALLY, FOR ME WOVOKA WAS ABOUT GATHERING UP ALL MY MOST POLITICAL SONGS—ESPECIALLY THE TITLE TRACK, ABOUT A 19TH-CENTURY INDIAN PROPHET. I REALLY DOVE INTO OUR HISTORY. BUT THAT YEAR, HISTORY CAUGHT UP WITH US.
1973? YOU MEAN WOUNDED KNEE?

VII
WOUNDED KNEE
(1973)

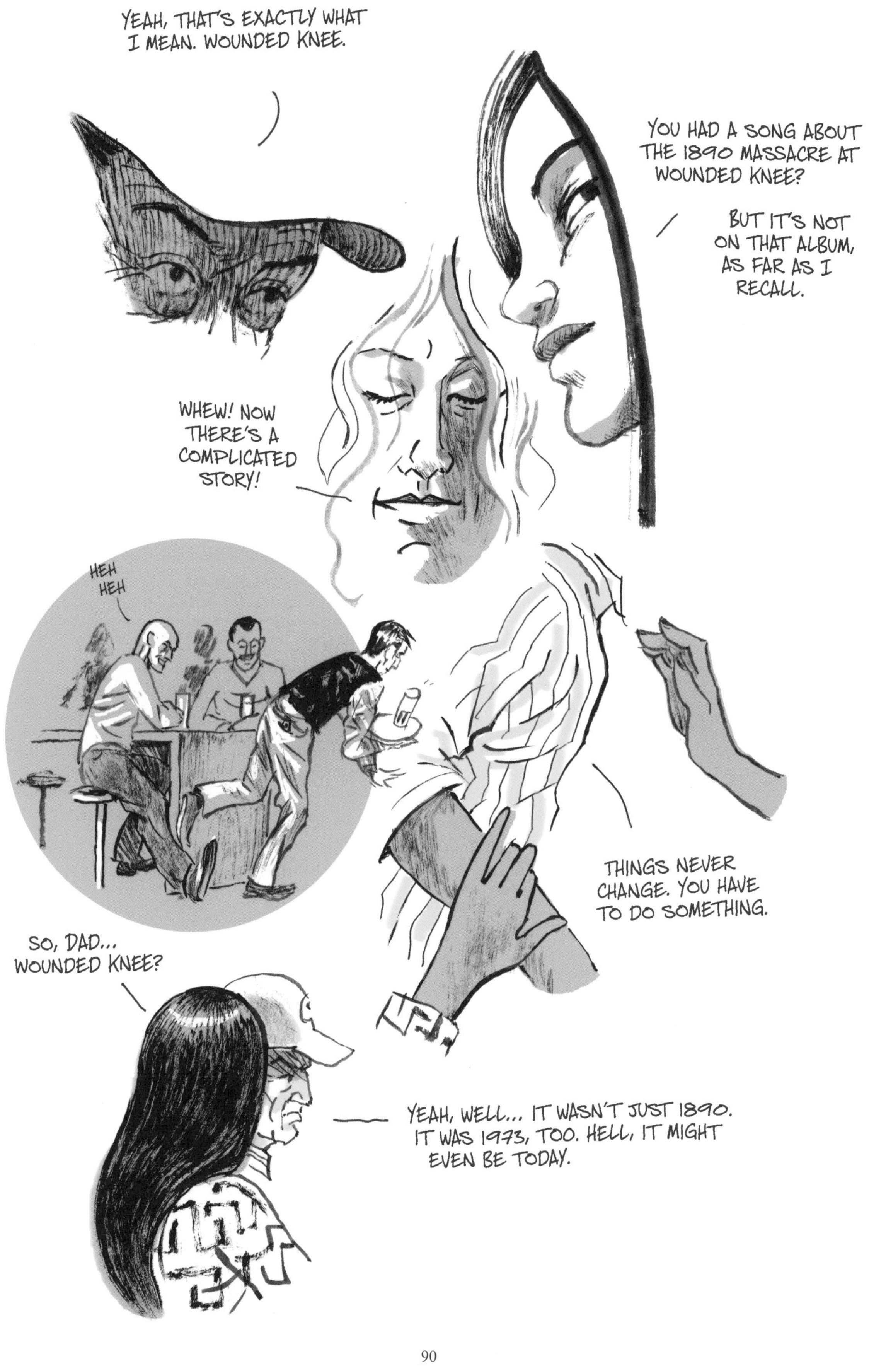
YEAH, THAT'S EXACTLY WHAT I MEAN. WOUNDED KNEE.
YOU HAD A SONG ABOUT THE 1890 MASSACRE AT WOUNDED KNEE?
BUT IT'S NOT ON THAT ALBUM, AS FAR AS I RECALL.
WHEW! NOW THERE'S A COMPLICATED STORY!
HEH HEH
THINGS NEVER CHANGE. YOU HAVE TO DO SOMETHING.
SO, DAD... WOUNDED KNEE?
YEAH, WELL... IT WASN'T JUST 1890. IT WAS 1973, TOO. HELL, IT MIGHT EVEN BE TODAY.

1890 REDBONE COMICS . 7

WOUNDED KNEE

THE GOVERNMENT ASKED THE LAKOTAS TO LAY DOWN THEIR ARMS, AND PROMISED THEY'D BE SAFE IN RETURN. THEN THE 7TH CAVALRY WIPED THEM ALL OUT. THREE HUNDRED MEN, WOMEN, AND CHILDREN WERE MURDERED. AS YOU KNOW, THIS MASS SLAUGHTER MARKED THE END OF THE INDIAN WARS.

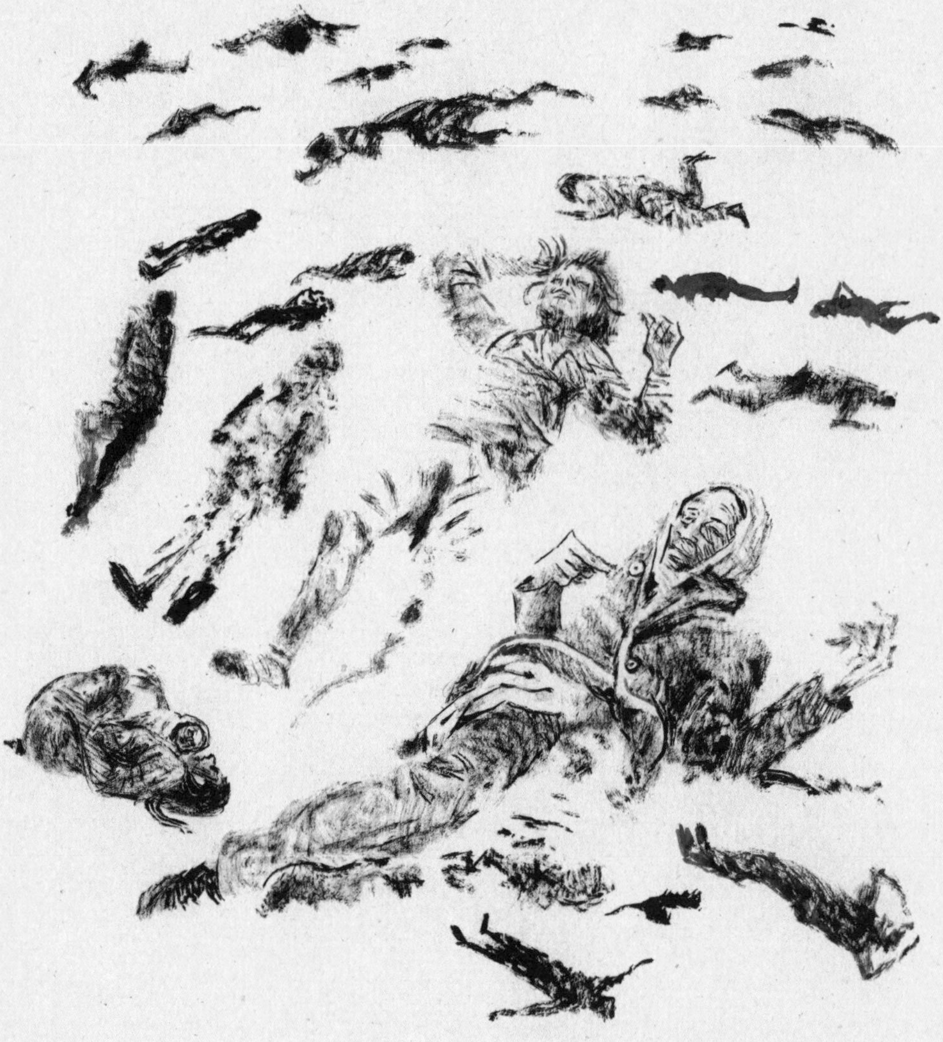

THE BATTLE OF 1973

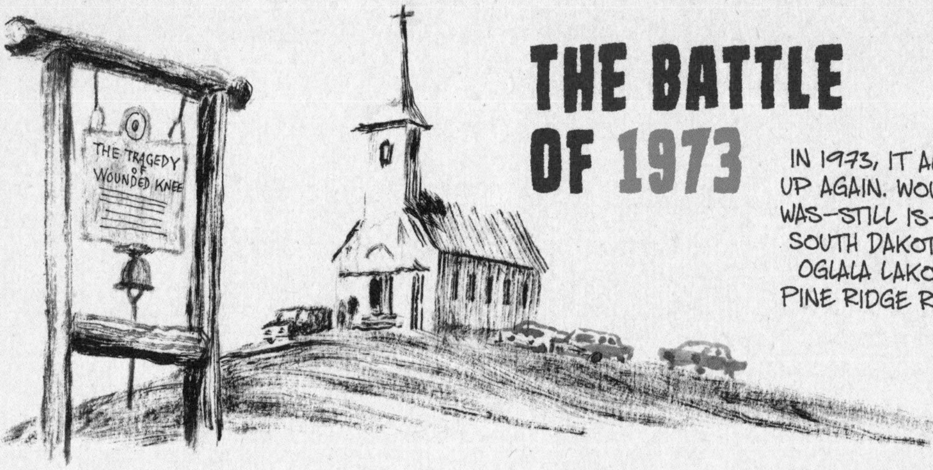
THE TRAGEDY OF WOUNDED KNEE

IN 1973, IT ALL STARTED UP AGAIN. WOUNDED KNEE WAS—STILL IS—A VERY POOR SOUTH DAKOTA VILLAGE OF OGLALA LAKOTAS ON THE PINE RIDGE RESERVATION.

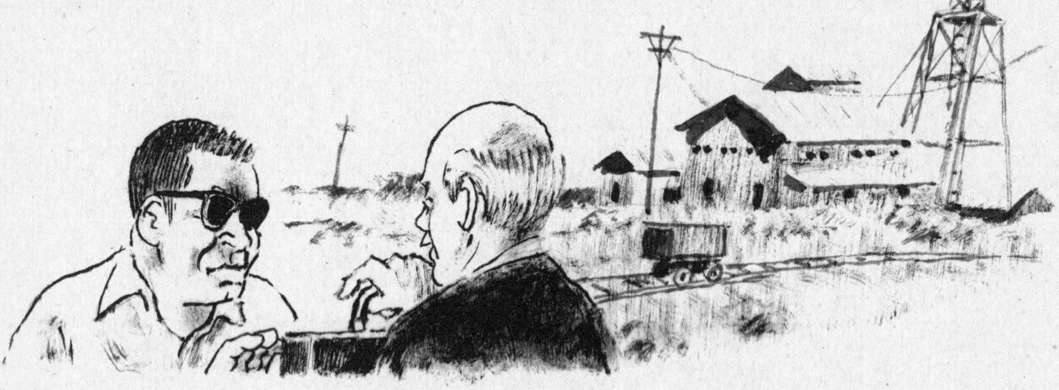

IN 1973, **DICK WILSON** WAS TRIBAL PRESIDENT AT PINE RIDGE. INSTEAD OF FIGHTING POVERTY, HE EMBEZZLED MONEY FOR HIS OWN GAIN. HE RAN THE SHOW ON THE RES, AND MADE LIFE HARD FOR EVERYONE. BRIBES, SELLING OFF TRIBAL LANDS TO MINING COMPANIES...

HE HAD HIS OWN PRIVATE MILITIA, THE GOONS*, TO ROUGH UP ANYONE WHO OPPOSED HIM. NOT THAT LIFE WAS BETTER IN THE NEARBY TOWNS. RACIST INCIDENTS WERE ON THE RISE, RAPES AND MURDERS OFTEN WENT UNPUNISHED.

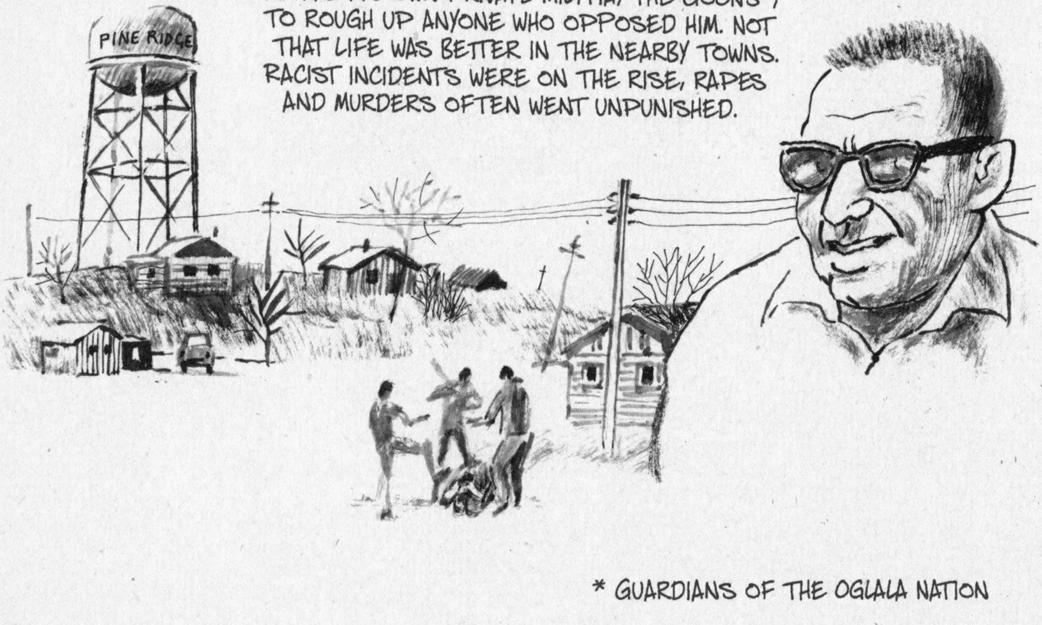
PINE RIDGE

* GUARDIANS OF THE OGLALA NATION

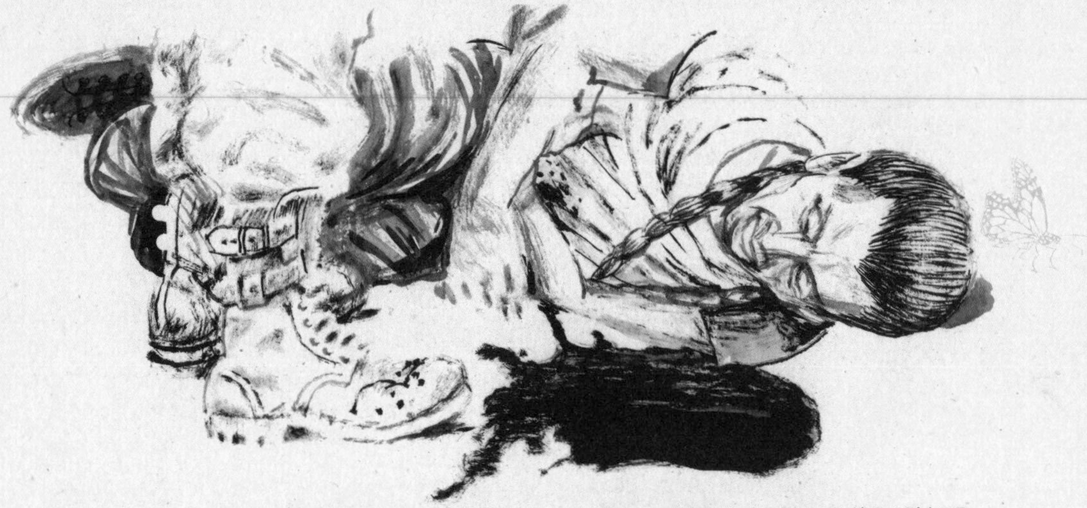

IN BUFFALO GAP, ONE HUNDRED TEN MILES FROM WOUNDED KNEE, A WHITE MAN KILLED TWENTY-YEAR-OLD OGLALA **WESLEY BAD HEART BULL.** THE MURDERER WAS CHARGED WITH "INVOLUNTARY MANSLAUGHTER" BY A RACIST AND PARTISAN COURT.

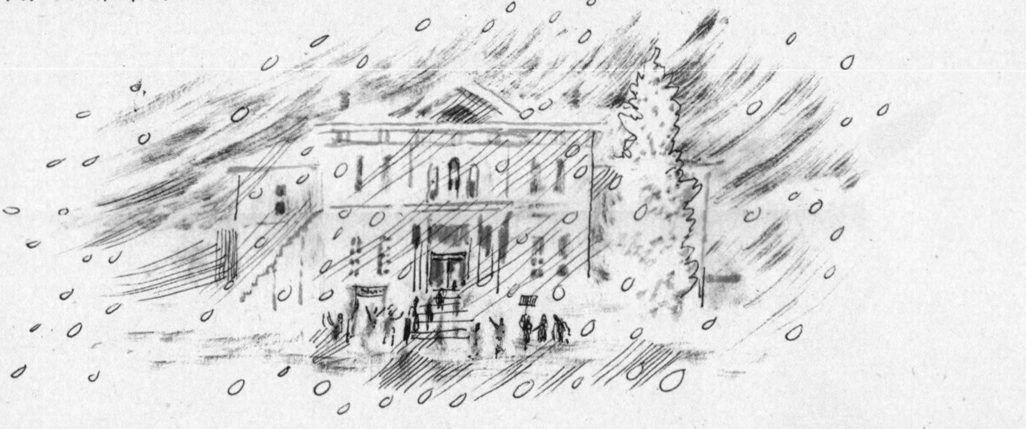

FOUR AIM REPRESENTATIVES MET WITH THE JUDGE IN CUSTER. TWO HUNDRED PROTESTERS WERE WAITING OUTSIDE. A POLICEMAN KEPT WESLEY'S MOTHER FROM GOING INSIDE BY HITTING HER

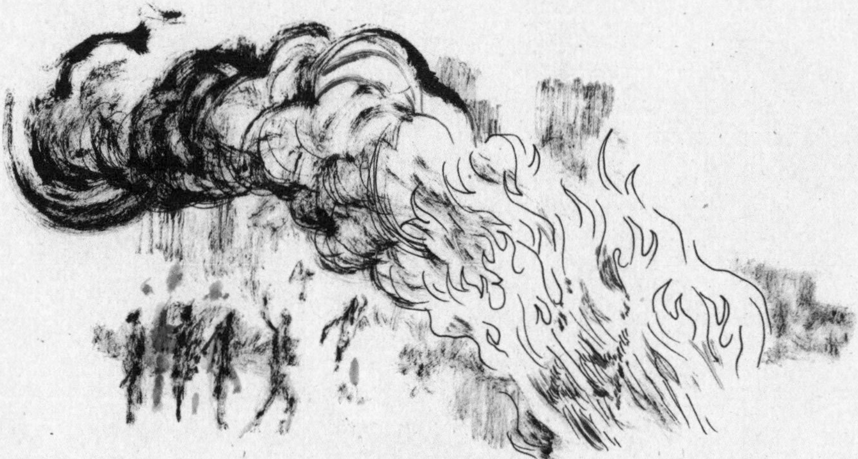

THAT'S ALL IT TOOK TO START A RIOT. THIRTY PEOPLE WERE ARRESTED BY NINETY POLICE OFFICERS SPOILING FOR A FIGHT. NATURALLY, TENSIONS MOUNTED AFTER THAT. PEOPLE ON THE RESERVATION HAD HAD ENOUGH.

THE TRIBAL COUNCIL AT PINE RIDGE DEMANDED WILSON'S IMPEACHMENT, BUT THE GOVERNMENT INTERVENED. HIS ABUSES OF POWER ONLY GOT WORSE, AND HE WAS NEVER SEEN WITHOUT HIS GOONS. TO TOP IT ALL OFF, HE ASKED FOR, AND RECEIVED, THE PROTECTION OF THE U.S. MARSHALS.

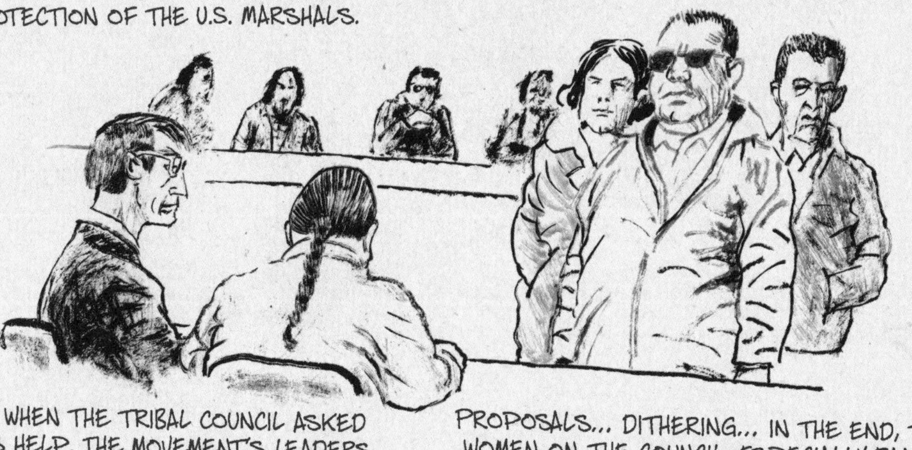

THAT WAS WHEN THE TRIBAL COUNCIL ASKED FOR AIM'S HELP. THE MOVEMENT'S LEADERS, MY FRIENDS RUSSELL MEANS AND DENNIS BANKS, WERE PRESENT. NEGOTIATIONS BOGGED DOWN.

PROPOSALS... DITHERING... IN THE END, THE WOMEN ON THE COUNCIL, ESPECIALLY **ELLEN MOVES CAMP,** CALLED FOR ACTION. RATHER THAN GO TO PINE RIDGE, WHERE THEIR ENEMIES WERE WAITING, THEY WOULD OCCUPY WOUNDED KNEE, A SYMBOL OF INJUSTICE TO INDIANS.

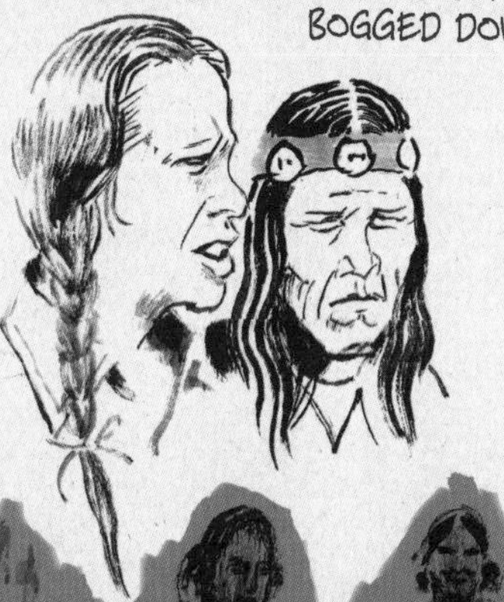

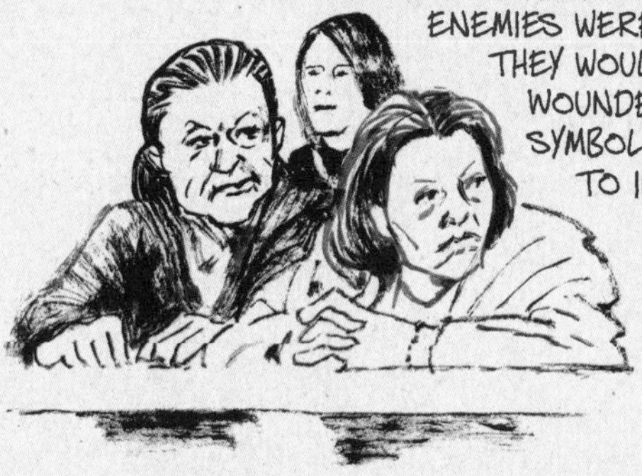

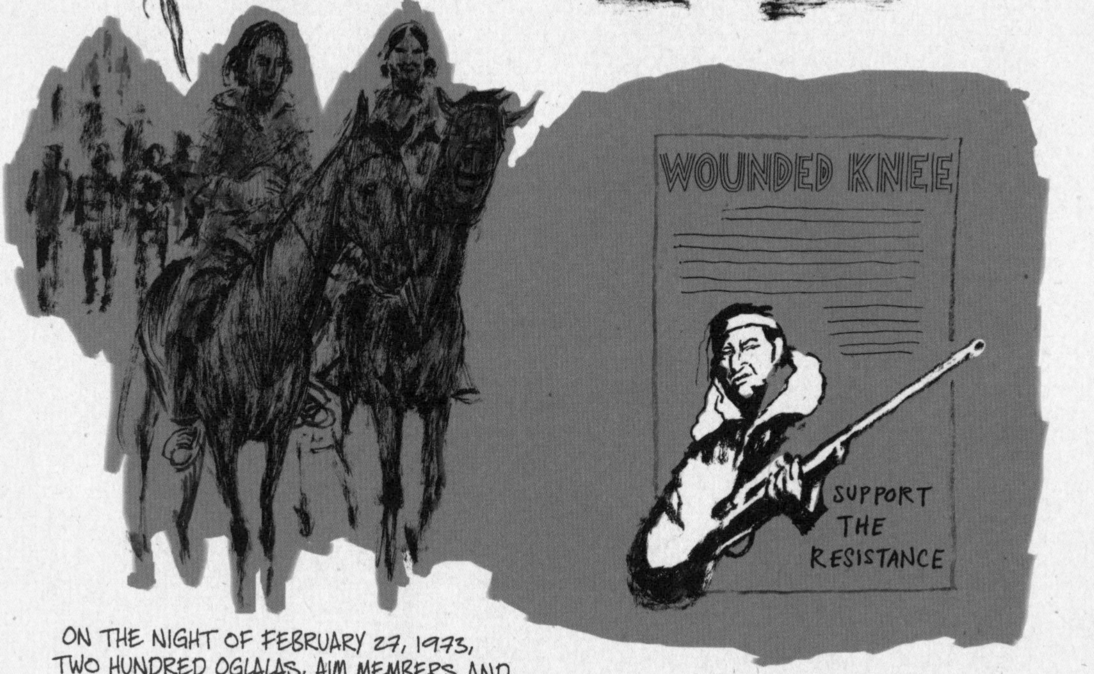
WOUNDED KNEE
SUPPORT THE RESISTANCE

ON THE NIGHT OF FEBRUARY 27, 1973, TWO HUNDRED OGLALAS, AIM MEMBERS AND THEIR SUPPORTERS FROM ALL OVER SHOWED UP IN CARS, ON FOOT, AND ON HORSEBACK AT THIS SITE OF INDIAN OPPRESSION.

WOUNDED KNEE WAS OCCUPIED. THE SIEGE BEGAN.

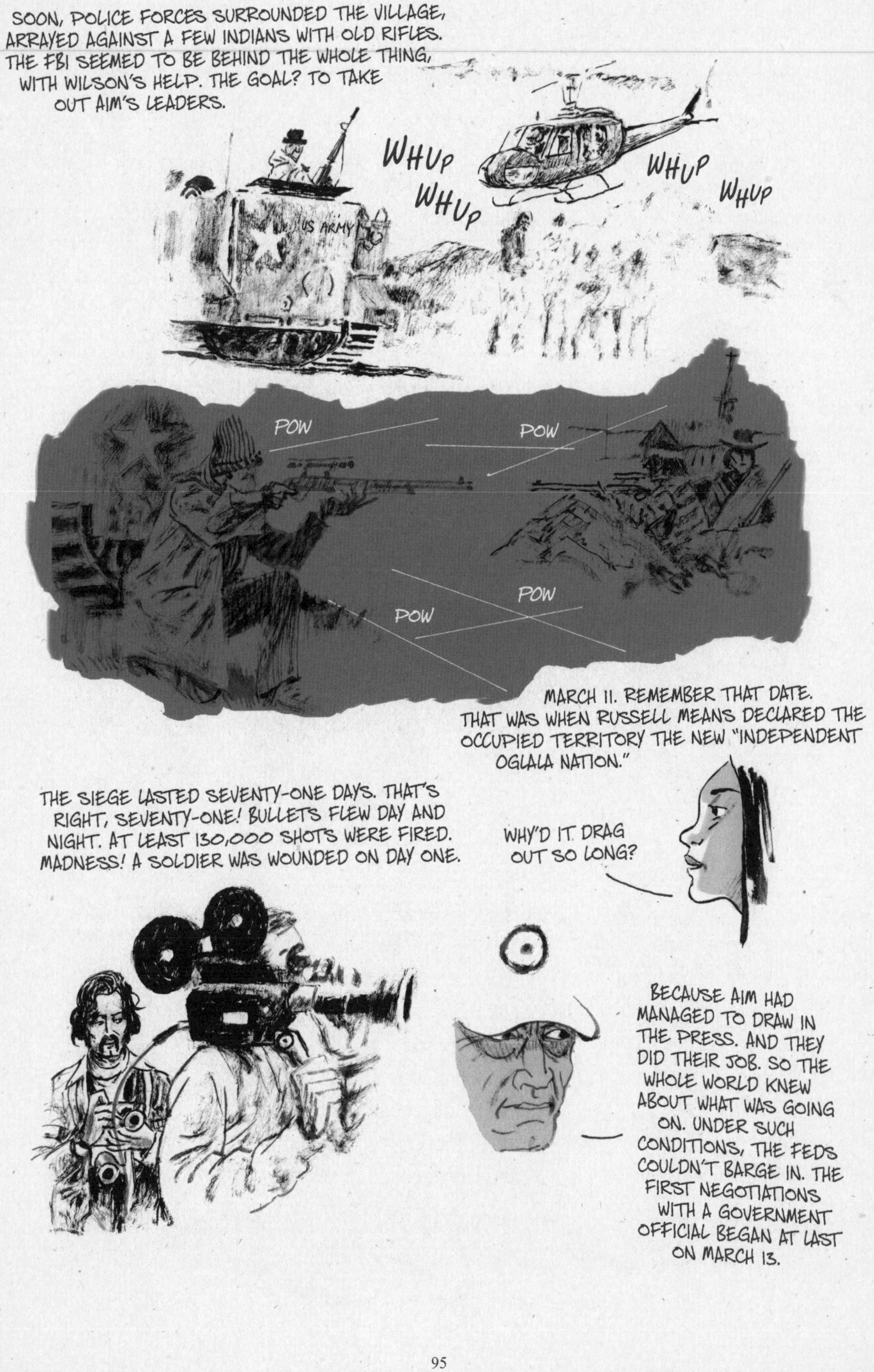
SOON, POLICE FORCES SURROUNDED THE VILLAGE, ARRAYED AGAINST A FEW INDIANS WITH OLD RIFLES. THE FBI SEEMED TO BE BEHIND THE WHOLE THING, WITH WILSON'S HELP. THE GOAL? TO TAKE OUT AIM'S LEADERS.
US ARMY
WHUP
WHUP
WHUP
WHUP
POW
POW
POW
POW
MARCH 11. REMEMBER THAT DATE. THAT WAS WHEN RUSSELL MEANS DECLARED THE OCCUPIED TERRITORY THE NEW "INDEPENDENT OGLALA NATION."
THE SIEGE LASTED SEVENTY-ONE DAYS. THAT'S RIGHT, SEVENTY-ONE! BULLETS FLEW DAY AND NIGHT. AT LEAST 130,000 SHOTS WERE FIRED. MADNESS! A SOLDIER WAS WOUNDED ON DAY ONE.
WHY'D IT DRAG OUT SO LONG?
BECAUSE AIM HAD MANAGED TO DRAW IN THE PRESS. AND THEY DID THEIR JOB. SO THE WHOLE WORLD KNEW ABOUT WHAT WAS GOING ON. UNDER SUCH CONDITIONS, THE FEDS COULDN'T BARGE IN. THE FIRST NEGOTIATIONS WITH A GOVERNMENT OFFICIAL BEGAN AT LAST ON MARCH 13.

DESPITE THIS INITIAL CONTACT, IT REALLY WAS A WAR. IT WAS WINTER. THE FEDS HAD BLOCKADED EVERYTHING, CUT OFF ELECTRICITY. GETTING SUPPLIES BECAME DIFFICULT. THE PRESS WERE KEPT BACK.

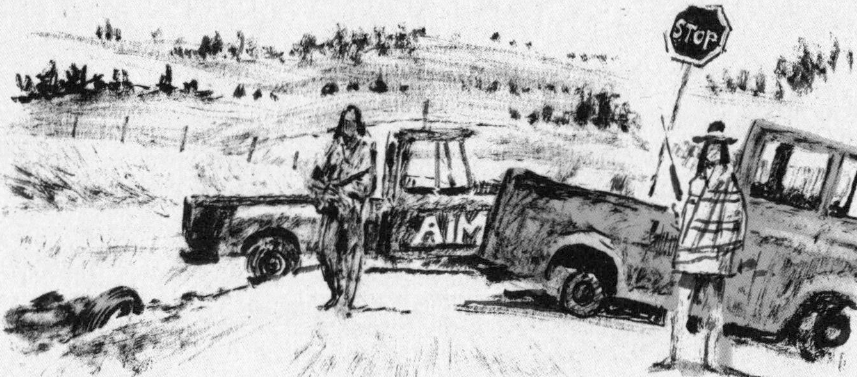
STOP
AIM

AND PUBLIC OPINION?

THAT PLAYED AN IMPORTANT ROLE. MANY CELEBRITIES SPOKE OUT FOR AIM.

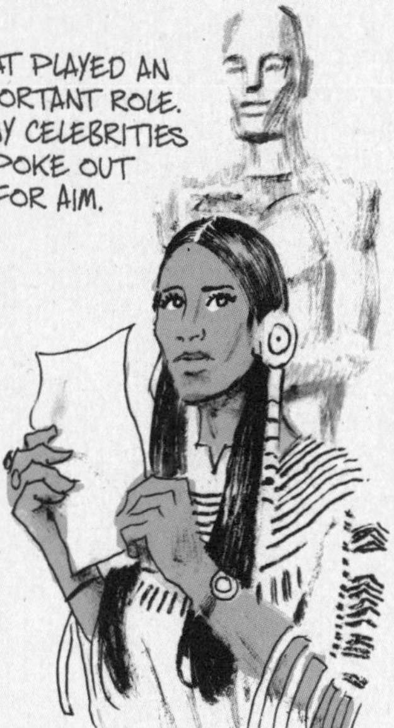

IN MARCH 1973, MARLON BRANDO WON AN OSCAR FOR **THE GODFATHER,** BUT HE SENT ACTRESS **SACHEEN LITTLEFEATHER** TO REFUSE IT FOR HIM, AND TO SPEAK FOR THE LAKOTAS INSTEAD.

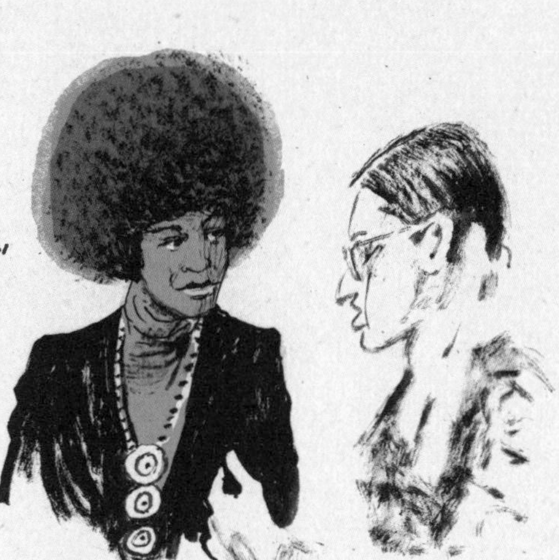

HE WASN'T ALONE. **JANE FONDA** AND **JOHNNY CASH,** AMONG OTHERS, ALSO MADE STATEMENTS. **ANGELA DAVIS** VISITED THE SCENE TO SEE THE REBELS. BUT THE FEDS TURNED HER BACK AS AN "UNDESIRABLE."

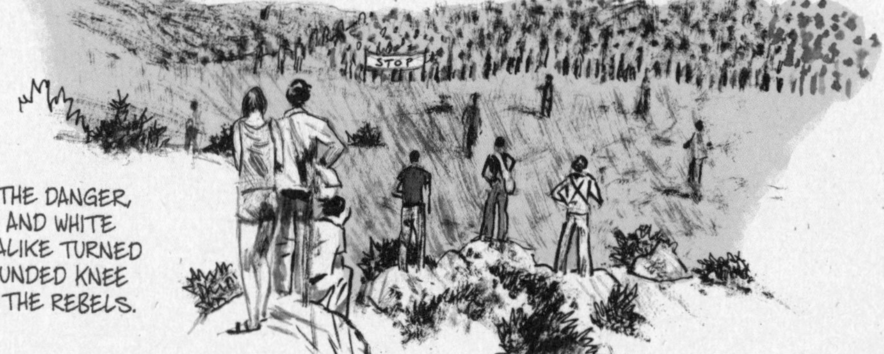
STOP

BRAVING THE DANGER, INDIANS AND WHITE PEOPLE ALIKE TURNED UP AT WOUNDED KNEE TO BACK THE REBELS.

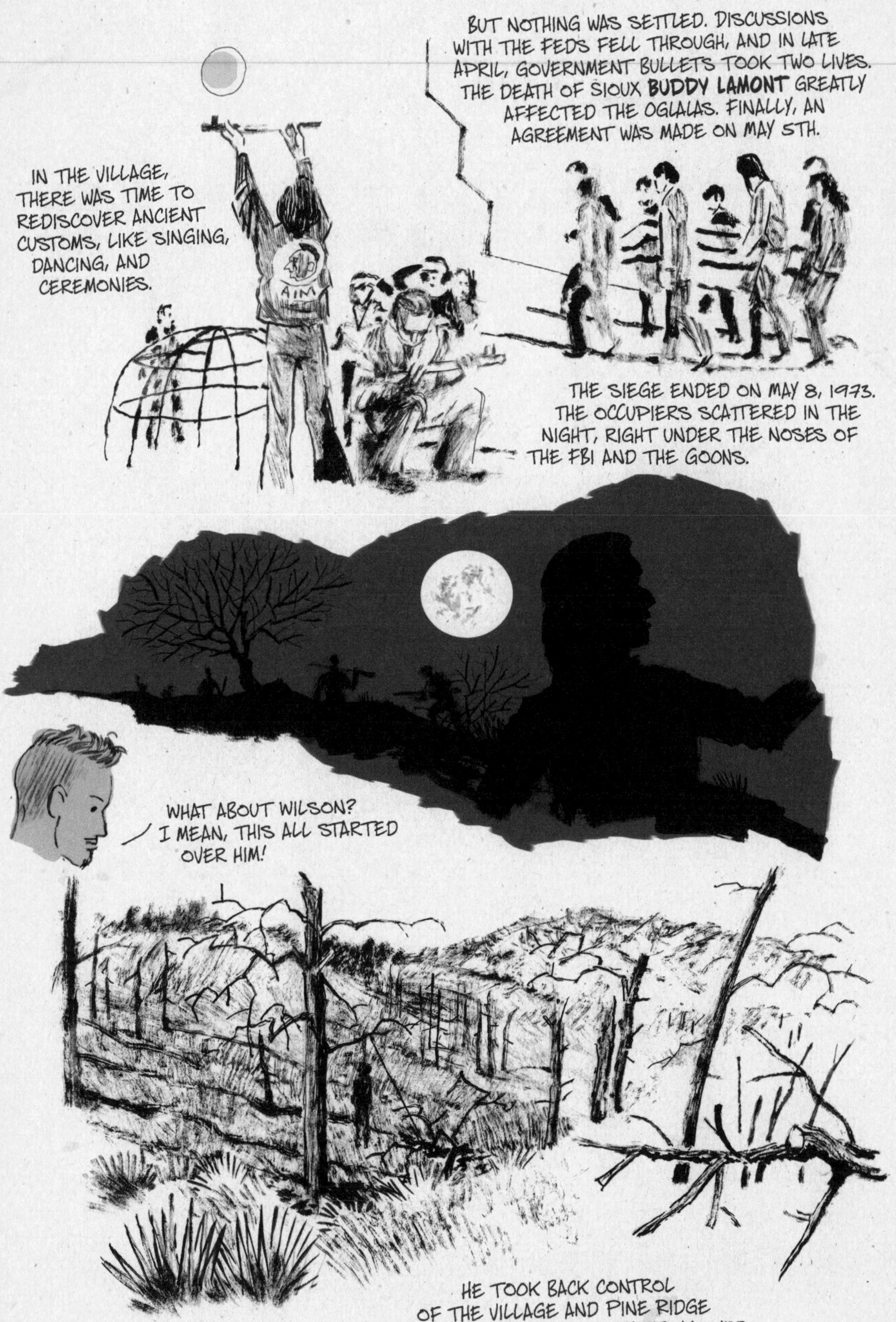
IN THE VILLAGE, THERE WAS TIME TO REDISCOVER ANCIENT CUSTOMS, LIKE SINGING, DANCING, AND CEREMONIES.
AIM
BUT NOTHING WAS SETTLED. DISCUSSIONS WITH THE FEDS FELL THROUGH, AND IN LATE APRIL, GOVERNMENT BULLETS TOOK TWO LIVES. THE DEATH OF SIOUX **BUDDY LAMONT** GREATLY AFFECTED THE OGLALAS. FINALLY, AN AGREEMENT WAS MADE ON MAY 5TH.
THE SIEGE ENDED ON MAY 8, 1973. THE OCCUPIERS SCATTERED IN THE NIGHT, RIGHT UNDER THE NOSES OF THE FBI AND THE GOONS.
WHAT ABOUT WILSON? I MEAN, THIS ALL STARTED OVER HIM!
HE TOOK BACK CONTROL OF THE VILLAGE AND PINE RIDGE RESERVATION. IN THE YEARS THAT FOLLOWED, MORE THAN FIFTY OF HIS OPPONENTS DISAPPEARED. HE NEVER HAD ANY MORE TROUBLES.

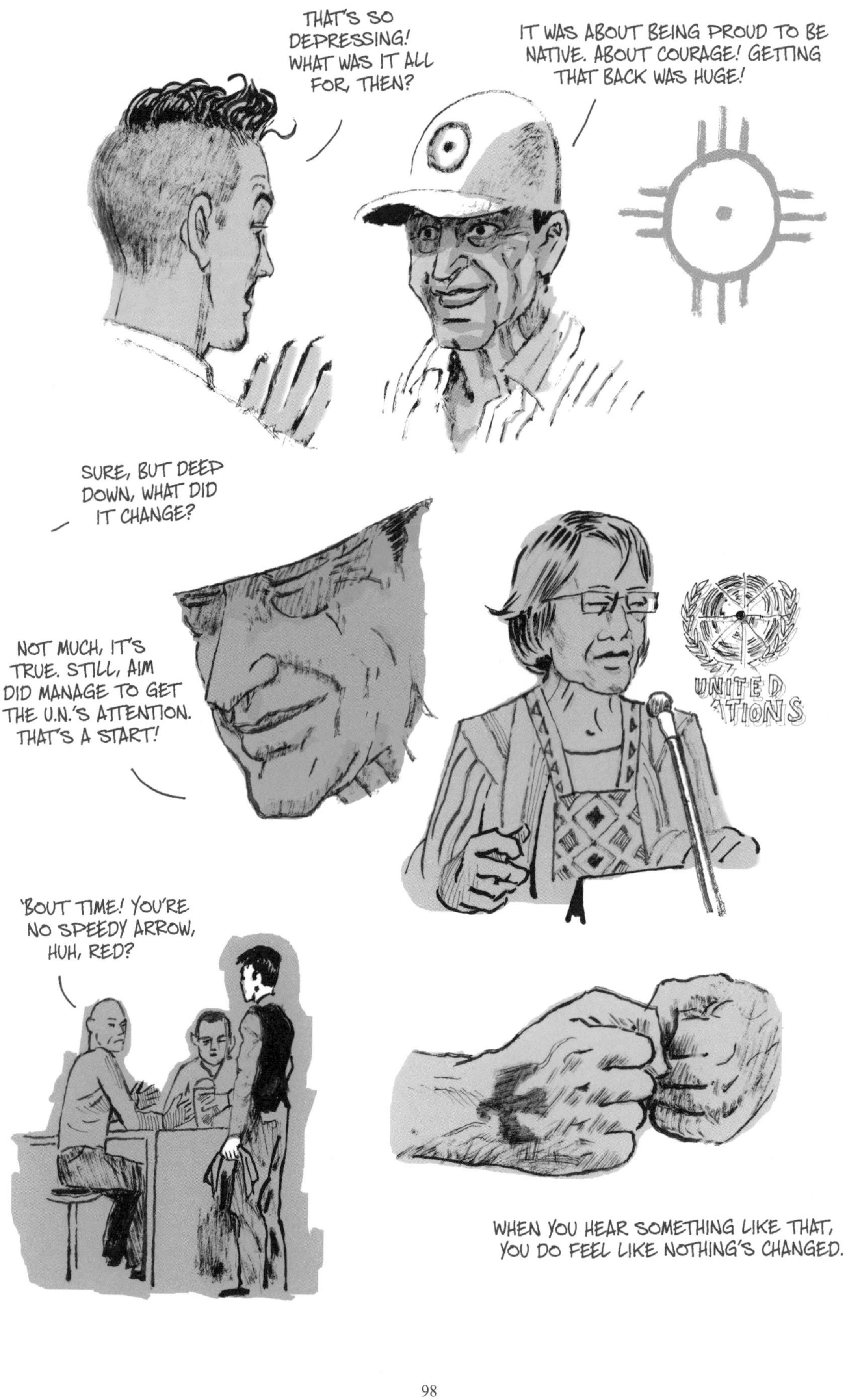
THAT'S SO DEPRESSING! WHAT WAS IT ALL FOR, THEN?
IT WAS ABOUT BEING PROUD TO BE NATIVE. ABOUT COURAGE! GETTING THAT BACK WAS HUGE!
SURE, BUT DEEP DOWN, WHAT DID IT CHANGE?
NOT MUCH, IT'S TRUE. STILL, AIM DID MANAGE TO GET THE U.N.'S ATTENTION. THAT'S A START!
UNITED NATIONS
'BOUT TIME! YOU'RE NO SPEEDY ARROW, HUH, RED?
WHEN YOU HEAR SOMETHING LIKE THAT, YOU DO FEEL LIKE NOTHING'S CHANGED.

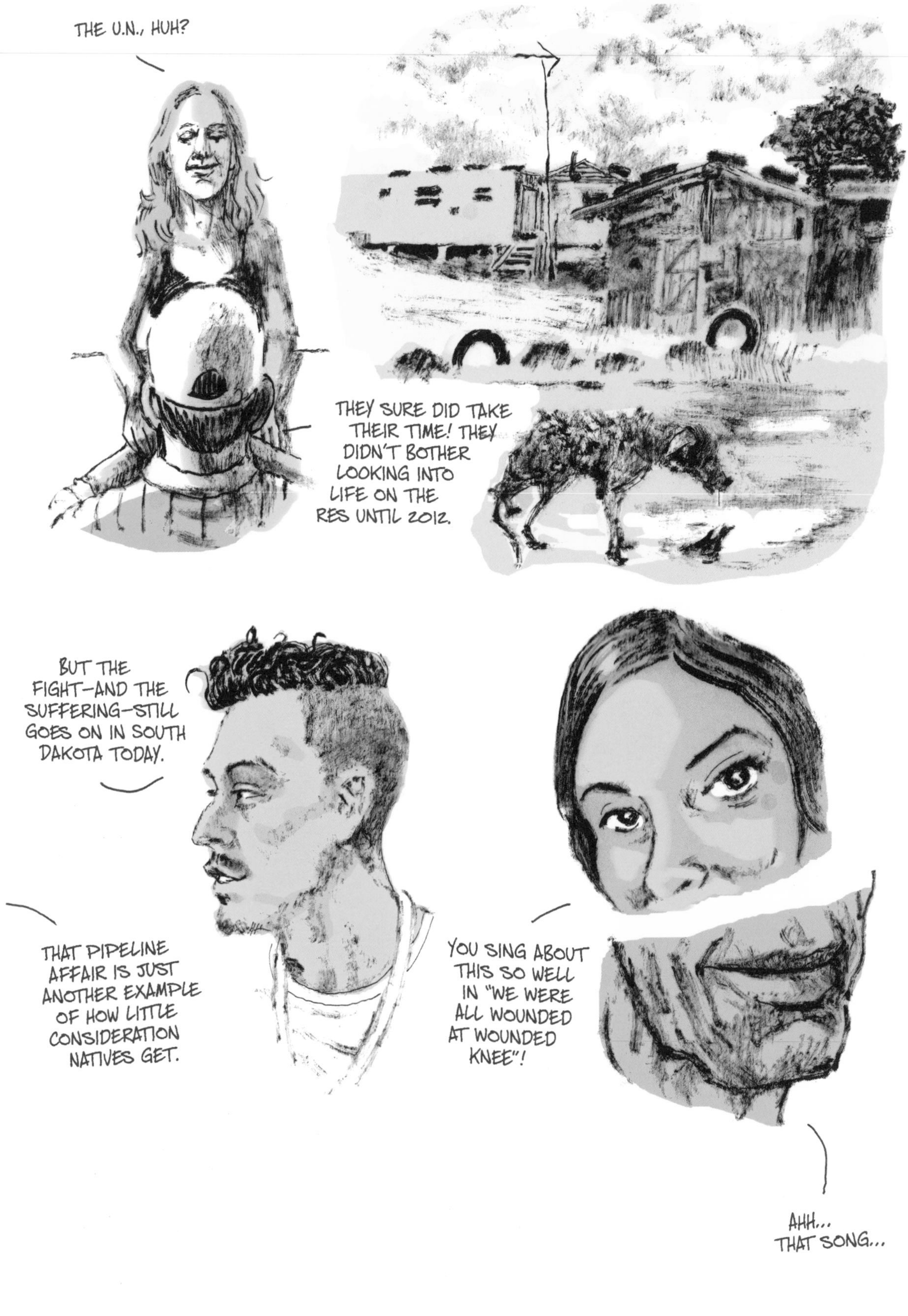
THE U.N., HUH?
THEY SURE DID TAKE THEIR TIME! THEY DIDN'T BOTHER LOOKING INTO LIFE ON THE RES UNTIL 2012.
BUT THE FIGHT—AND THE SUFFERING—STILL GOES ON IN SOUTH DAKOTA TODAY.
THAT PIPELINE AFFAIR IS JUST ANOTHER EXAMPLE OF HOW LITTLE CONSIDERATION NATIVES GET.
YOU SING ABOUT THIS SO WELL IN "WE WERE ALL WOUNDED AT WOUNDED KNEE"!
AHH... THAT SONG...

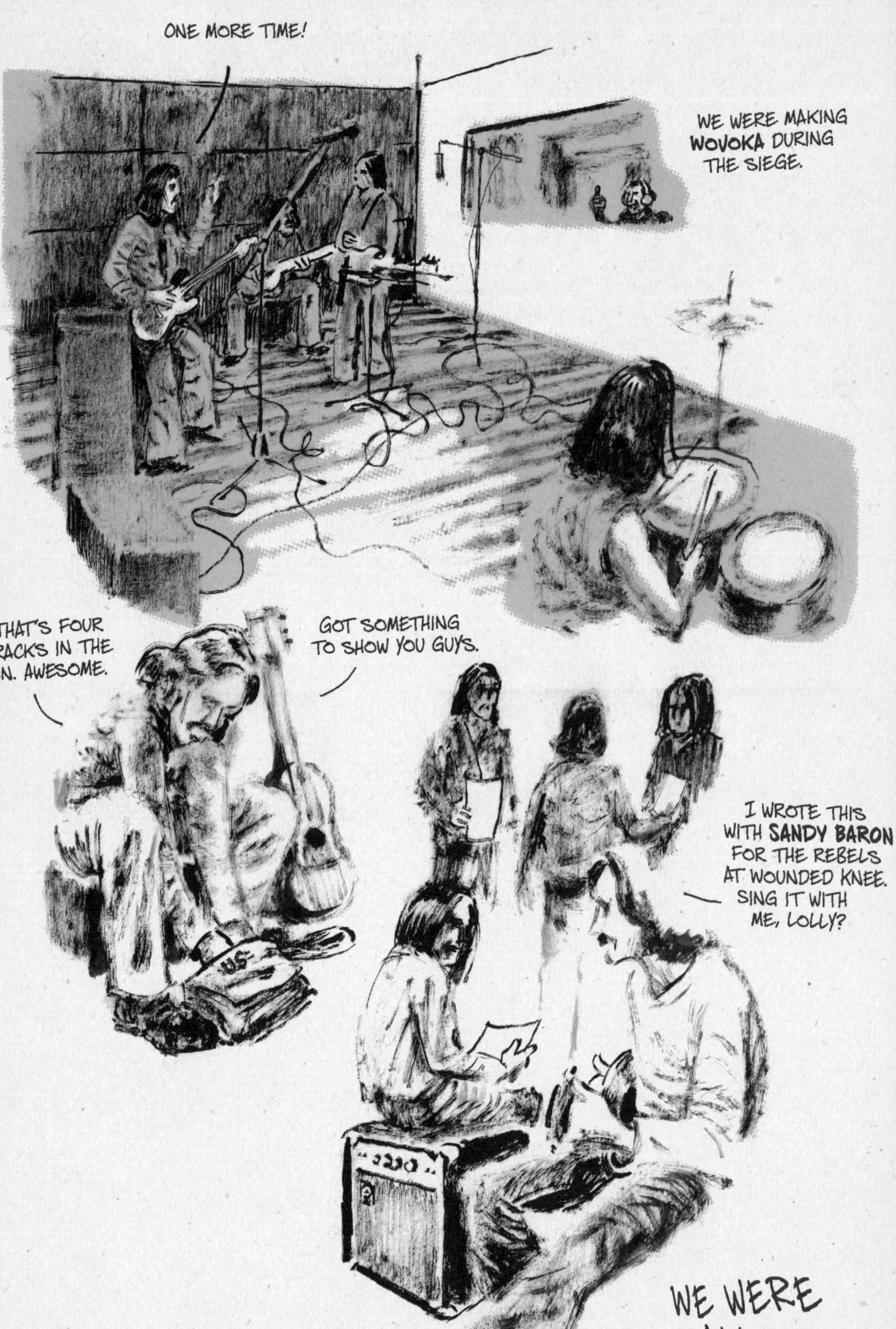
ONE MORE TIME!
WE WERE MAKING **WOVOKA** DURING THE SIEGE.
THAT'S FOUR TRACKS IN THE CAN. AWESOME.
GOT SOMETHING TO SHOW YOU GUYS.
I WROTE THIS WITH **SANDY BARON** FOR THE REBELS AT WOUNDED KNEE. SING IT WITH ME, LOLLY?
WE WERE ALL...

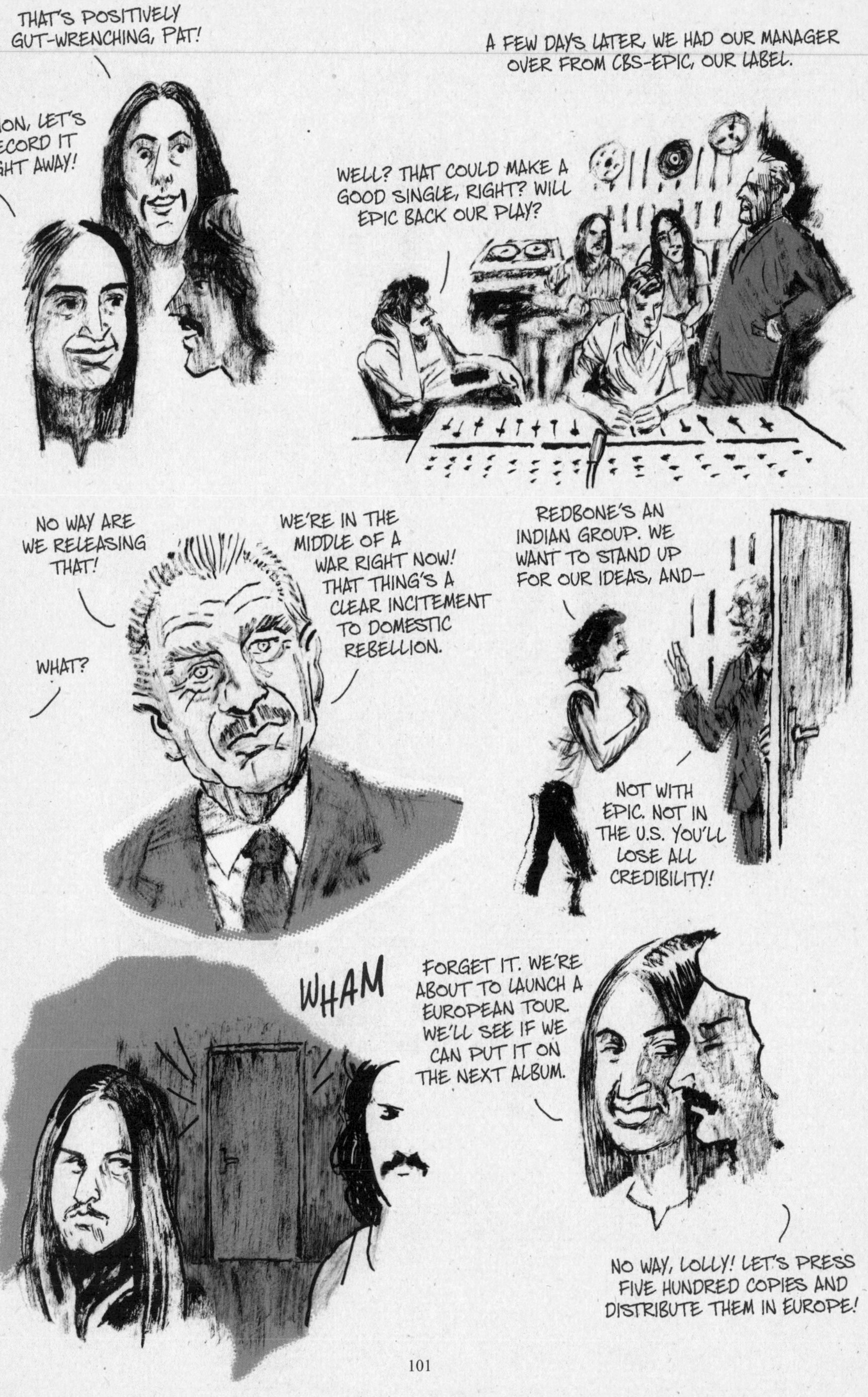
THAT'S POSITIVELY GUT-WRENCHING, PAT!
C'MON, LET'S RECORD IT RIGHT AWAY!
A FEW DAYS LATER, WE HAD OUR MANAGER OVER FROM CBS-EPIC, OUR LABEL.
WELL? THAT COULD MAKE A GOOD SINGLE, RIGHT? WILL EPIC BACK OUR PLAY?
NO WAY ARE WE RELEASING THAT!
WHAT?
WE'RE IN THE MIDDLE OF A WAR RIGHT NOW! THAT THING'S A CLEAR INCITEMENT TO DOMESTIC REBELLION.
REDBONE'S AN INDIAN GROUP. WE WANT TO STAND UP FOR OUR IDEAS, AND—
NOT WITH EPIC. NOT IN THE U.S. YOU'LL LOSE ALL CREDIBILITY!
WHAM
FORGET IT. WE'RE ABOUT TO LAUNCH A EUROPEAN TOUR. WE'LL SEE IF WE CAN PUT IT ON THE NEXT ALBUM.
NO WAY, LOLLY! LET'S PRESS FIVE HUNDRED COPIES AND DISTRIBUTE THEM IN EUROPE!

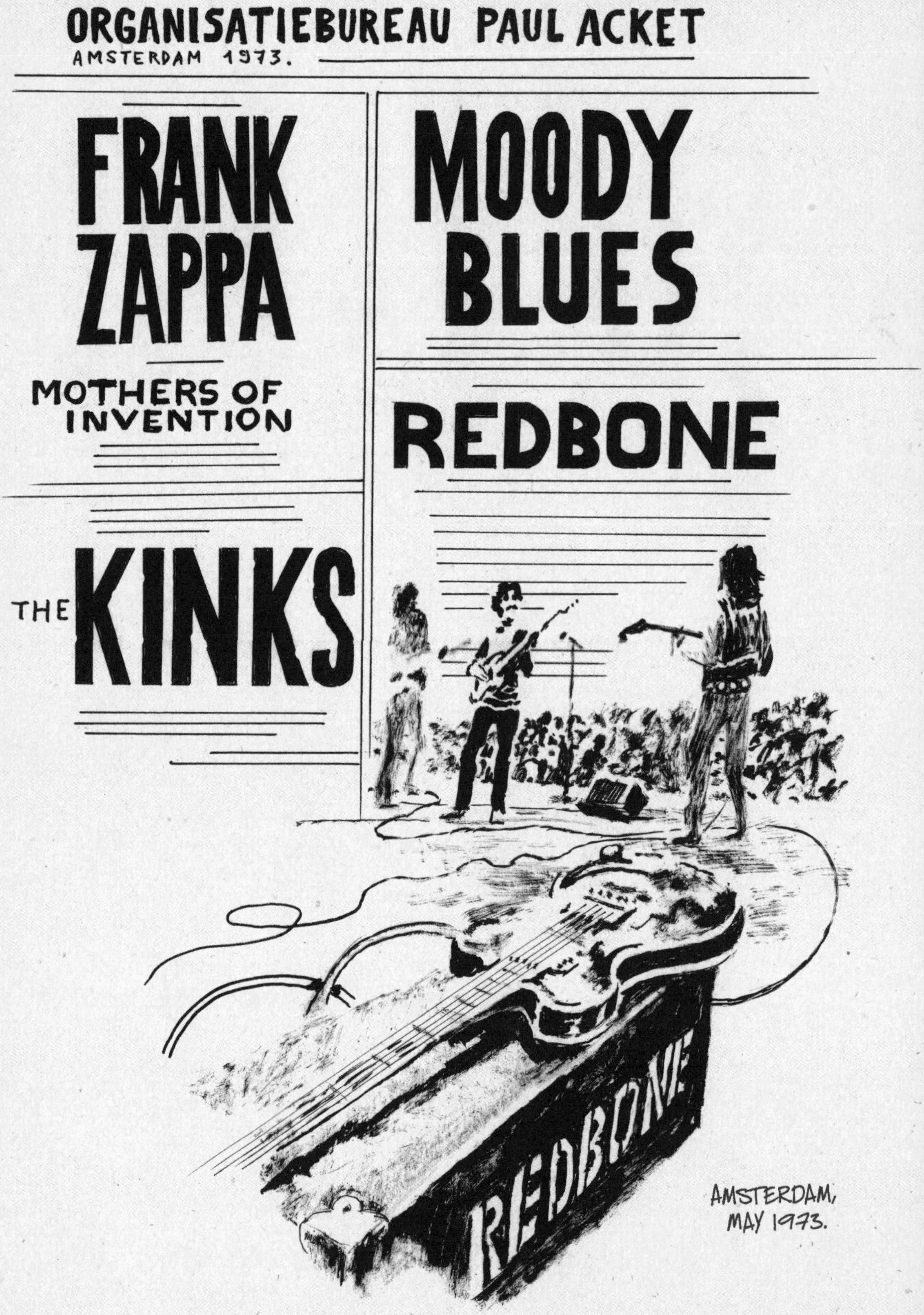

ORGANISATIEBUREAU PAUL ACKET
AMSTERDAM 1973.
FRANK ZAPPA
MOTHERS OF INVENTION
MOODY BLUES
REDBONE
THE KINKS
REDBONE
AMSTERDAM, MAY 1973.

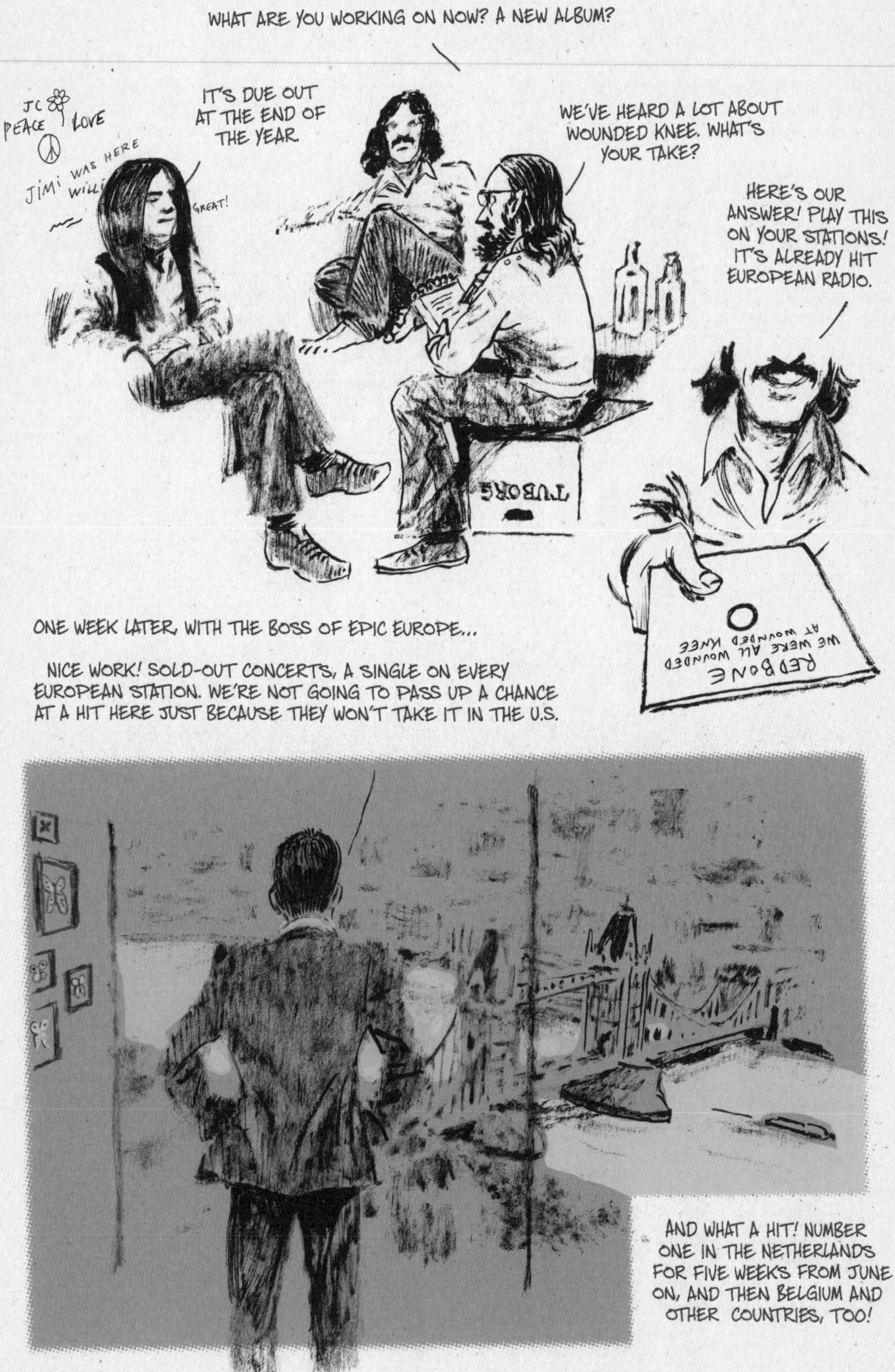
WHAT ARE YOU WORKING ON NOW? A NEW ALBUM?
IT'S DUE OUT AT THE END OF THE YEAR.
JC
PEACE
LOVE
JIMI WAS HERE
GREAT!
WE'VE HEARD A LOT ABOUT WOUNDED KNEE. WHAT'S YOUR TAKE?
HERE'S OUR ANSWER! PLAY THIS ON YOUR STATIONS! IT'S ALREADY HIT EUROPEAN RADIO.
REDBONE
WE WERE ALL WOUNDED AT WOUNDED KNEE
ONE WEEK LATER, WITH THE BOSS OF EPIC EUROPE...
NICE WORK! SOLD-OUT CONCERTS, A SINGLE ON EVERY EUROPEAN STATION. WE'RE NOT GOING TO PASS UP A CHANCE AT A HIT HERE JUST BECAUSE THEY WON'T TAKE IT IN THE U.S.
AND WHAT A HIT! NUMBER ONE IN THE NETHERLANDS FOR FIVE WEEKS FROM JUNE ON, AND THEN BELGIUM AND OTHER COUNTRIES, TOO!

BUT IN THE U.S., THE SONG WAS DEFINITIVELY BANNED. I REMEMBER AT SOME CONCERTS...

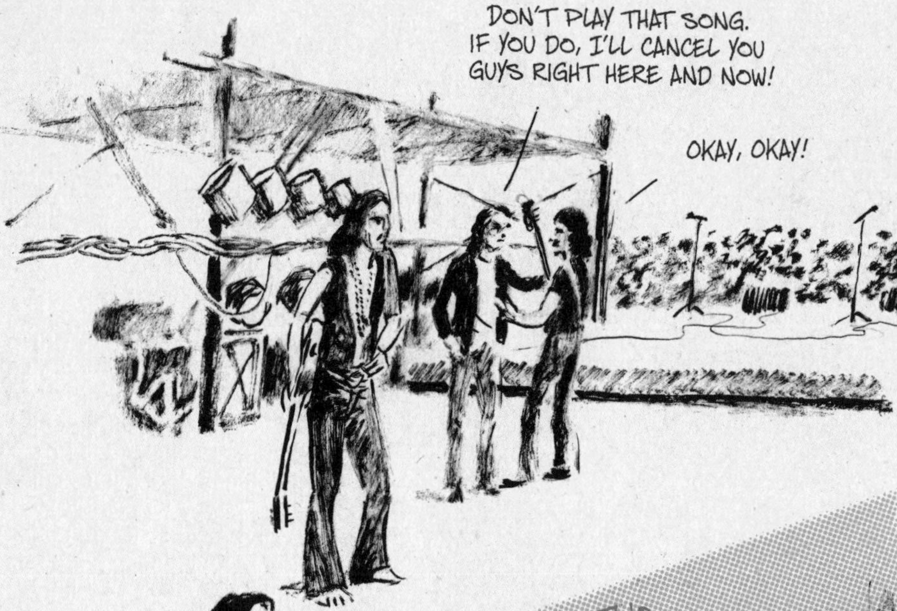
DON'T PLAY THAT SONG. IF YOU DO, I'LL CANCEL YOU GUYS RIGHT HERE AND NOW!
OKAY, OKAY!

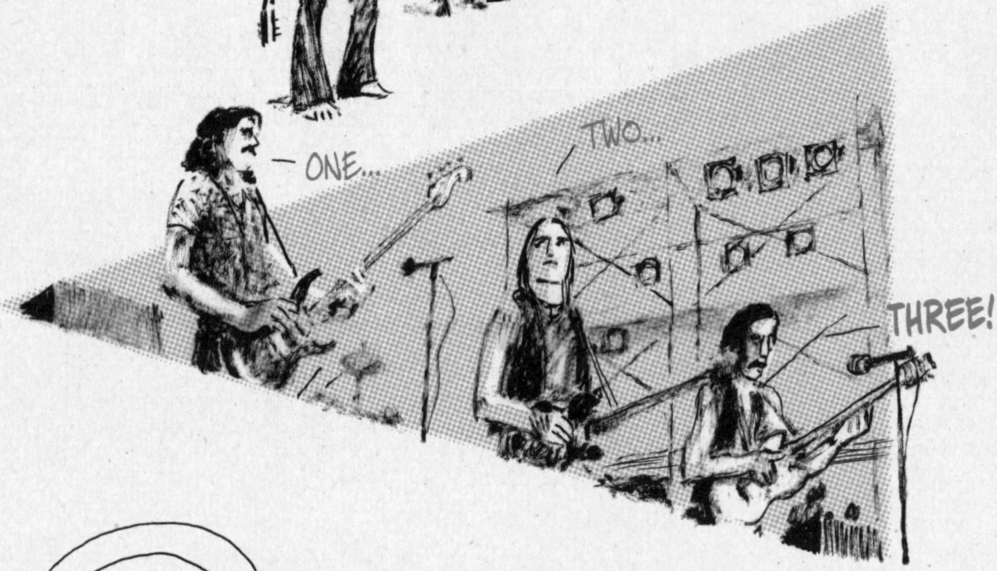
ONE...
TWO...
THREE!

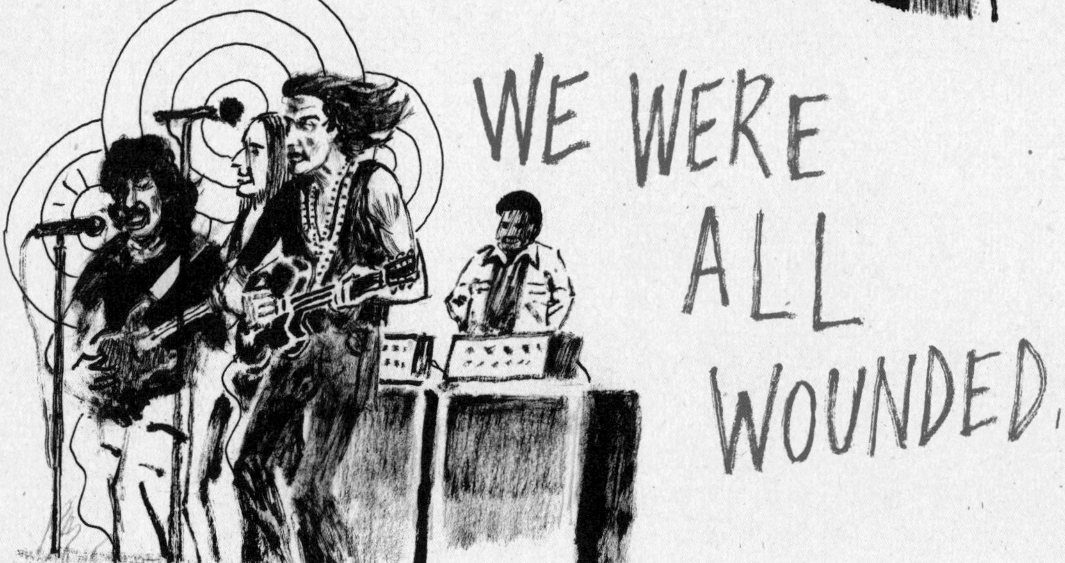
WE WERE ALL WOUNDED...

VIII
THE END OF REDBONE
(1976)

I THINK "WE WERE ALL WOUNDED AT WOUNDED KNEE" COST US OUR CAREER.

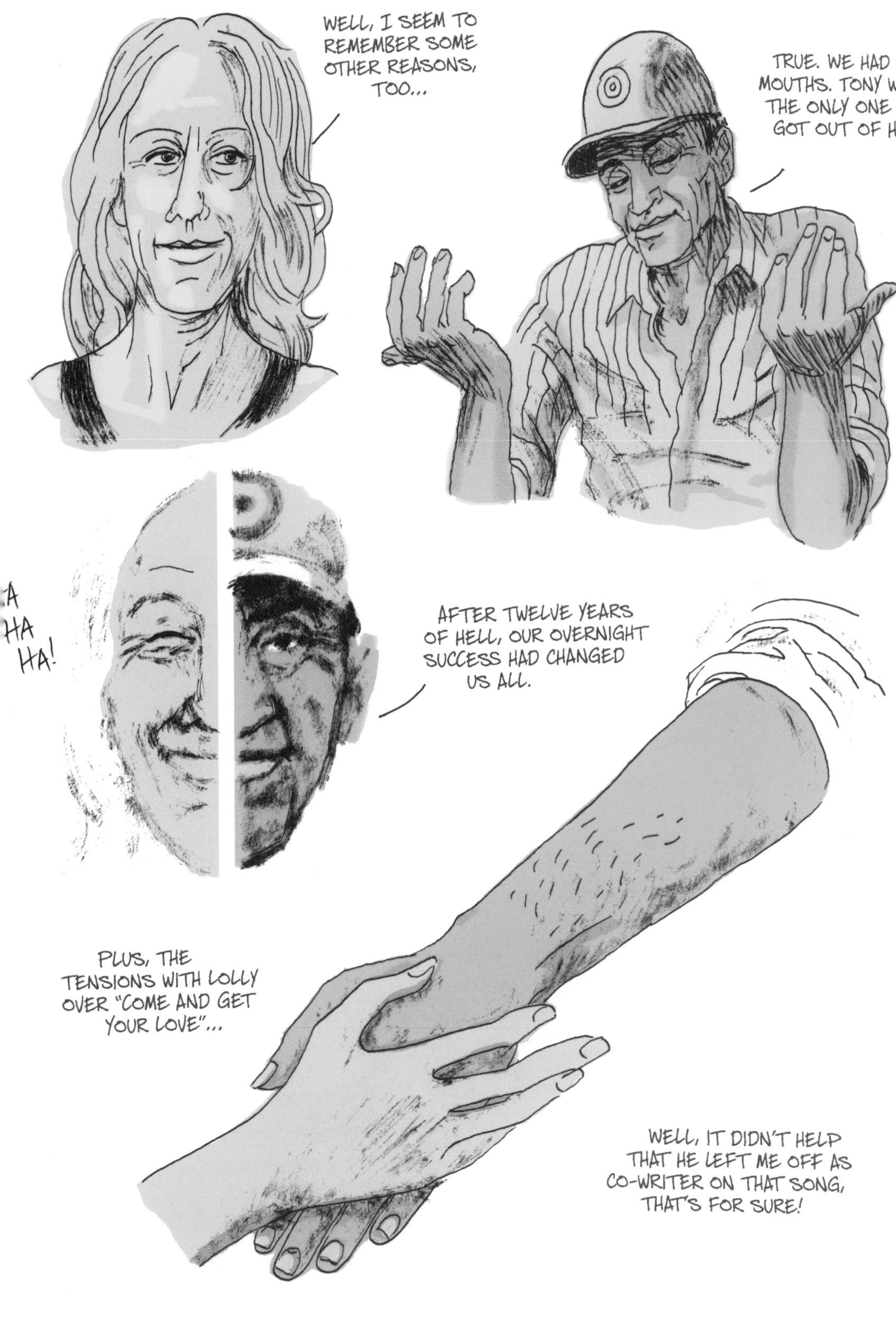

WELL, I SEEM TO REMEMBER SOME OTHER REASONS, TOO...
TRUE. WE HAD BIG MOUTHS. TONY WASN'T THE ONLY ONE WHO GOT OUT OF HAND!
A HA HA!
AFTER TWELVE YEARS OF HELL, OUR OVERNIGHT SUCCESS HAD CHANGED US ALL.
PLUS, THE TENSIONS WITH LOLLY OVER "COME AND GET YOUR LOVE"...
WELL, IT DIDN'T HELP THAT HE LEFT ME OFF AS CO-WRITER ON THAT SONG, THAT'S FOR SURE!

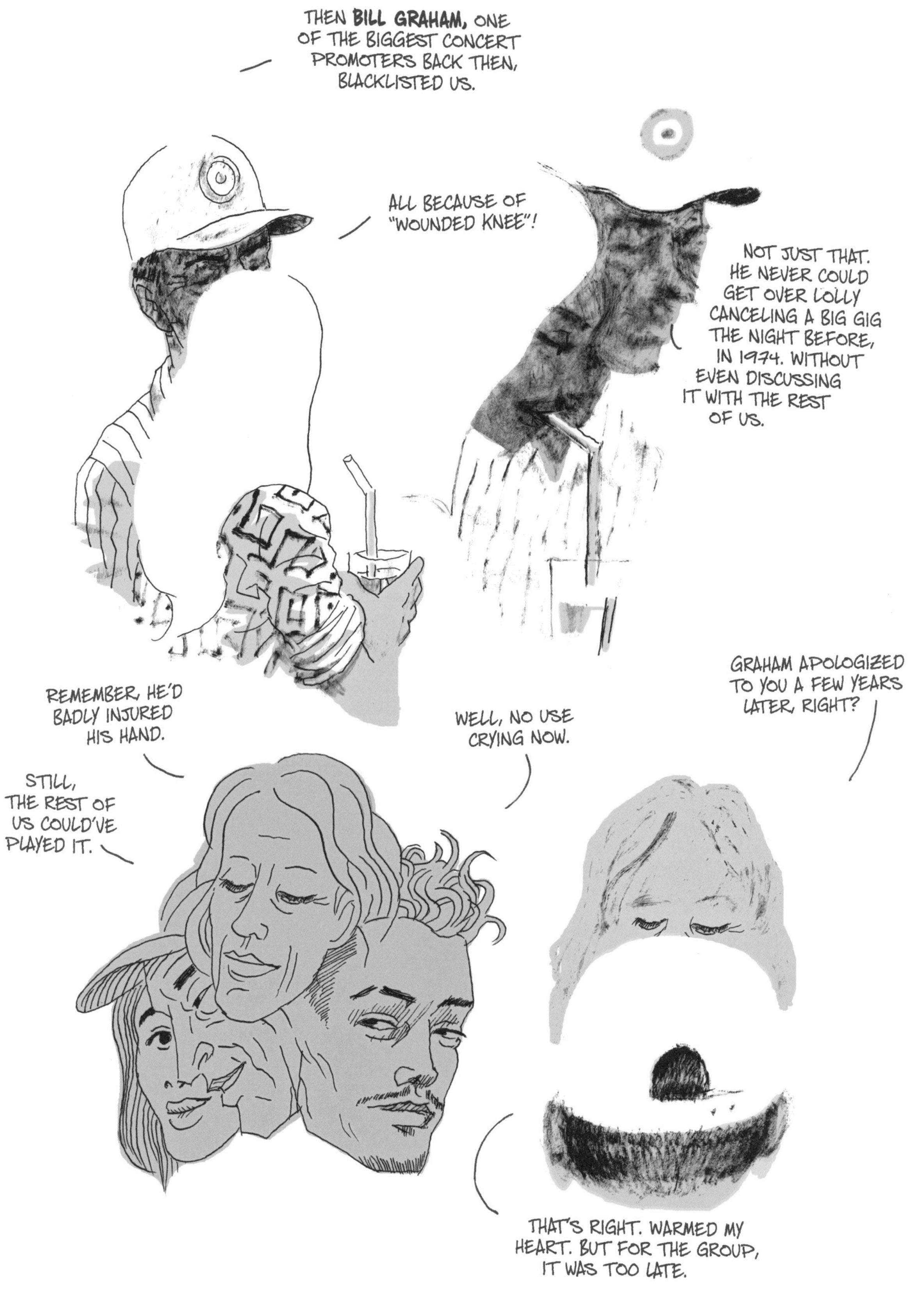
THEN **BILL GRAHAM,** ONE OF THE BIGGEST CONCERT PROMOTERS BACK THEN, BLACKLISTED US.
ALL BECAUSE OF "WOUNDED KNEE"!
NOT JUST THAT. HE NEVER COULD GET OVER LOLLY CANCELING A BIG GIG THE NIGHT BEFORE, IN 1974. WITHOUT EVEN DISCUSSING IT WITH THE REST OF US.
REMEMBER, HE'D BADLY INJURED HIS HAND.
STILL, THE REST OF US COULD'VE PLAYED IT.
WELL, NO USE CRYING NOW.
GRAHAM APOLOGIZED TO YOU A FEW YEARS LATER, RIGHT?
THAT'S RIGHT. WARMED MY HEART. BUT FOR THE GROUP, IT WAS TOO LATE.

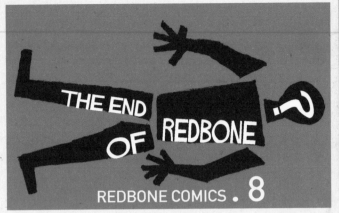

THE END OF REDBONE

REDBONE COMICS . 8

IN 1973, WE TOURED LIKE CRAZY. EVERY MAJOR EUROPEAN NETWORK WANTED US ONSTAGE. I REMEMBER A FRENCH SHOW* WHERE THEY OVERLAID POP COLORS ON ALL THE IMAGES.

THEY'RE REAL INDIANS, AND THEY'RE ON THE WARPATH. BUT INSTEAD OF BEING ANGRY LIKE THEIR BROTHERS BACK IN AMERICA...

...THEY SING SONGS.

THEY ARE...
REDBONE!

POISON IVY,
POISON IVY,
LATE AT NIGHT
WHILE YOU'RE
SLEEPING
POISON IVY
COMES A
CREEPING
ALL AROUND

* "TOP À" BROADCAST ON MAY 5, 1973, HOSTED BY FRENCH SINGER GILBERT BÉCAUD

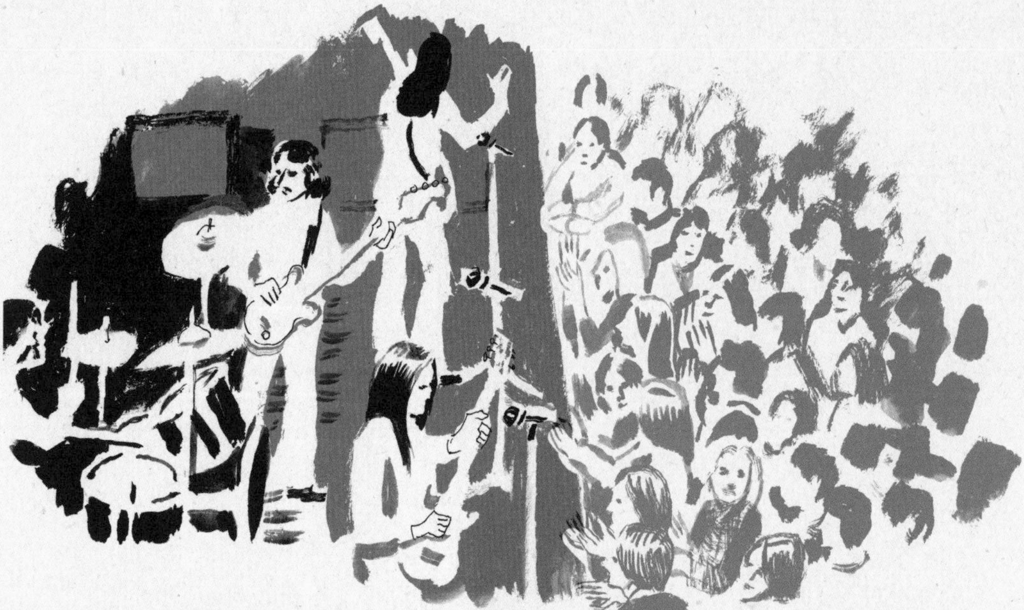

THEN, THERE WERE TENSIONS WITHIN THE GROUP. IT HAPPENED GRADUALLY. WE DIDN'T REALIZE IT RIGHT AWAY. WHEN OUR ALBUM **BEADED DREAMS THROUGH TURQUOISE EYES** DIDN'T DO SO WELL, THE GROUP FELL APART.

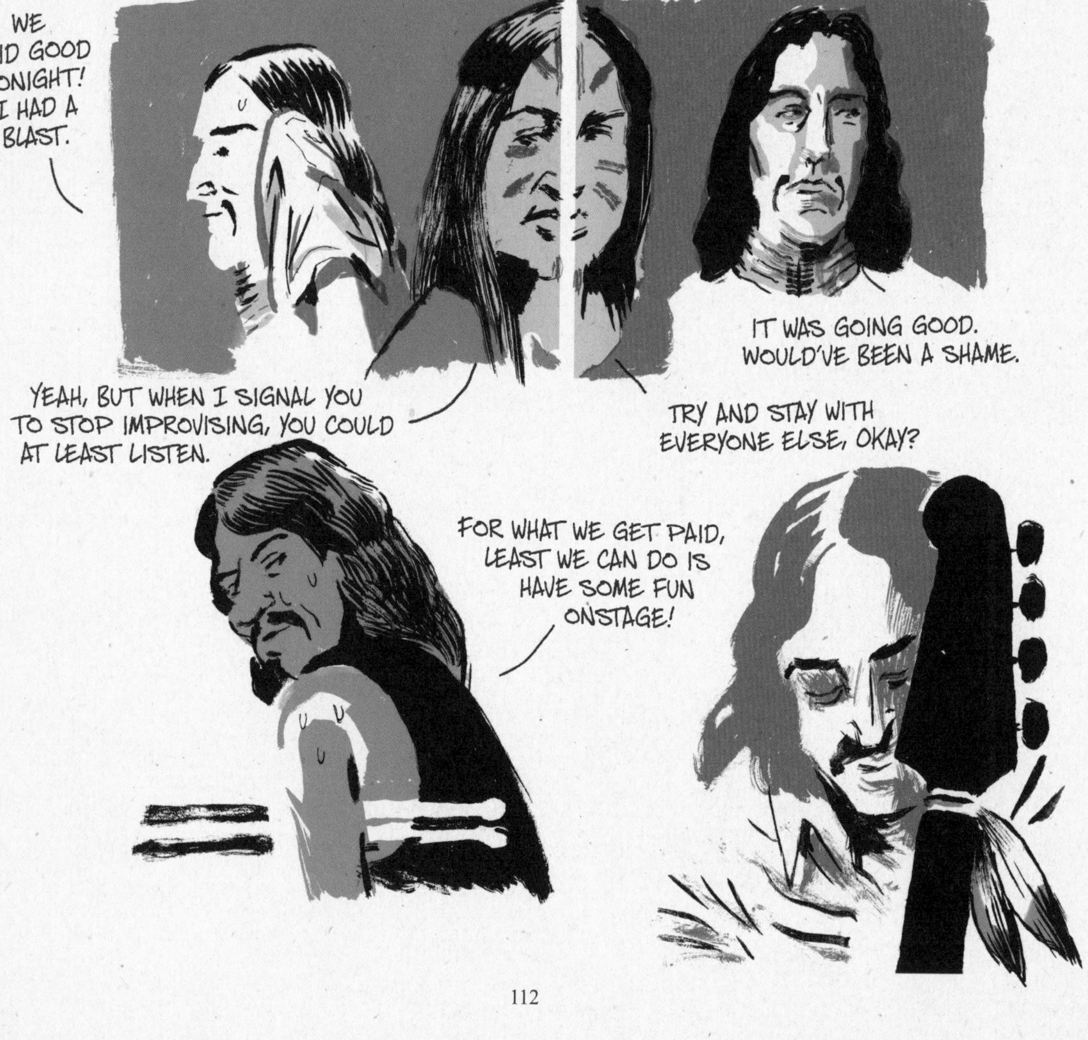
WE DID GOOD TONIGHT! I HAD A BLAST.
YEAH, BUT WHEN I SIGNAL YOU TO STOP IMPROVISING, YOU COULD AT LEAST LISTEN.
IT WAS GOING GOOD. WOULD'VE BEEN A SHAME.
TRY AND STAY WITH EVERYONE ELSE, OKAY?
FOR WHAT WE GET PAID, LEAST WE CAN DO IS HAVE SOME FUN ONSTAGE!

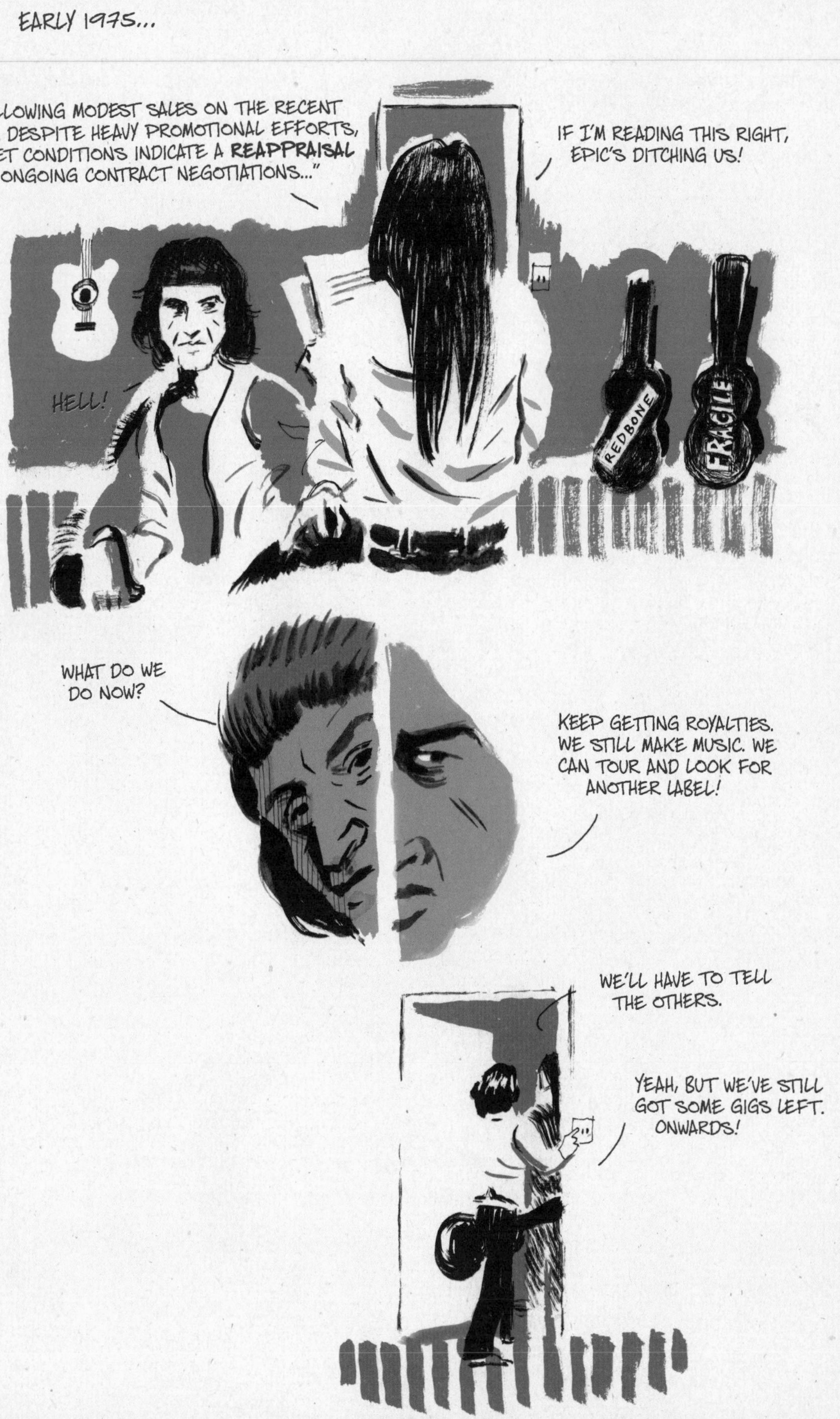
EARLY 1975...
"FOLLOWING MODEST SALES ON THE RECENT ALBUM DESPITE HEAVY PROMOTIONAL EFFORTS, MARKET CONDITIONS INDICATE A **REAPPRAISAL** OF ONGOING CONTRACT NEGOTIATIONS..."
IF I'M READING THIS RIGHT, EPIC'S DITCHING US!
HELL!
REDBONE
FRAGILE
WHAT DO WE DO NOW?
KEEP GETTING ROYALTIES. WE STILL MAKE MUSIC. WE CAN TOUR AND LOOK FOR ANOTHER LABEL!
WE'LL HAVE TO TELL THE OTHERS.
YEAH, BUT WE'VE STILL GOT SOME GIGS LEFT. ONWARDS!

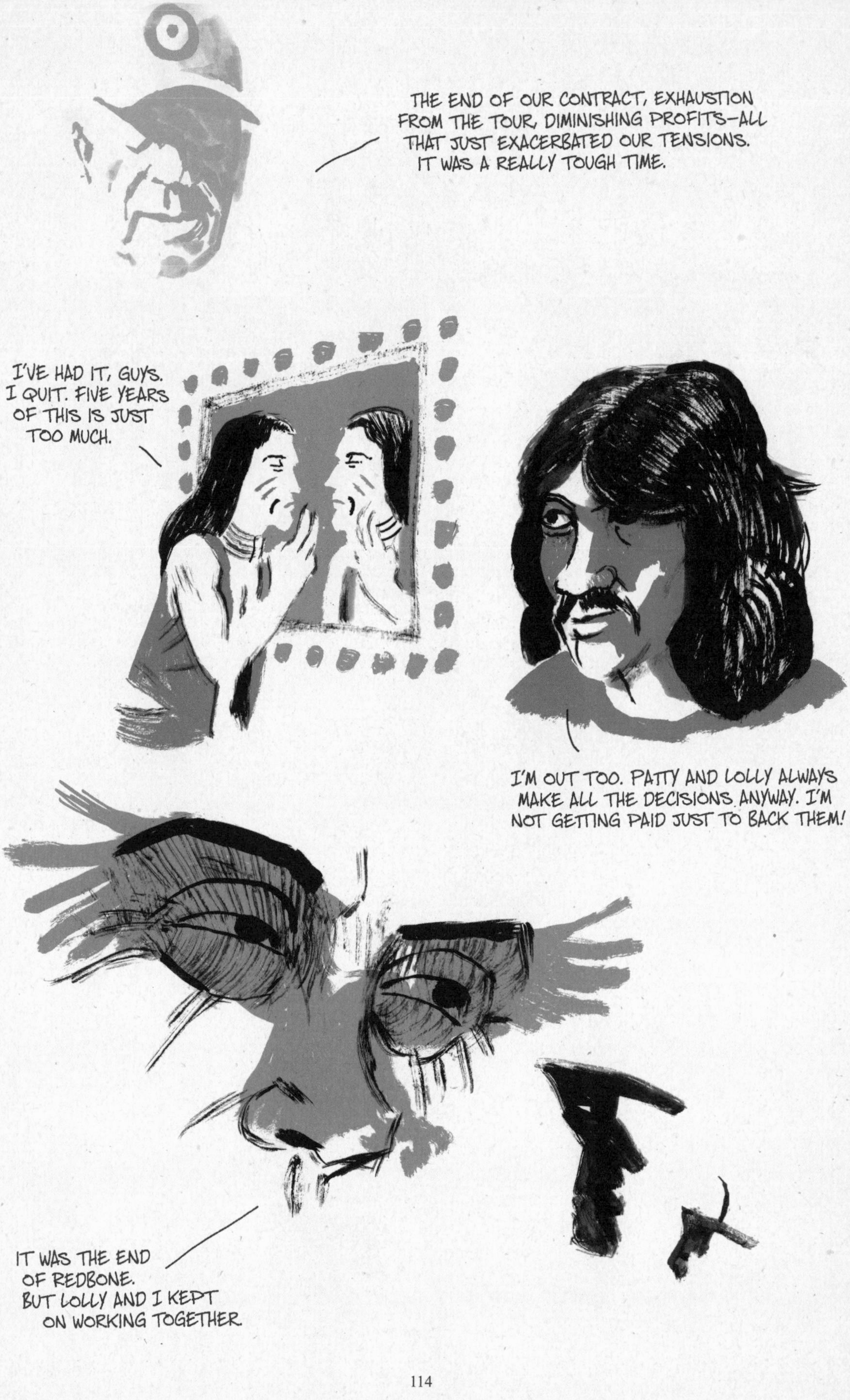
THE END OF OUR CONTRACT, EXHAUSTION FROM THE TOUR, DIMINISHING PROFITS—ALL THAT JUST EXACERBATED OUR TENSIONS. IT WAS A REALLY TOUGH TIME.
I'VE HAD IT, GUYS. I QUIT. FIVE YEARS OF THIS IS JUST TOO MUCH.
I'M OUT TOO. PATTY AND LOLLY ALWAYS MAKE ALL THE DECISIONS ANYWAY. I'M NOT GETTING PAID JUST TO BACK THEM!
IT WAS THE END OF REDBONE. BUT LOLLY AND I KEPT ON WORKING TOGETHER.

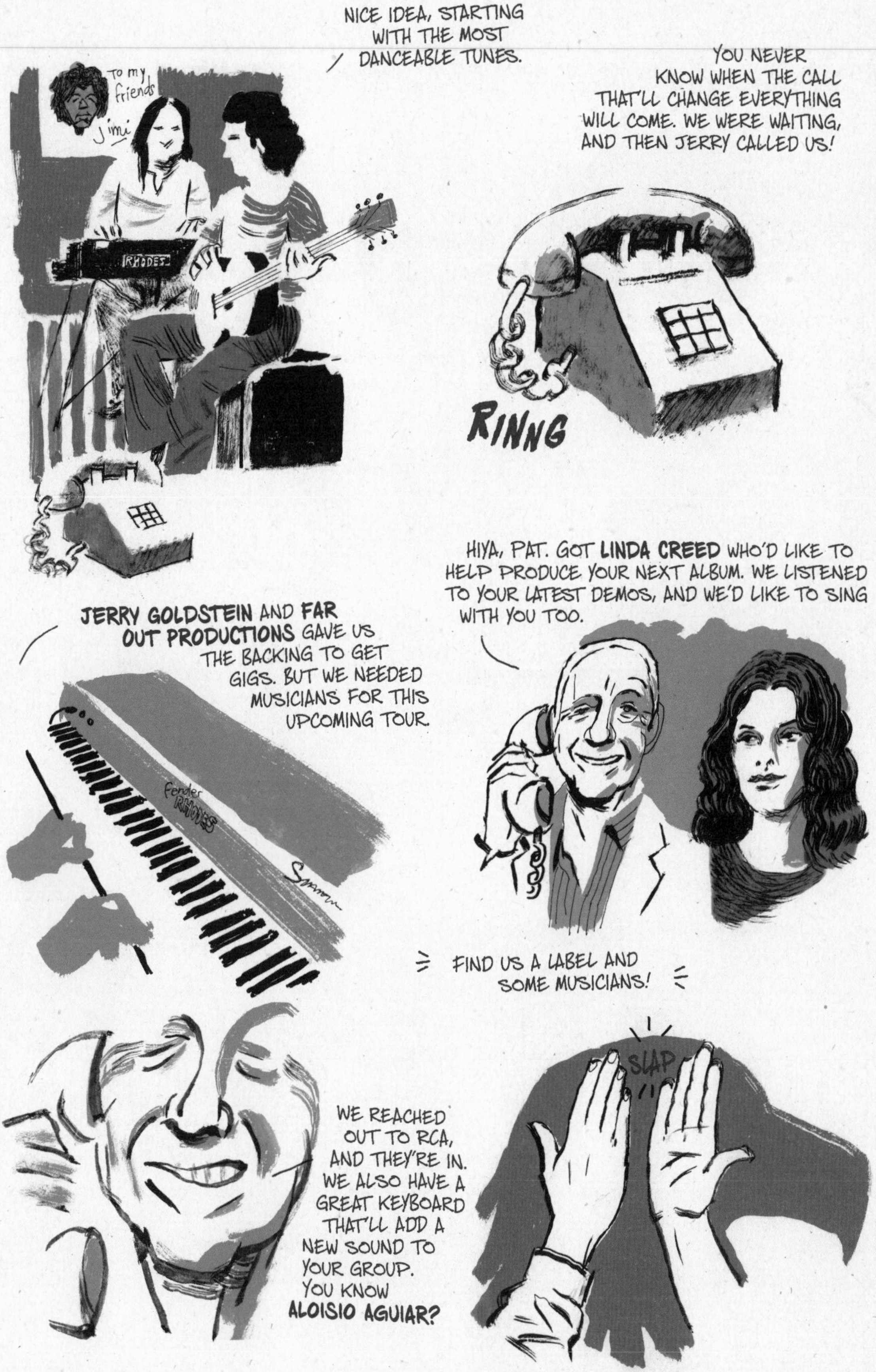
NICE IDEA, STARTING WITH THE MOST DANCEABLE TUNES.
To my friends Jimi
RHODES
YOU NEVER KNOW WHEN THE CALL THAT'LL CHANGE EVERYTHING WILL COME. WE WERE WAITING, AND THEN JERRY CALLED US!
RINNG
JERRY GOLDSTEIN AND FAR OUT PRODUCTIONS GAVE US THE BACKING TO GET GIGS. BUT WE NEEDED MUSICIANS FOR THIS UPCOMING TOUR.
Fender RHODES
HIYA, PAT. GOT LINDA CREED WHO'D LIKE TO HELP PRODUCE YOUR NEXT ALBUM. WE LISTENED TO YOUR LATEST DEMOS, AND WE'D LIKE TO SING WITH YOU TOO.
FIND US A LABEL AND SOME MUSICIANS!
WE REACHED OUT TO RCA, AND THEY'RE IN. WE ALSO HAVE A GREAT KEYBOARD THAT'LL ADD A NEW SOUND TO YOUR GROUP. YOU KNOW ALOISIO AGUIAR?
SLAP

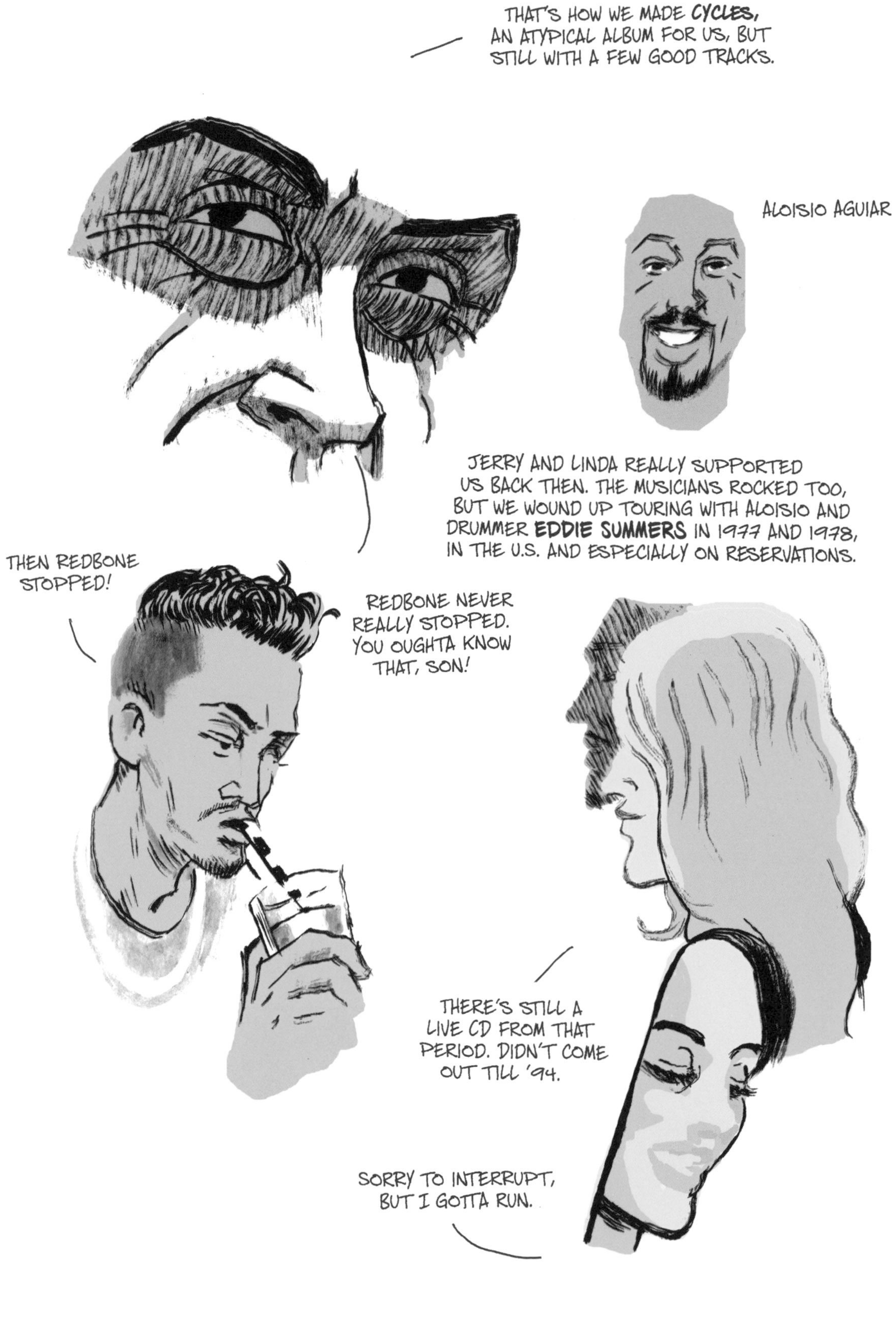
THAT'S HOW WE MADE **CYCLES**, AN ATYPICAL ALBUM FOR US, BUT STILL WITH A FEW GOOD TRACKS.
ALOISIO AGUIAR
JERRY AND LINDA REALLY SUPPORTED US BACK THEN. THE MUSICIANS ROCKED TOO, BUT WE WOUND UP TOURING WITH ALOISIO AND DRUMMER **EDDIE SUMMERS** IN 1977 AND 1978, IN THE U.S. AND ESPECIALLY ON RESERVATIONS.
THEN REDBONE STOPPED!
REDBONE NEVER REALLY STOPPED. YOU OUGHTA KNOW THAT, SON!
THERE'S STILL A LIVE CD FROM THAT PERIOD. DIDN'T COME OUT TILL '94.
SORRY TO INTERRUPT, BUT I GOTTA RUN.

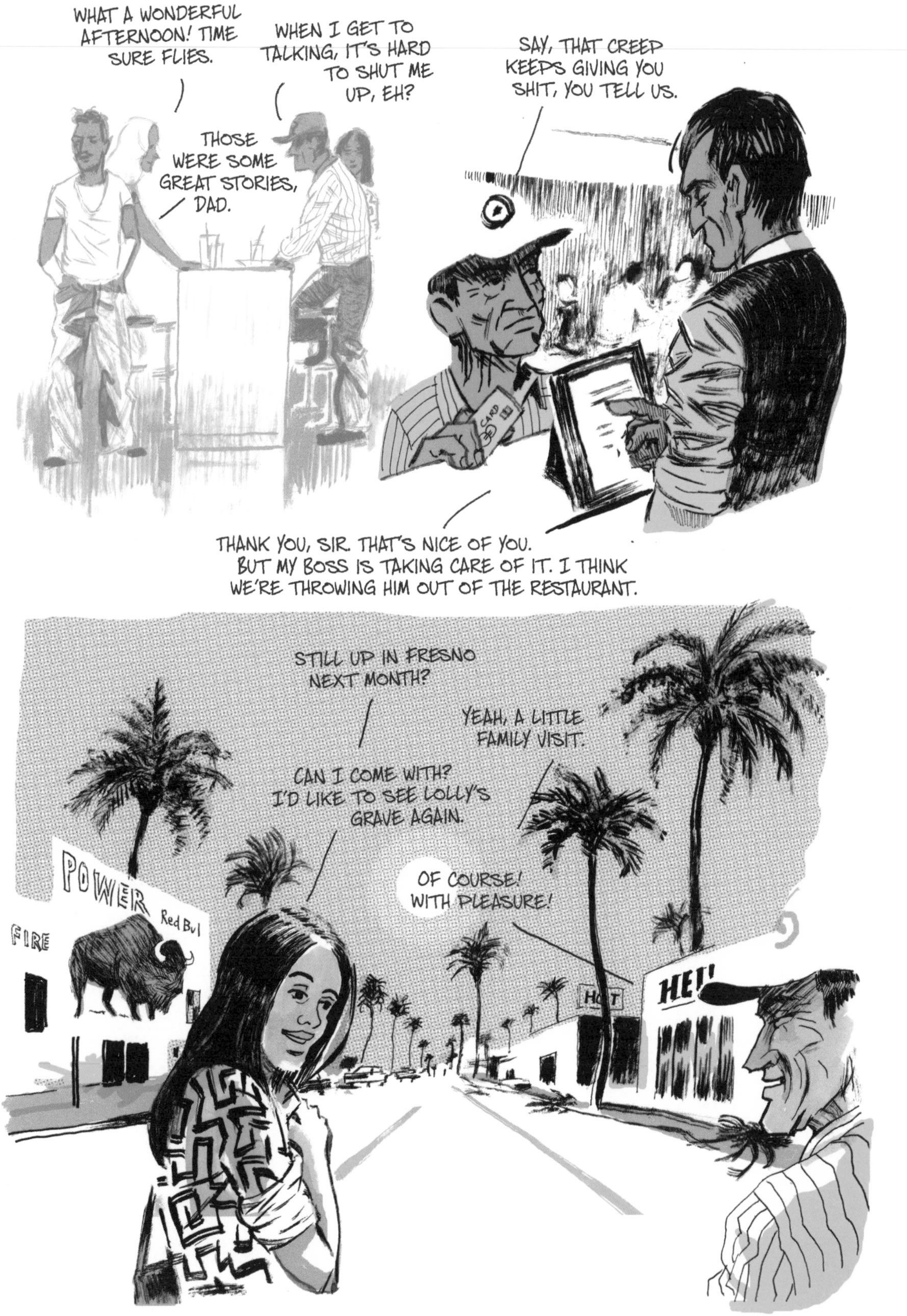
WHAT A WONDERFUL AFTERNOON! TIME SURE FLIES.
WHEN I GET TO TALKING, IT'S HARD TO SHUT ME UP, EH?
THOSE WERE SOME GREAT STORIES, DAD.
SAY, THAT CREEP KEEPS GIVING YOU SHIT, YOU TELL US.
CARD
THANK YOU, SIR. THAT'S NICE OF YOU. BUT MY BOSS IS TAKING CARE OF IT. I THINK WE'RE THROWING HIM OUT OF THE RESTAURANT.
STILL UP IN FRESNO NEXT MONTH?
YEAH, A LITTLE FAMILY VISIT.
CAN I COME WITH? I'D LIKE TO SEE LOLLY'S GRAVE AGAIN.
OF COURSE! WITH PLEASURE!
POWER
Red Bul
FIRE

IX
AFTER REDBONE
(1990-2018)

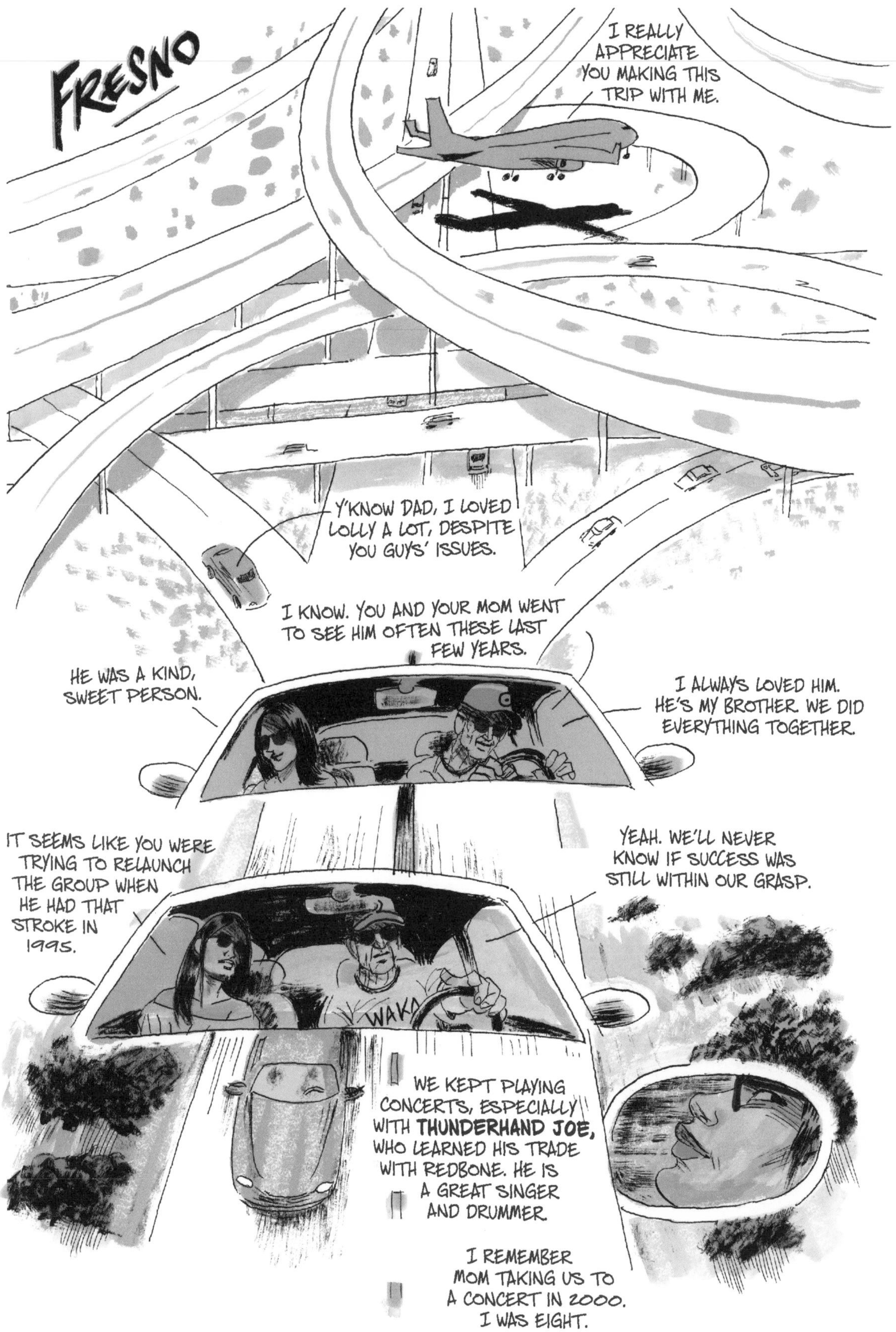
FRESNO
I REALLY APPRECIATE YOU MAKING THIS TRIP WITH ME.
Y'KNOW DAD, I LOVED LOLLY A LOT, DESPITE YOU GUYS' ISSUES.
I KNOW. YOU AND YOUR MOM WENT TO SEE HIM OFTEN THESE LAST FEW YEARS.
HE WAS A KIND, SWEET PERSON.
I ALWAYS LOVED HIM. HE'S MY BROTHER. WE DID EVERYTHING TOGETHER.
IT SEEMS LIKE YOU WERE TRYING TO RELAUNCH THE GROUP WHEN HE HAD THAT STROKE IN 1995.
YEAH. WE'LL NEVER KNOW IF SUCCESS WAS STILL WITHIN OUR GRASP.
WAKA
WE KEPT PLAYING CONCERTS, ESPECIALLY WITH THUNDERHAND JOE, WHO LEARNED HIS TRADE WITH REDBONE. HE IS A GREAT SINGER AND DRUMMER.
I REMEMBER MOM TAKING US TO A CONCERT IN 2000. I WAS EIGHT.

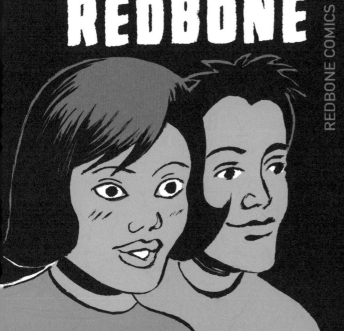

AFTER REDBONE

REDBONE COMICS · 9

$ 2.50
¢ 2.95 CAN

Redbo

INDIAN MATTERS

SPOTLIGHT 29
CASINO. 2000

DID YOU SEE YOUR DAD? WHAT A ROCK STAR!

'YOU'VE GOT THE POWER' SHOW HER WHAT LOVE IS

REDBONE

AND NOW, I'D LIKE TO INTRODUCE...

...TWO WONDERFUL PEOPLE WHO MEAN A GREAT DEAL TO ME.

FANTASTICS BOOKS

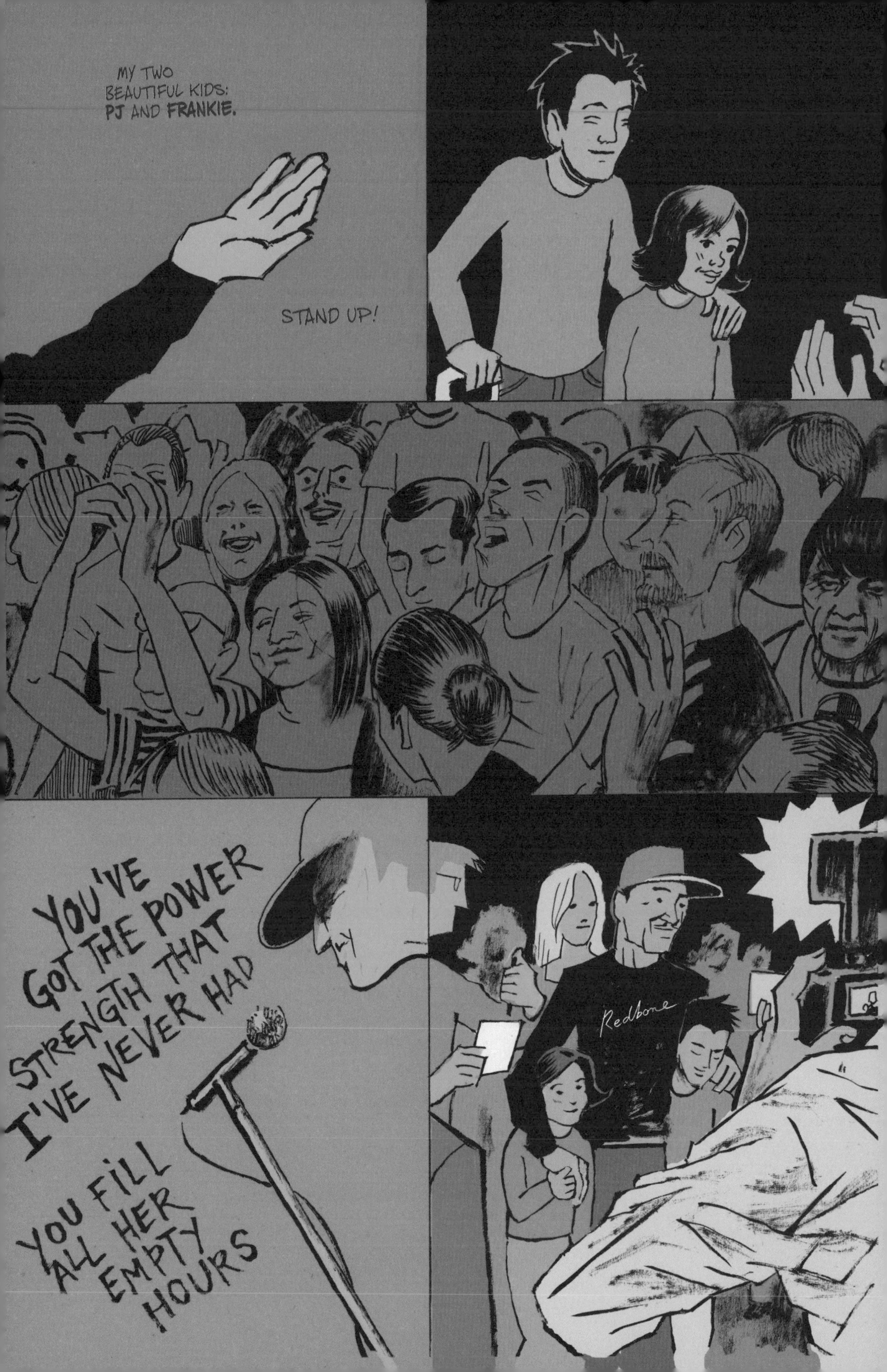
MY TWO BEAUTIFUL KIDS: PJ AND FRANKIE.
STAND UP!
YOU'VE GOT THE POWER
STRENGTH THAT I'VE NEVER HAD
YOU FILL ALL HER EMPTY HOURS
Redbone

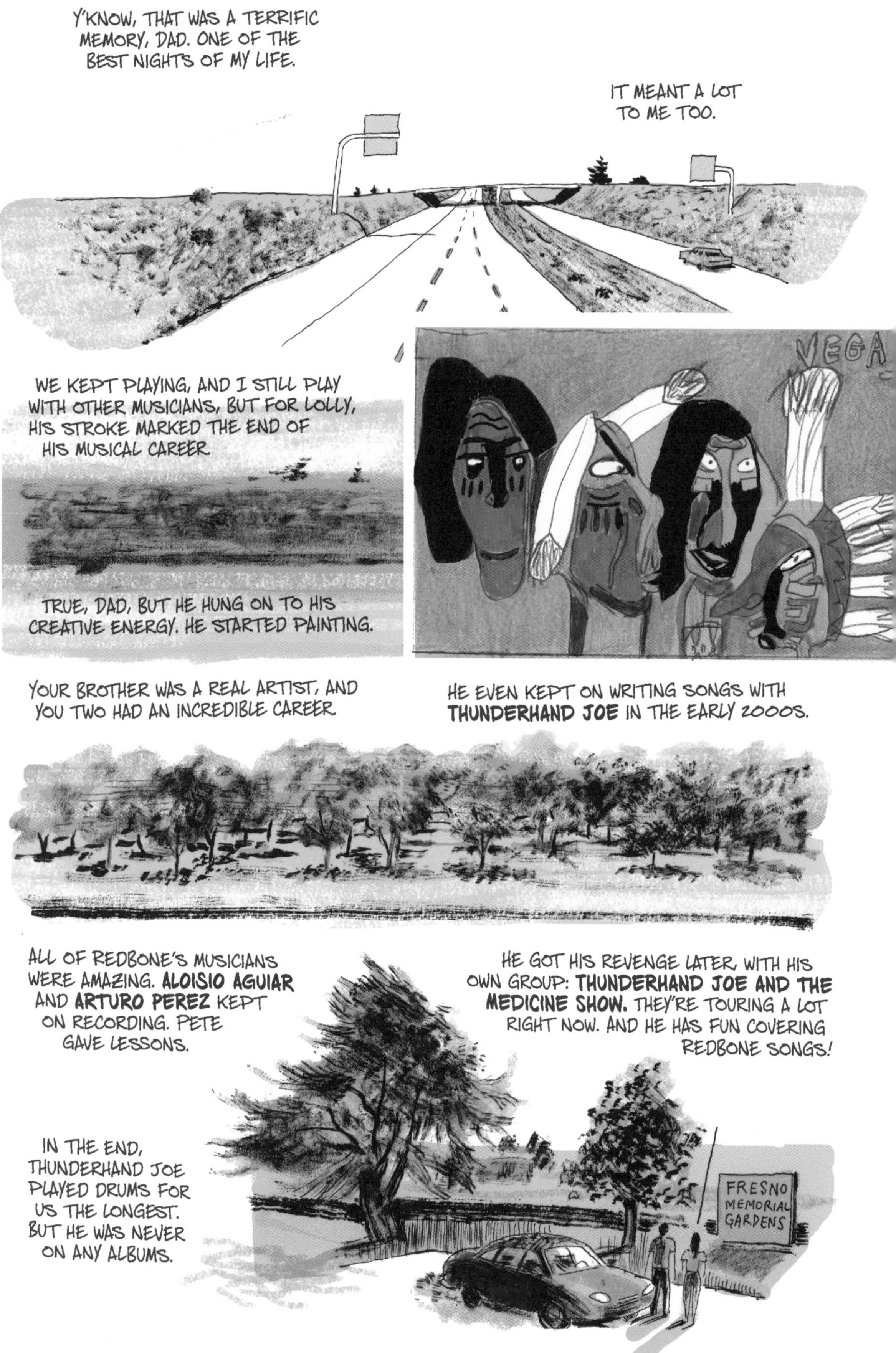
Y'KNOW, THAT WAS A TERRIFIC MEMORY, DAD. ONE OF THE BEST NIGHTS OF MY LIFE.
IT MEANT A LOT TO ME TOO.
WE KEPT PLAYING, AND I STILL PLAY WITH OTHER MUSICIANS, BUT FOR LOLLY, HIS STROKE MARKED THE END OF HIS MUSICAL CAREER.
TRUE, DAD, BUT HE HUNG ON TO HIS CREATIVE ENERGY. HE STARTED PAINTING.
VEGA
YOUR BROTHER WAS A REAL ARTIST, AND YOU TWO HAD AN INCREDIBLE CAREER.
HE EVEN KEPT ON WRITING SONGS WITH **THUNDERHAND JOE** IN THE EARLY 2000S.
ALL OF REDBONE'S MUSICIANS WERE AMAZING. **ALOISIO AGUIAR** AND **ARTURO PEREZ** KEPT ON RECORDING. PETE GAVE LESSONS.
HE GOT HIS REVENGE LATER, WITH HIS OWN GROUP: **THUNDERHAND JOE AND THE MEDICINE SHOW.** THEY'RE TOURING A LOT RIGHT NOW. AND HE HAS FUN COVERING REDBONE SONGS!
IN THE END, THUNDERHAND JOE PLAYED DRUMS FOR US THE LONGEST. BUT HE WAS NEVER ON ANY ALBUMS.
FRESNO MEMORIAL GARDENS

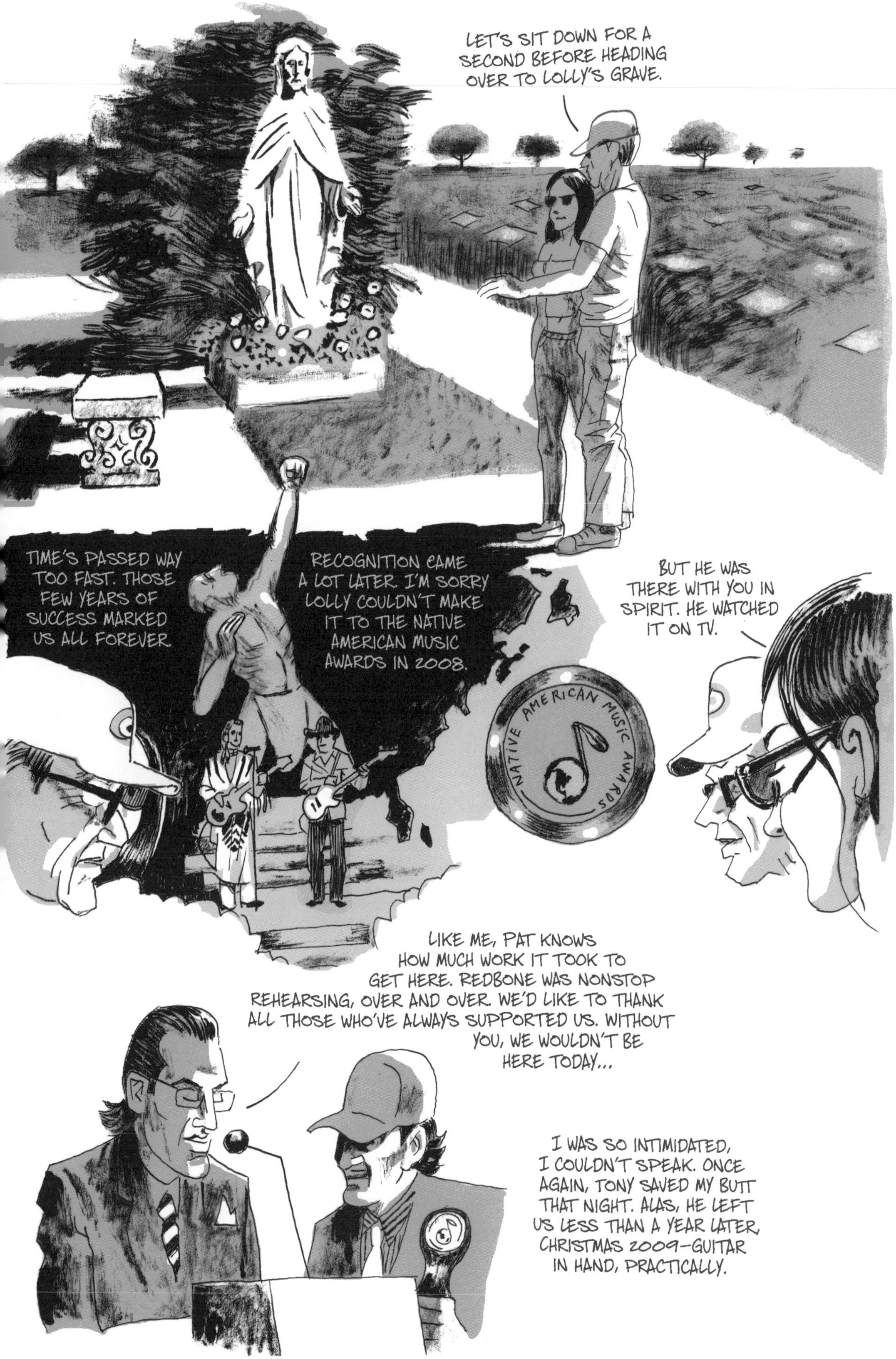

LET'S SIT DOWN FOR A SECOND BEFORE HEADING OVER TO LOLLY'S GRAVE.
TIME'S PASSED WAY TOO FAST. THOSE FEW YEARS OF SUCCESS MARKED US ALL FOREVER.
RECOGNITION CAME A LOT LATER. I'M SORRY LOLLY COULDN'T MAKE IT TO THE NATIVE AMERICAN MUSIC AWARDS IN 2008.
NATIVE AMERICAN MUSIC AWARDS
BUT HE WAS THERE WITH YOU IN SPIRIT. HE WATCHED IT ON TV.
LIKE ME, PAT KNOWS HOW MUCH WORK IT TOOK TO GET HERE. REDBONE WAS NONSTOP REHEARSING, OVER AND OVER. WE'D LIKE TO THANK ALL THOSE WHO'VE ALWAYS SUPPORTED US. WITHOUT YOU, WE WOULDN'T BE HERE TODAY...
I WAS SO INTIMIDATED, I COULDN'T SPEAK. ONCE AGAIN, TONY SAVED MY BUTT THAT NIGHT. ALAS, HE LEFT US LESS THAN A YEAR LATER, CHRISTMAS 2009—GUITAR IN HAND, PRACTICALLY.

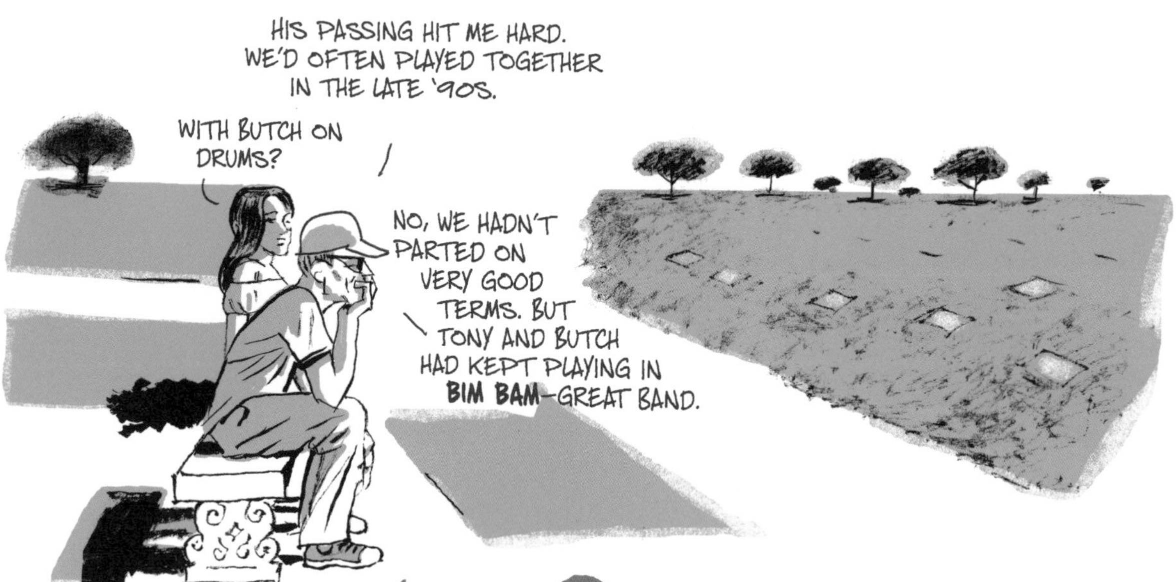
HIS PASSING HIT ME HARD. WE'D OFTEN PLAYED TOGETHER IN THE LATE '90S.
WITH BUTCH ON DRUMS?
NO, WE HADN'T PARTED ON VERY GOOD TERMS. BUT TONY AND BUTCH HAD KEPT PLAYING IN **BIM BAM**–GREAT BAND.

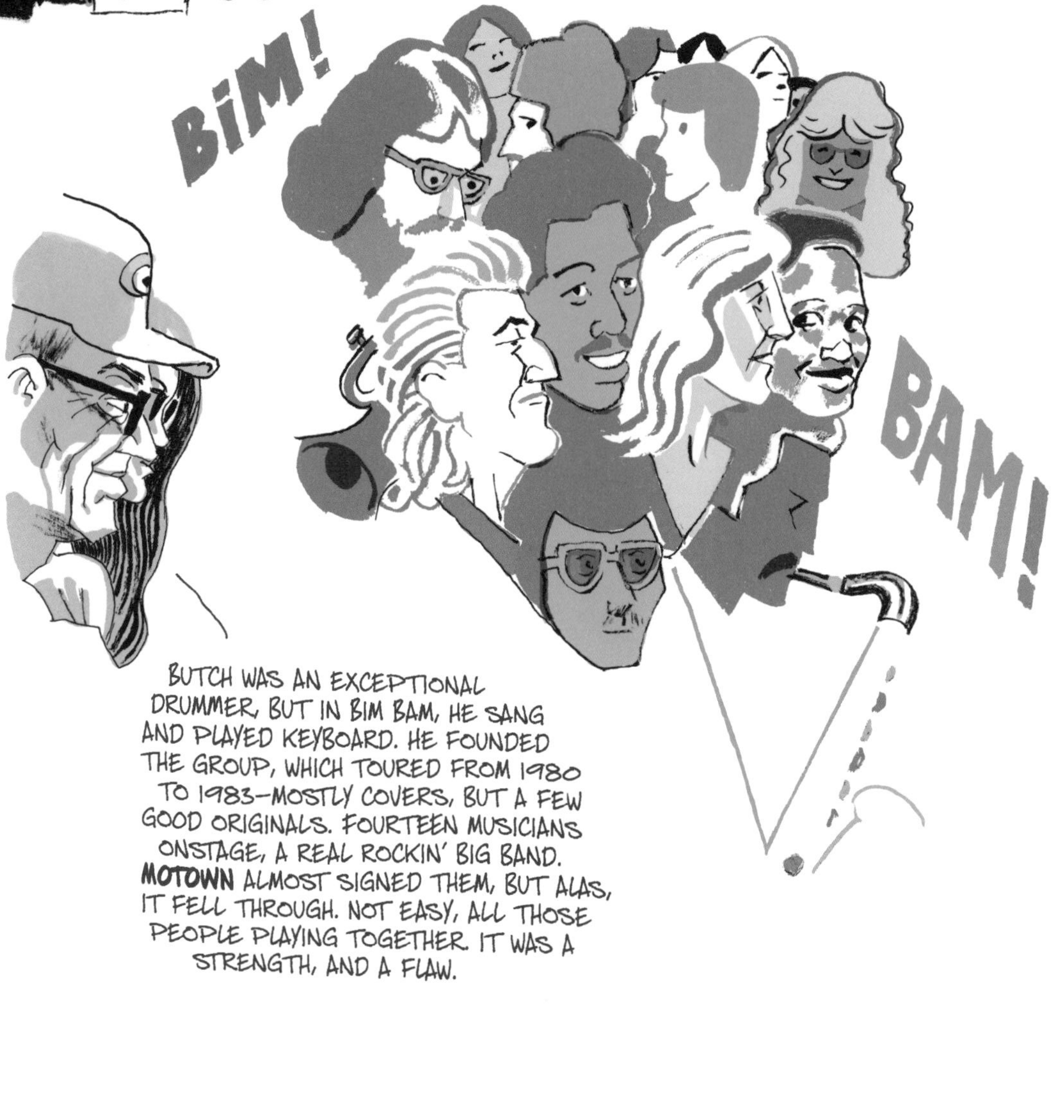
BIM!
BAM!
BUTCH WAS AN EXCEPTIONAL DRUMMER, BUT IN BIM BAM, HE SANG AND PLAYED KEYBOARD. HE FOUNDED THE GROUP, WHICH TOURED FROM 1980 TO 1983–MOSTLY COVERS, BUT A FEW GOOD ORIGINALS. FOURTEEN MUSICIANS ONSTAGE, A REAL ROCKIN' BIG BAND. **MOTOWN** ALMOST SIGNED THEM, BUT ALAS, IT FELL THROUGH. NOT EASY, ALL THOSE PEOPLE PLAYING TOGETHER. IT WAS A STRENGTH, AND A FLAW.

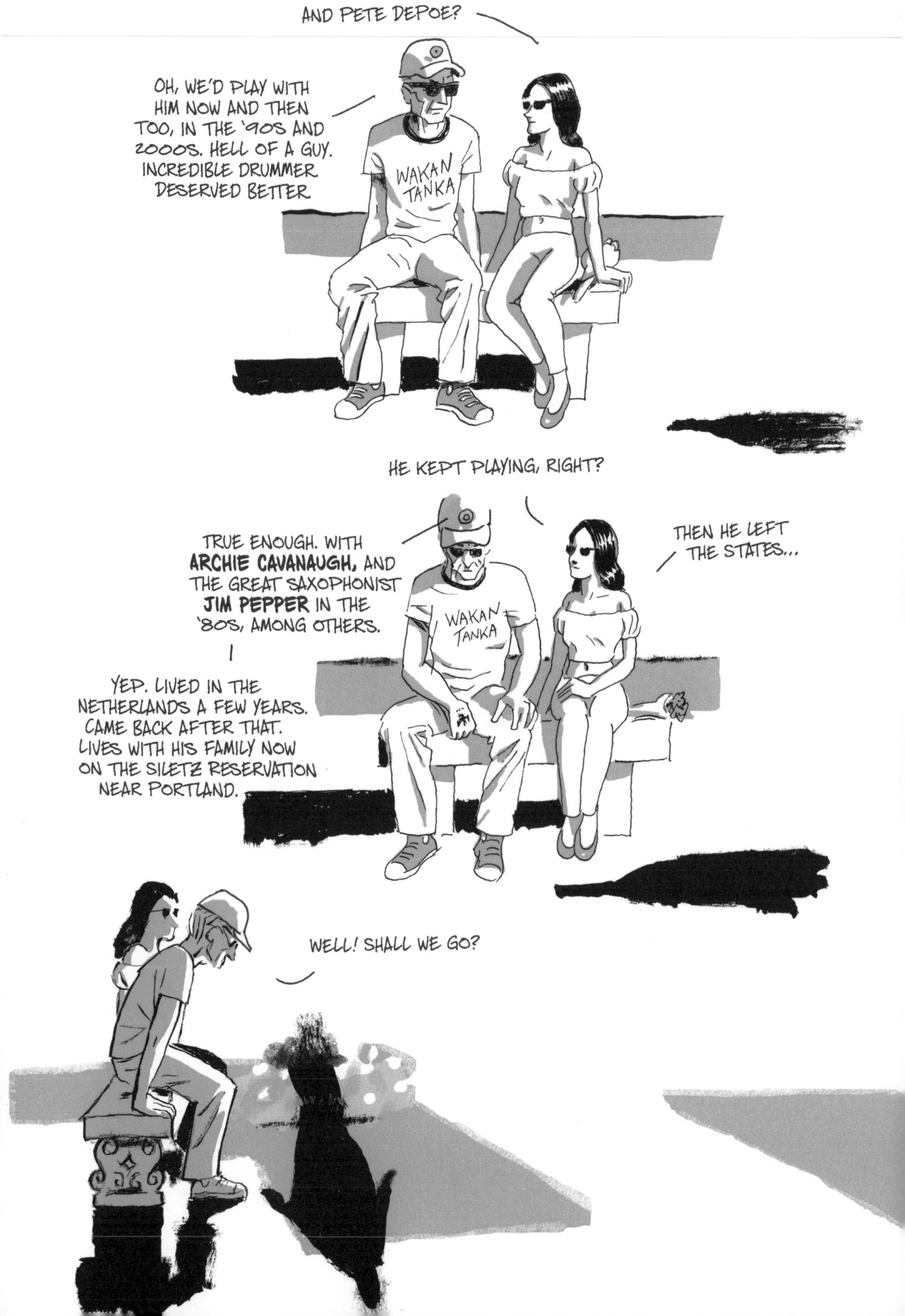
AND PETE DEPOE?
OH, WE'D PLAY WITH HIM NOW AND THEN TOO, IN THE '90S AND 2000S. HELL OF A GUY. INCREDIBLE DRUMMER. DESERVED BETTER.
HE KEPT PLAYING, RIGHT?
TRUE ENOUGH. WITH ARCHIE CAVANAUGH, AND THE GREAT SAXOPHONIST JIM PEPPER IN THE '80S, AMONG OTHERS.
THEN HE LEFT THE STATES...
YEP. LIVED IN THE NETHERLANDS A FEW YEARS. CAME BACK AFTER THAT. LIVES WITH HIS FAMILY NOW ON THE SILETZ RESERVATION NEAR PORTLAND.
WELL! SHALL WE GO?
WAKAN TANKA

X
CHILDHOOD
(1941-1959)

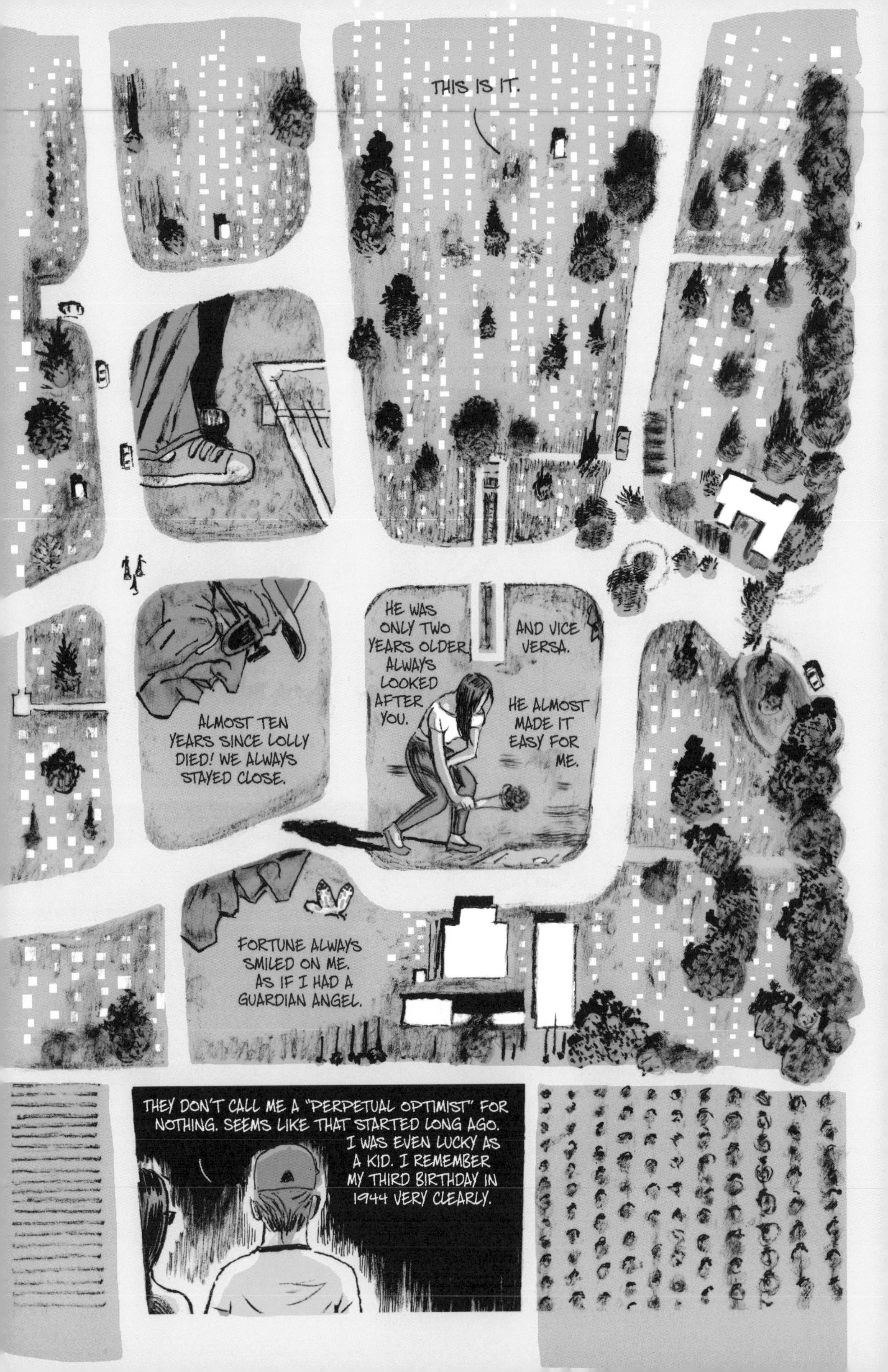
THIS IS IT.
ALMOST TEN YEARS SINCE LOLLY DIED! WE ALWAYS STAYED CLOSE.
HE WAS ONLY TWO YEARS OLDER ALWAYS LOOKED AFTER YOU.
AND VICE VERSA.
HE ALMOST MADE IT EASY FOR ME.
FORTUNE ALWAYS SMILED ON ME. AS IF I HAD A GUARDIAN ANGEL.
THEY DON'T CALL ME A "PERPETUAL OPTIMIST" FOR NOTHING. SEEMS LIKE THAT STARTED LONG AGO.
I WAS EVEN LUCKY AS A KID. I REMEMBER MY THIRD BIRTHDAY IN 1944 VERY CLEARLY.

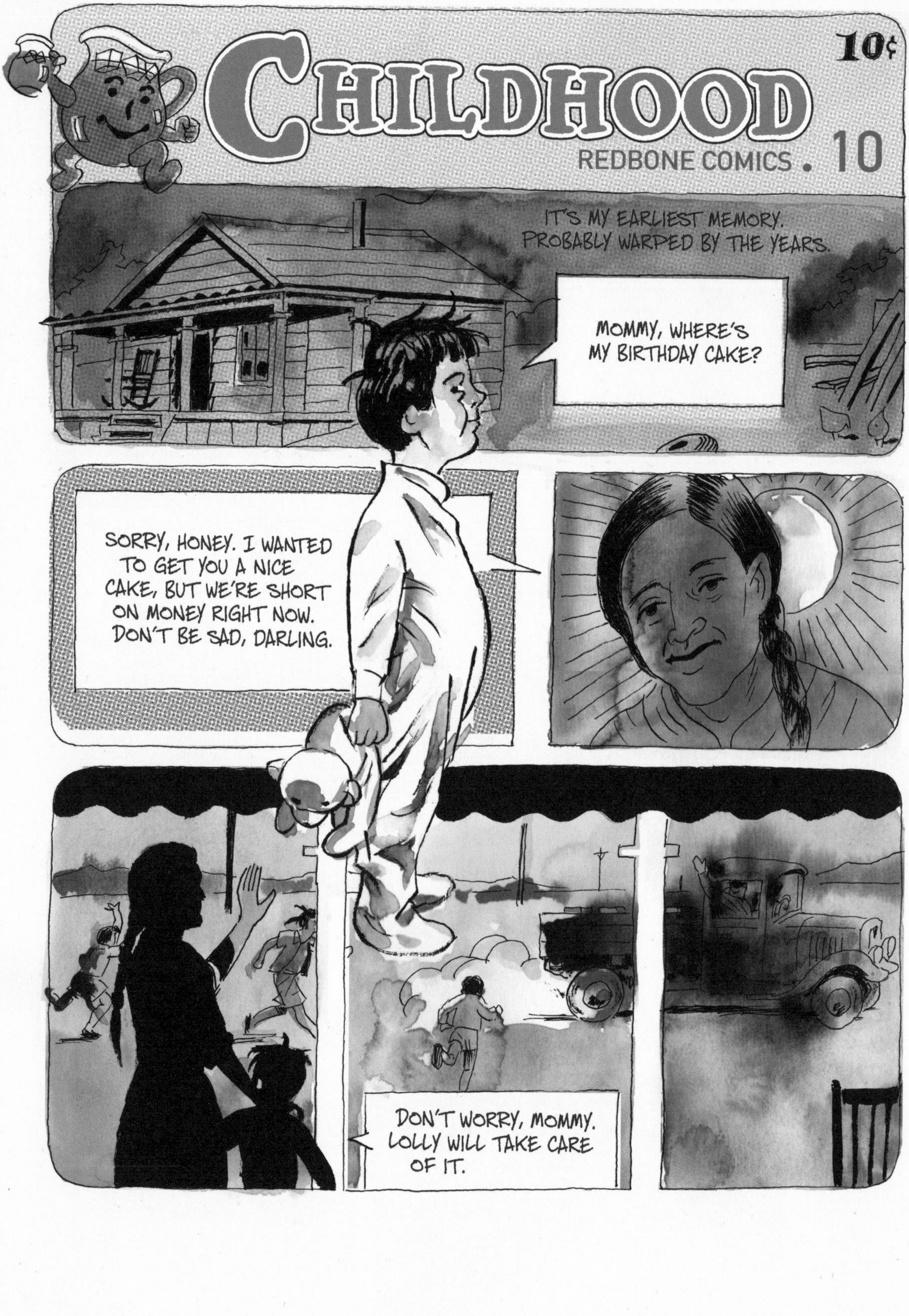
CHILDHOOD
10¢
REDBONE COMICS . 10
IT'S MY EARLIEST MEMORY. PROBABLY WARPED BY THE YEARS.
MOMMY, WHERE'S MY BIRTHDAY CAKE?
SORRY, HONEY. I WANTED TO GET YOU A NICE CAKE, BUT WE'RE SHORT ON MONEY RIGHT NOW. DON'T BE SAD, DARLING.
DON'T WORRY, MOMMY. LOLLY WILL TAKE CARE OF IT.

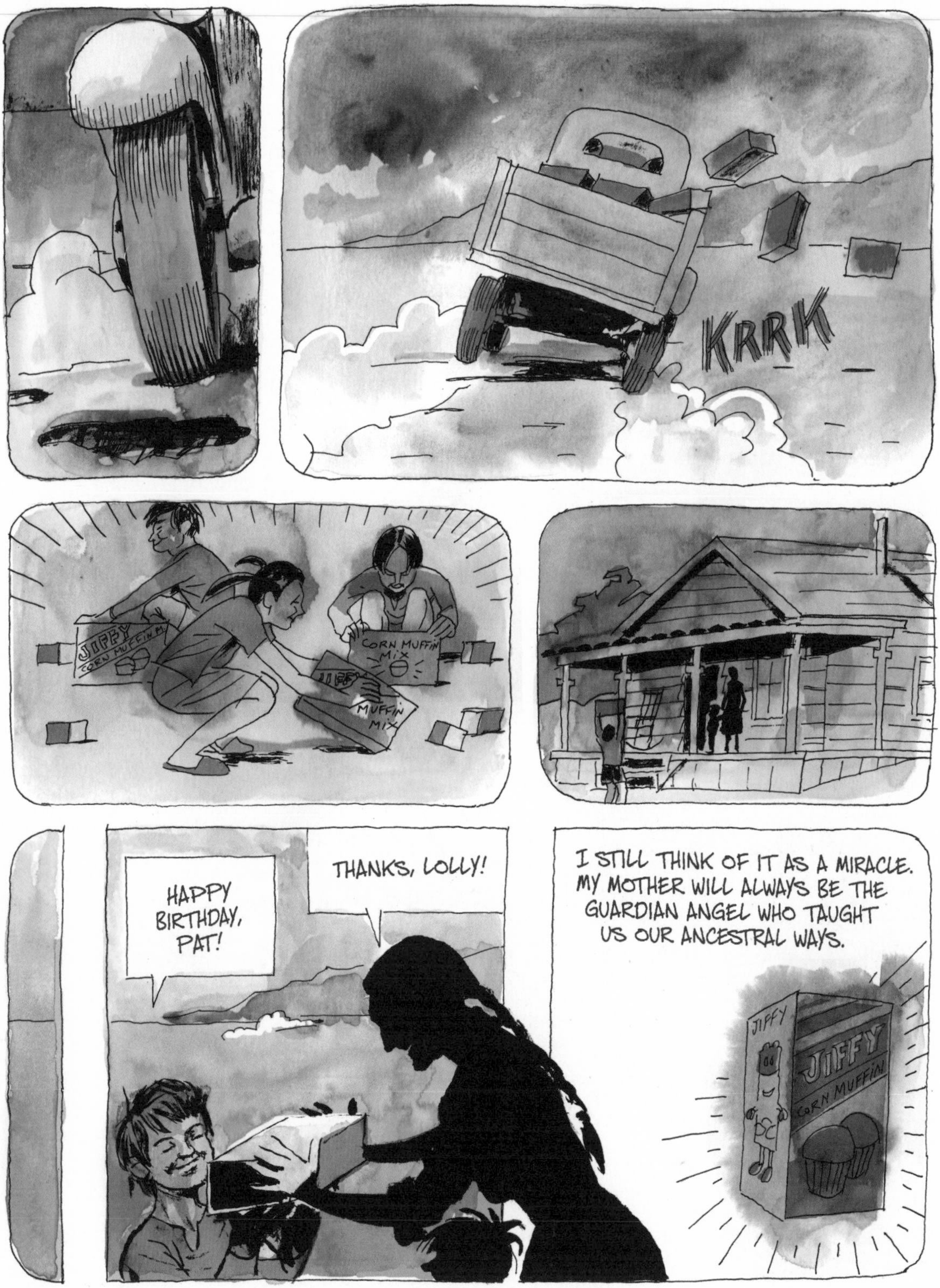
KRRK
JIFFY
CORN MUFFIN MIX
CORN MUFFIN MIX
JIFFY
MUFFIN MIX
HAPPY BIRTHDAY, PAT!
THANKS, LOLLY!
I STILL THINK OF IT AS A MIRACLE. MY MOTHER WILL ALWAYS BE THE GUARDIAN ANGEL WHO TAUGHT US OUR ANCESTRAL WAYS.
JIFFY
JIFFY
CORN MUFFIN

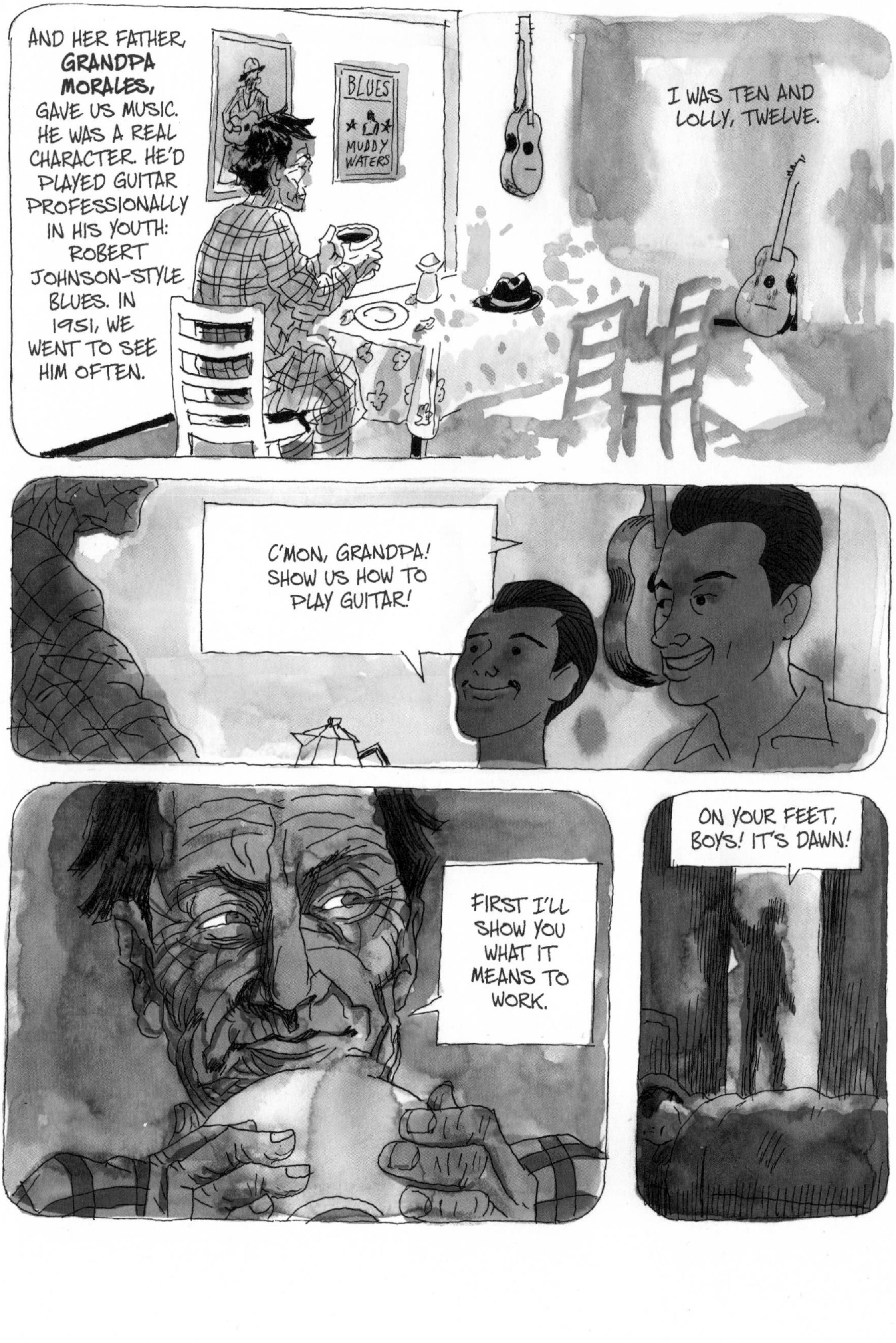
AND HER FATHER, **GRANDPA MORALES,** GAVE US MUSIC. HE WAS A REAL CHARACTER. HE'D PLAYED GUITAR PROFESSIONALLY IN HIS YOUTH: ROBERT JOHNSON-STYLE BLUES. IN 1951, WE WENT TO SEE HIM OFTEN.
BLUES
MUDDY WATERS
I WAS TEN AND LOLLY, TWELVE.
C'MON, GRANDPA! SHOW US HOW TO PLAY GUITAR!
FIRST I'LL SHOW YOU WHAT IT MEANS TO WORK.
ON YOUR FEET, BOYS! IT'S DAWN!

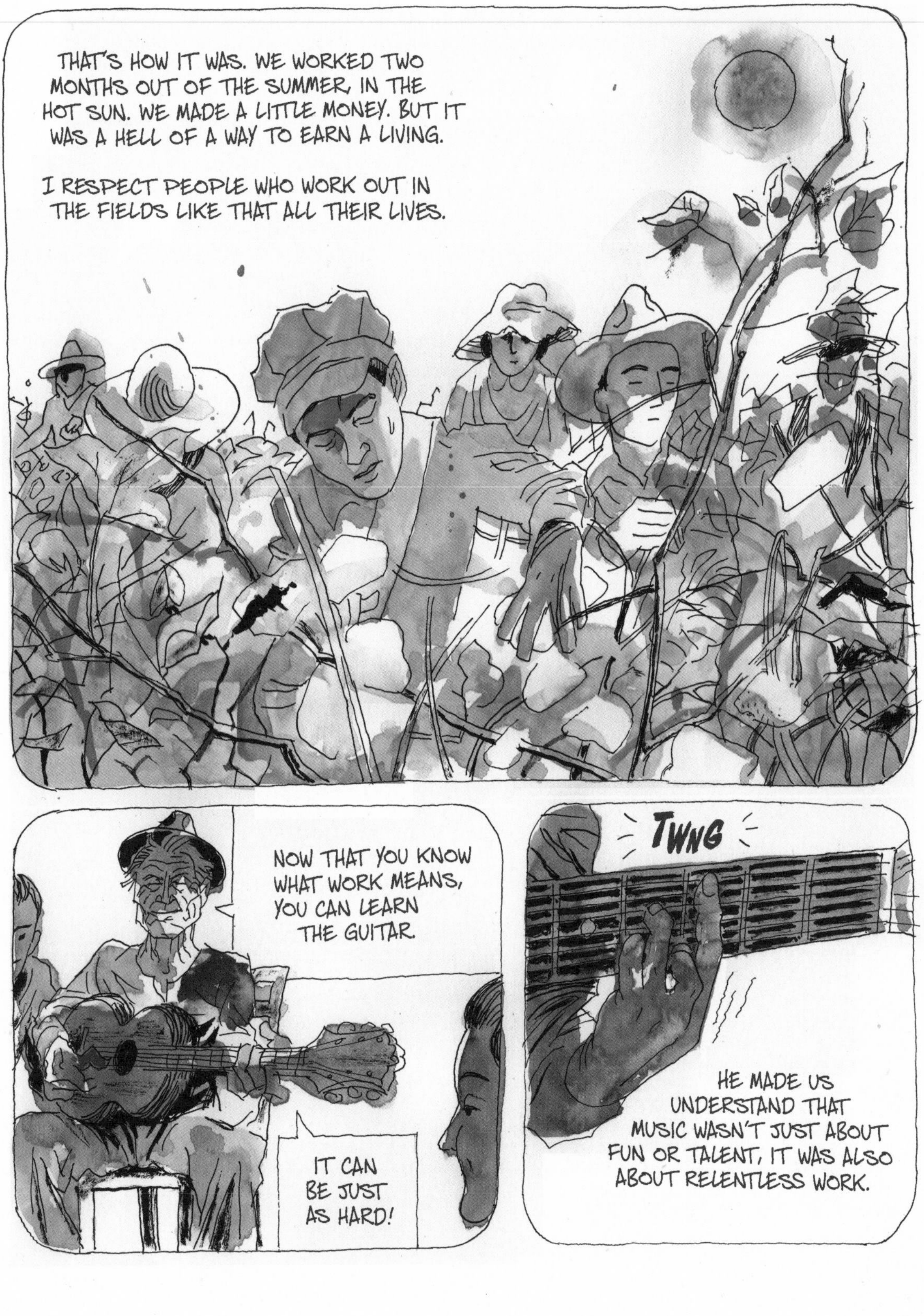
THAT'S HOW IT WAS. WE WORKED TWO MONTHS OUT OF THE SUMMER, IN THE HOT SUN. WE MADE A LITTLE MONEY. BUT IT WAS A HELL OF A WAY TO EARN A LIVING.
I RESPECT PEOPLE WHO WORK OUT IN THE FIELDS LIKE THAT ALL THEIR LIVES.
NOW THAT YOU KNOW WHAT WORK MEANS, YOU CAN LEARN THE GUITAR.
IT CAN BE JUST AS HARD!
TWNG
HE MADE US UNDERSTAND THAT MUSIC WASN'T JUST ABOUT FUN OR TALENT, IT WAS ALSO ABOUT RELENTLESS WORK.

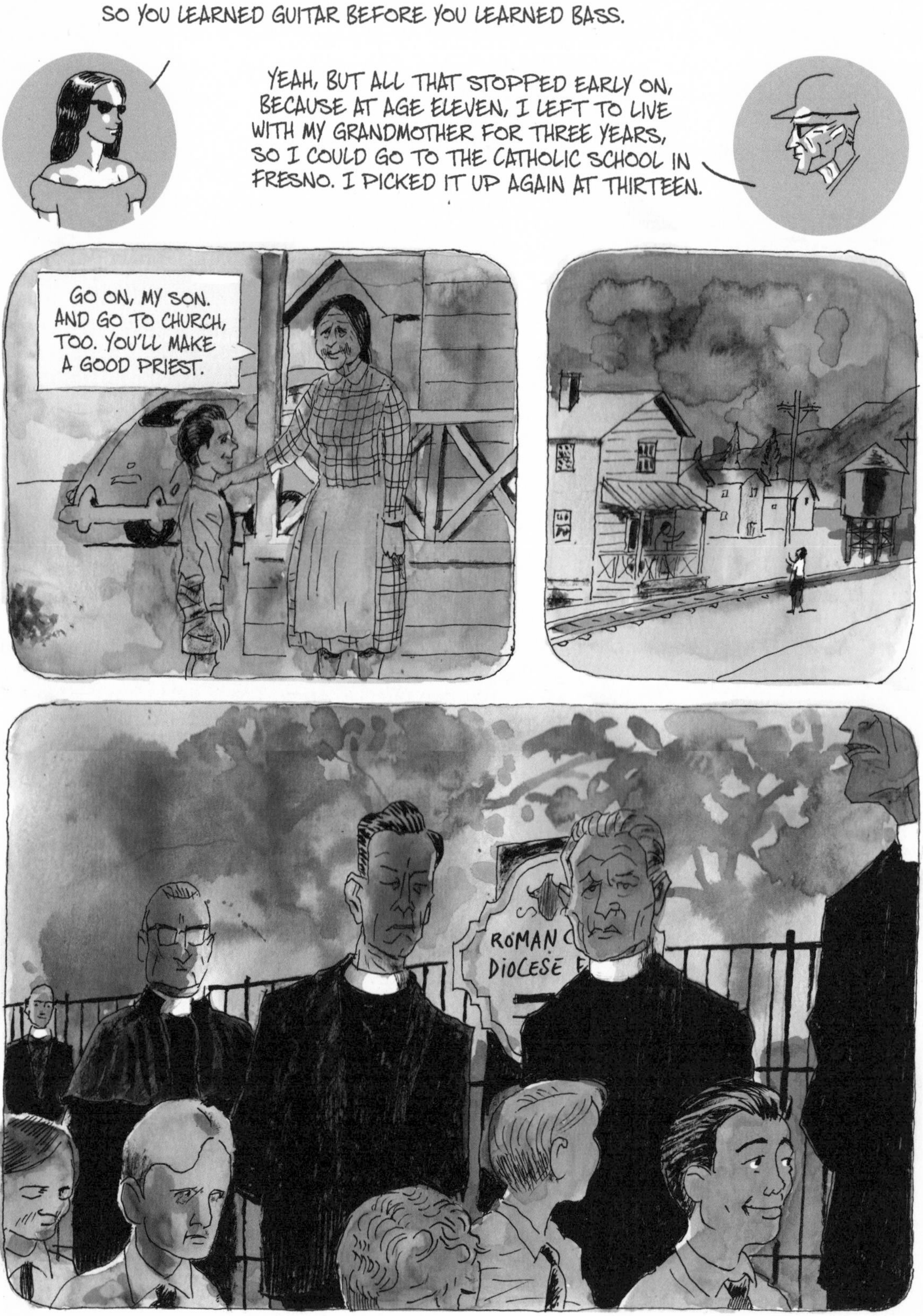

SO YOU LEARNED GUITAR BEFORE YOU LEARNED BASS.
YEAH, BUT ALL THAT STOPPED EARLY ON, BECAUSE AT AGE ELEVEN, I LEFT TO LIVE WITH MY GRANDMOTHER FOR THREE YEARS, SO I COULD GO TO THE CATHOLIC SCHOOL IN FRESNO. I PICKED IT UP AGAIN AT THIRTEEN.
GO ON, MY SON. AND GO TO CHURCH, TOO. YOU'LL MAKE A GOOD PRIEST.
ROMAN
DIOCESE

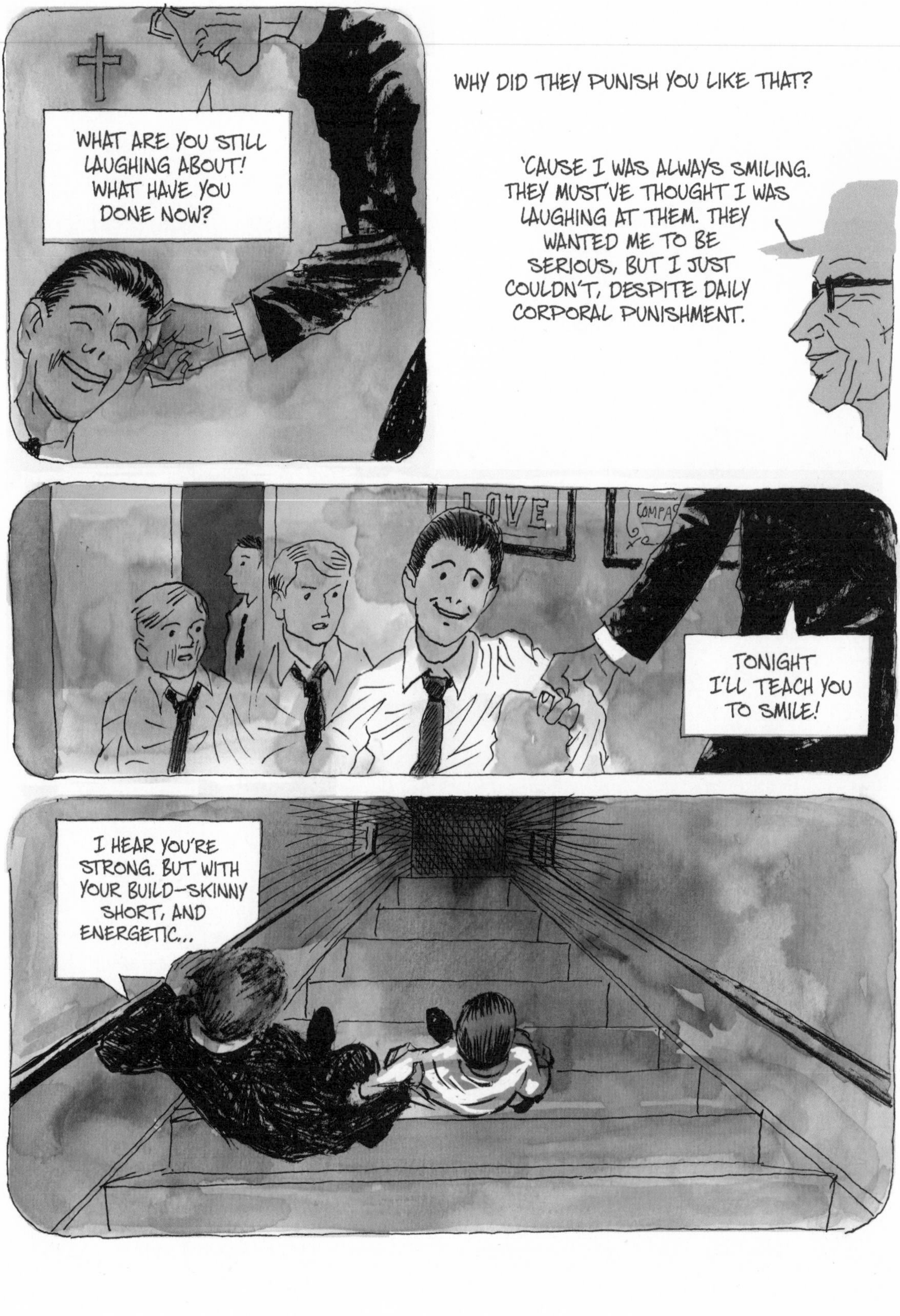
WHAT ARE YOU STILL LAUGHING ABOUT! WHAT HAVE YOU DONE NOW?
WHY DID THEY PUNISH YOU LIKE THAT?
'CAUSE I WAS ALWAYS SMILING. THEY MUST'VE THOUGHT I WAS LAUGHING AT THEM. THEY WANTED ME TO BE SERIOUS, BUT I JUST COULDN'T, DESPITE DAILY CORPORAL PUNISHMENT.
LOVE
TONIGHT I'LL TEACH YOU TO SMILE!
I HEAR YOU'RE STRONG. BUT WITH YOUR BUILD—SKINNY SHORT, AND ENERGETIC...

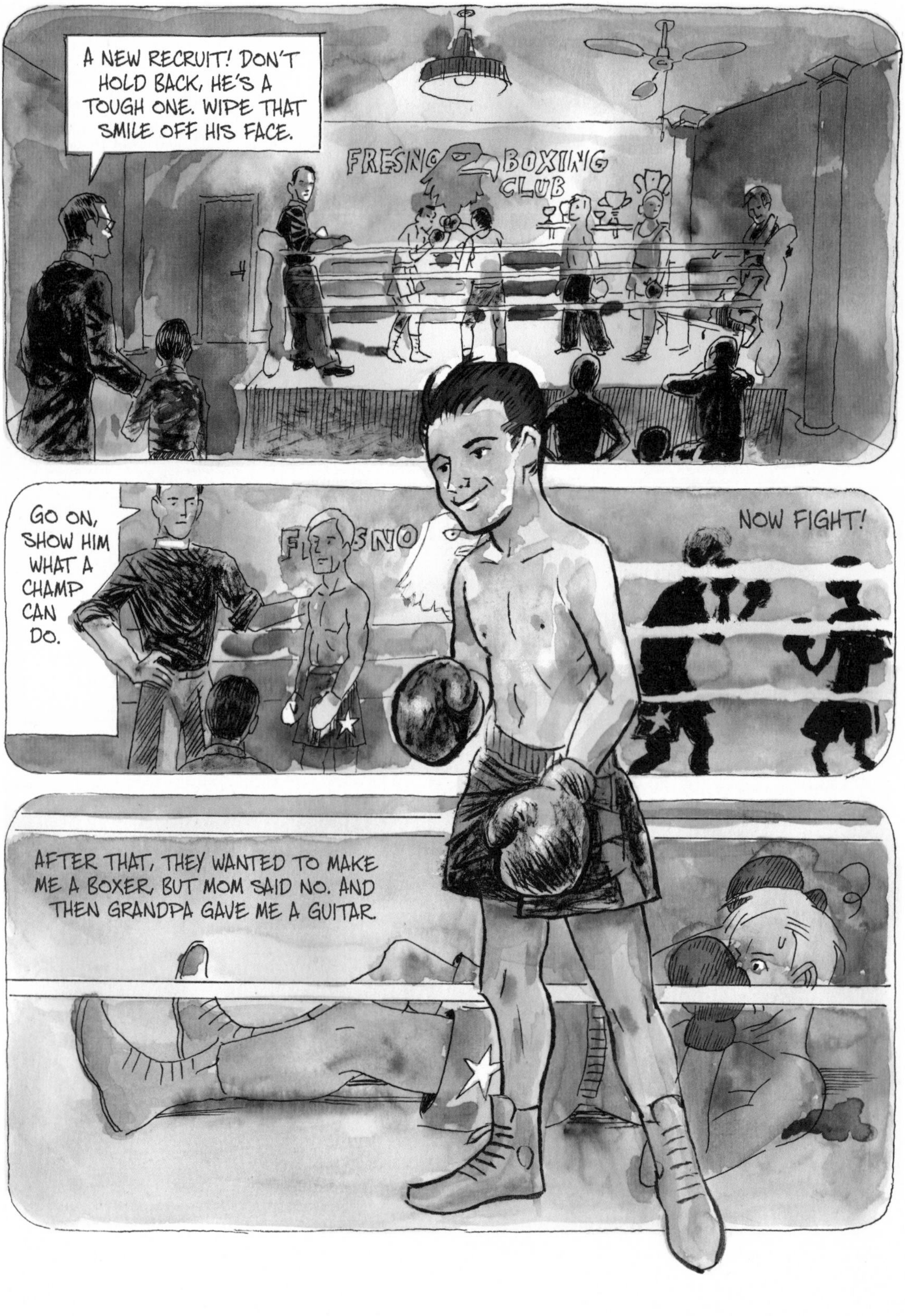
A NEW RECRUIT! DON'T HOLD BACK, HE'S A TOUGH ONE. WIPE THAT SMILE OFF HIS FACE.
FRESNO BOXING CLUB
GO ON, SHOW HIM WHAT A CHAMP CAN DO.
FRESNO
NOW FIGHT!
AFTER THAT, THEY WANTED TO MAKE ME A BOXER, BUT MOM SAID NO. AND THEN GRANDPA GAVE ME A GUITAR.

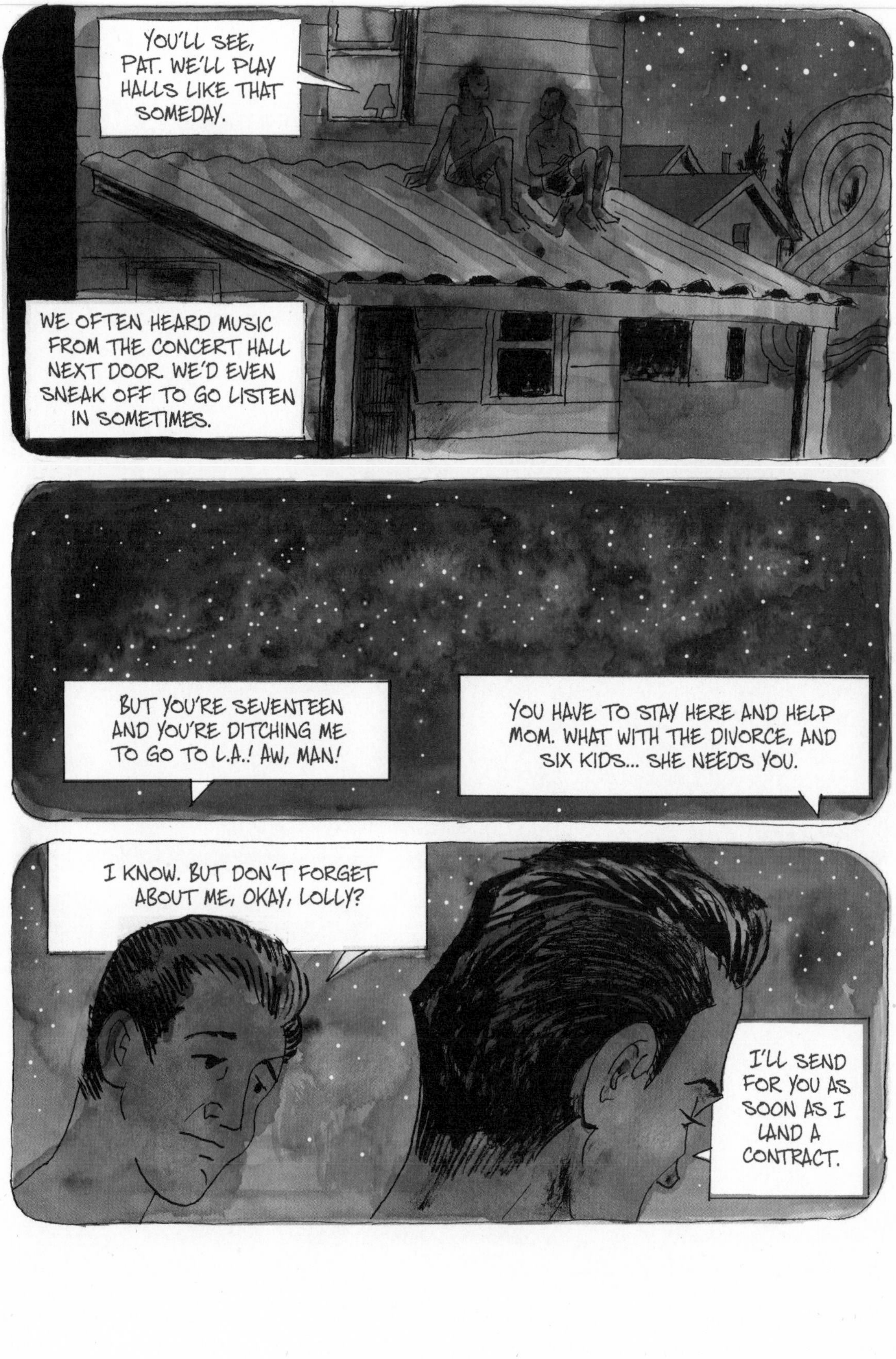
YOU'LL SEE, PAT. WE'LL PLAY HALLS LIKE THAT SOMEDAY.
WE OFTEN HEARD MUSIC FROM THE CONCERT HALL NEXT DOOR. WE'D EVEN SNEAK OFF TO GO LISTEN IN SOMETIMES.
BUT YOU'RE SEVENTEEN AND YOU'RE DITCHING ME TO GO TO L.A.! AW, MAN!
YOU HAVE TO STAY HERE AND HELP MOM. WHAT WITH THE DIVORCE, AND SIX KIDS... SHE NEEDS YOU.
I KNOW. BUT DON'T FORGET ABOUT ME, OKAY, LOLLY?
I'LL SEND FOR YOU AS SOON AS I LAND A CONTRACT.

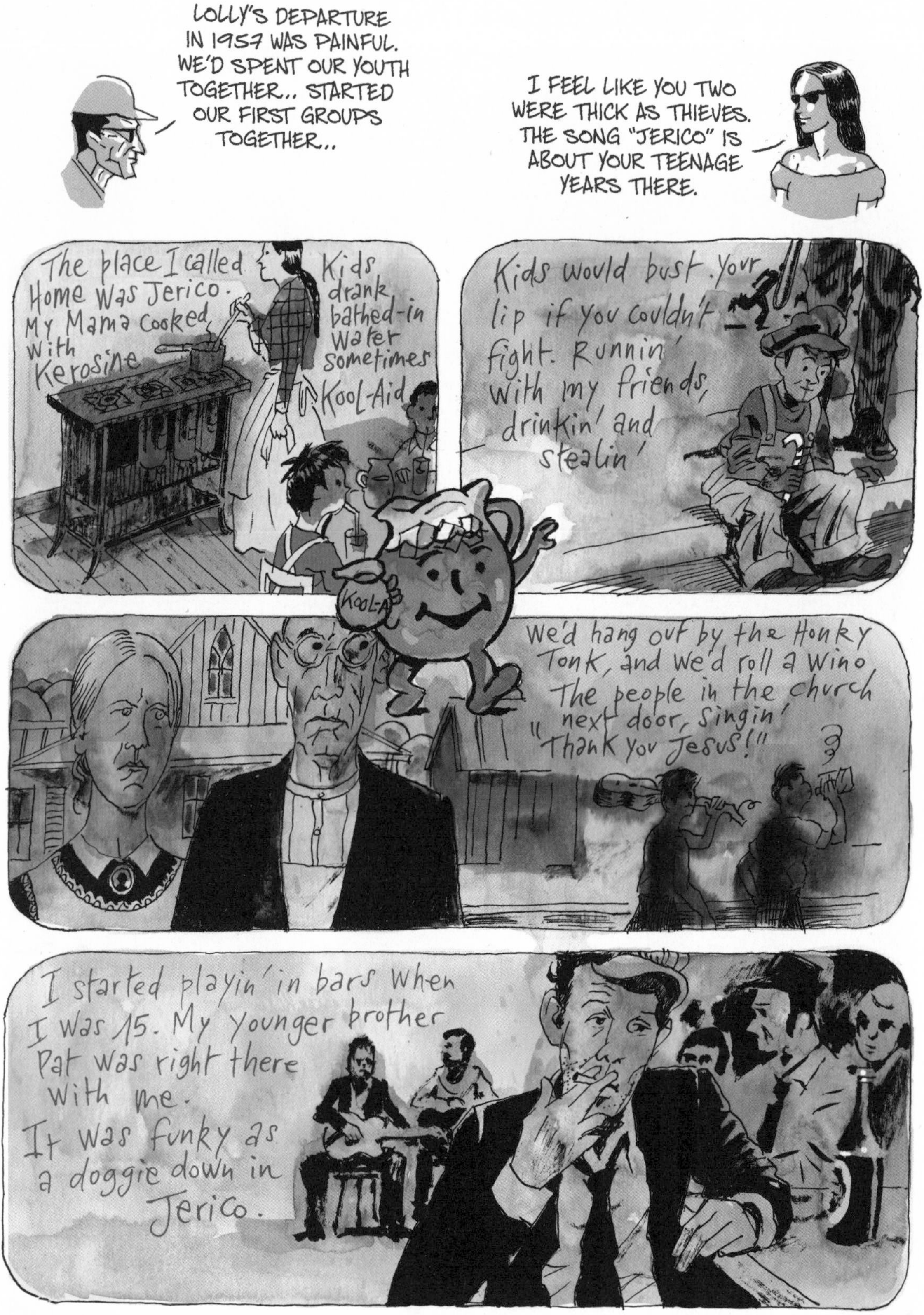
LOLLY'S DEPARTURE IN 1957 WAS PAINFUL. WE'D SPENT OUR YOUTH TOGETHER.. STARTED OUR FIRST GROUPS TOGETHER..
I FEEL LIKE YOU TWO WERE THICK AS THIEVES. THE SONG "JERICO" IS ABOUT YOUR TEENAGE YEARS THERE.
The place I called Home was Jerico. My Mama cooked with Kerosine
Kids drank bathed-in water sometimes Kool-Aid
Kids would bust your lip if you couldn't fight. Runnin' with my friends, drinkin' and stealin'
We'd hang out by the Honky Tonk, and we'd roll a wino
The people in the church next door, singin' "Thank you Jesus!"
I started playin' in bars when I was 15. My younger brother Pat was right there with me.
It was funky as a doggie down in Jerico.

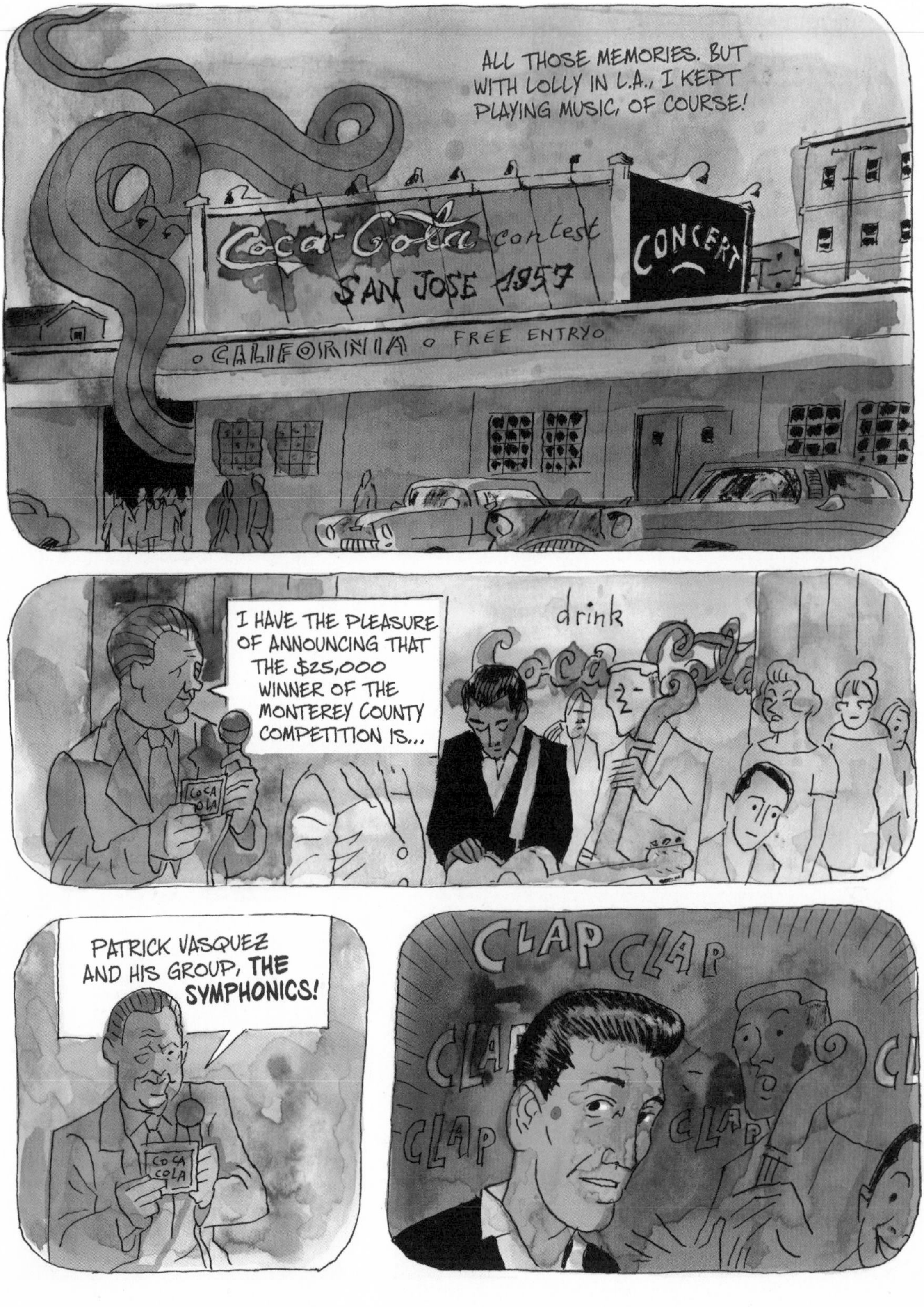
ALL THOSE MEMORIES. BUT WITH LOLLY IN L.A., I KEPT PLAYING MUSIC, OF COURSE!
Coca-Cola contest
SAN JOSE 1957
CONCERT
CALIFORNIA
FREE ENTRY
I HAVE THE PLEASURE OF ANNOUNCING THAT THE $25,000 WINNER OF THE MONTEREY COUNTY COMPETITION IS...
drink
COCA COLA
PATRICK VASQUEZ AND HIS GROUP, THE SYMPHONICS!
COCA COLA
CLAP CLAP
CLAP
CLAP
CLAP

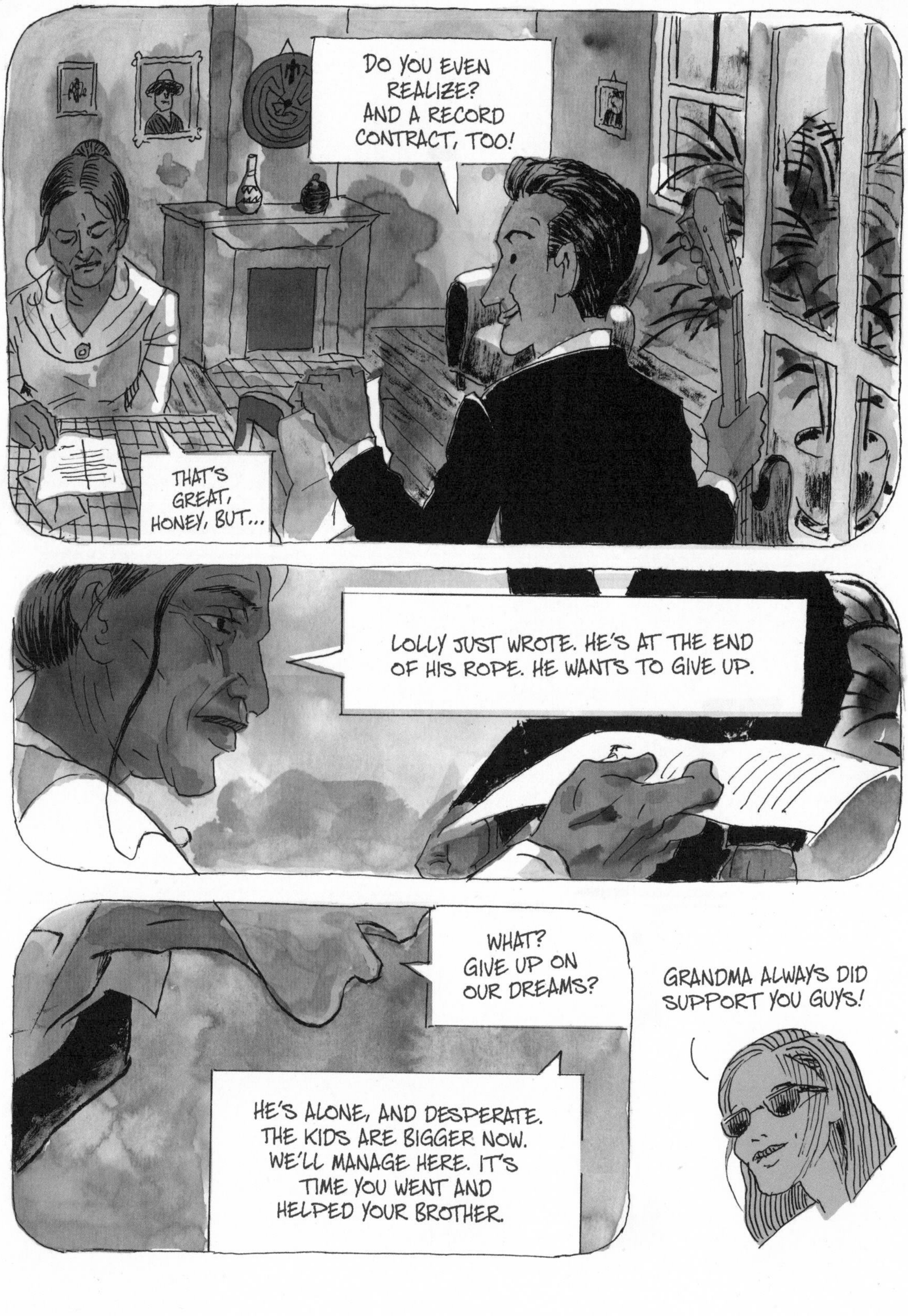
DO YOU EVEN REALIZE? AND A RECORD CONTRACT, TOO!
THAT'S GREAT, HONEY, BUT...
LOLLY JUST WROTE. HE'S AT THE END OF HIS ROPE. HE WANTS TO GIVE UP.
WHAT? GIVE UP ON OUR DREAMS?
HE'S ALONE, AND DESPERATE. THE KIDS ARE BIGGER NOW. WE'LL MANAGE HERE. IT'S TIME YOU WENT AND HELPED YOUR BROTHER.
GRANDMA ALWAYS DID SUPPORT YOU GUYS!

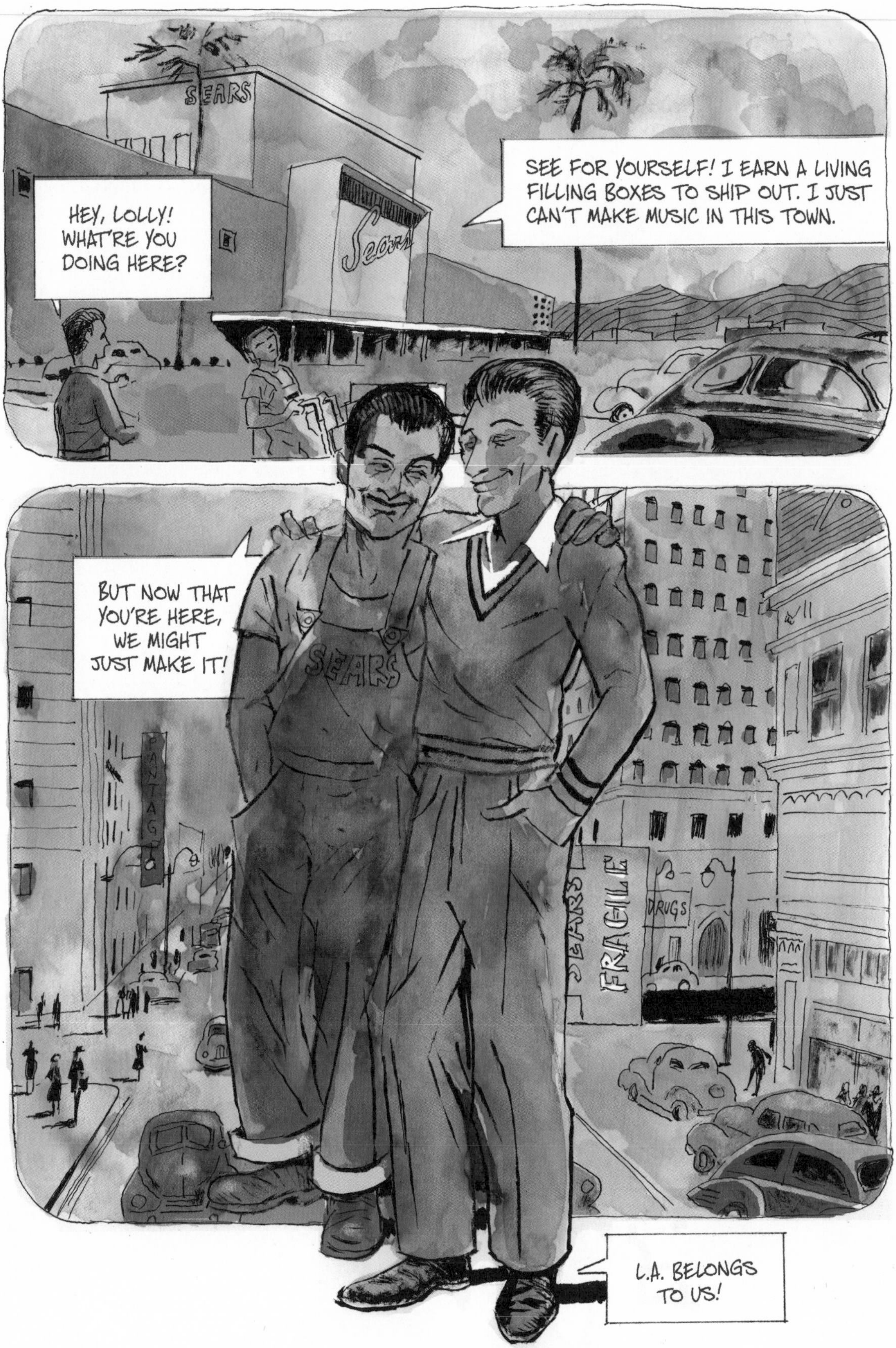
HEY, LOLLY! WHAT'RE YOU DOING HERE?
SEE FOR YOURSELF! I EARN A LIVING FILLING BOXES TO SHIP OUT. I JUST CAN'T MAKE MUSIC IN THIS TOWN.
BUT NOW THAT YOU'RE HERE, WE MIGHT JUST MAKE IT!
L.A. BELONGS TO US!
SEARS
DRUGS
FRAGILE

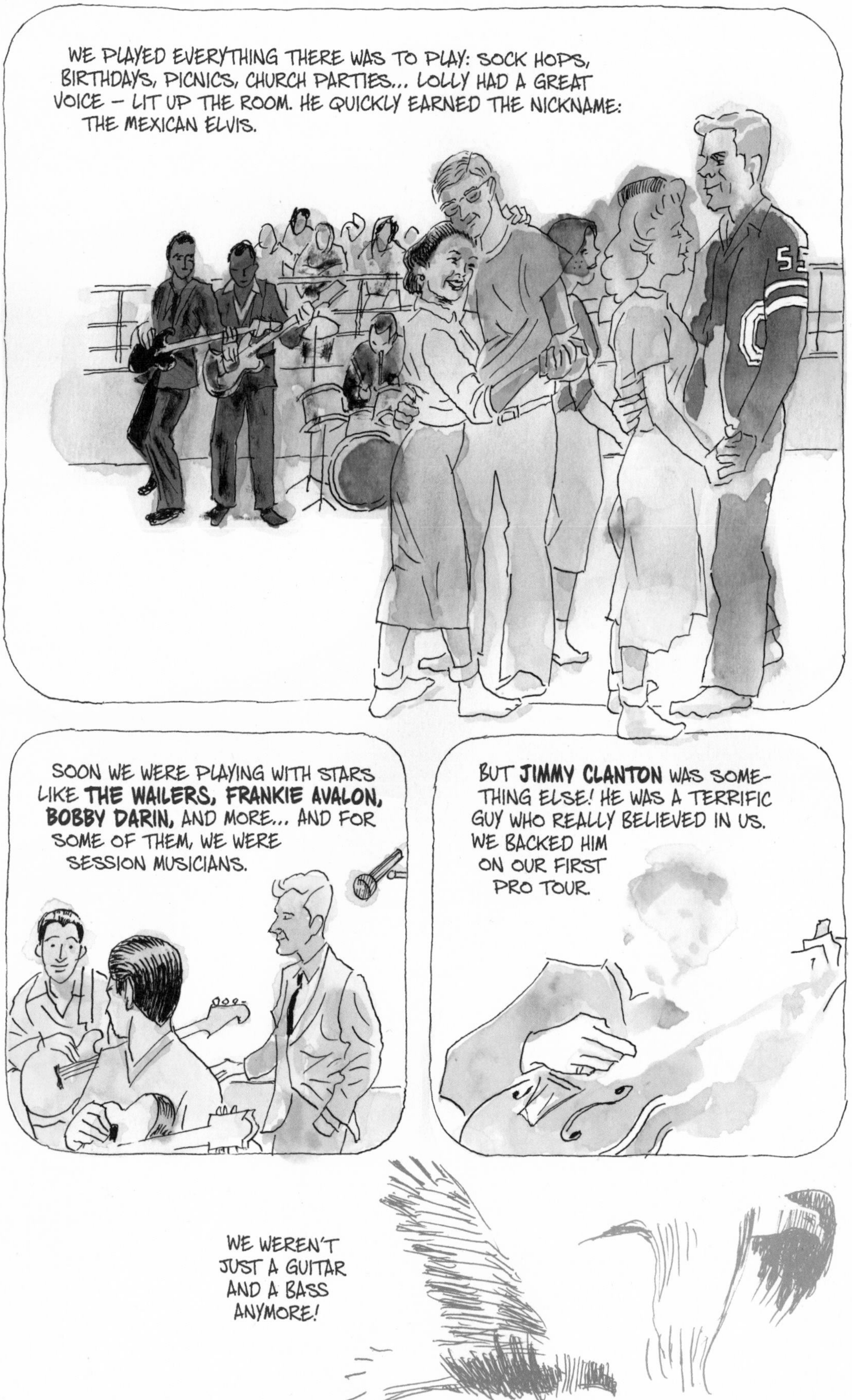
WE PLAYED EVERYTHING THERE WAS TO PLAY: SOCK HOPS, BIRTHDAYS, PICNICS, CHURCH PARTIES... LOLLY HAD A GREAT VOICE – LIT UP THE ROOM. HE QUICKLY EARNED THE NICKNAME: THE MEXICAN ELVIS.
SOON WE WERE PLAYING WITH STARS LIKE **THE WAILERS, FRANKIE AVALON, BOBBY DARIN,** AND MORE... AND FOR SOME OF THEM, WE WERE SESSION MUSICIANS.
BUT **JIMMY CLANTON** WAS SOMETHING ELSE! HE WAS A TERRIFIC GUY WHO REALLY BELIEVED IN US. WE BACKED HIM ON OUR FIRST PRO TOUR.
WE WEREN'T JUST A GUITAR AND A BASS ANYMORE!

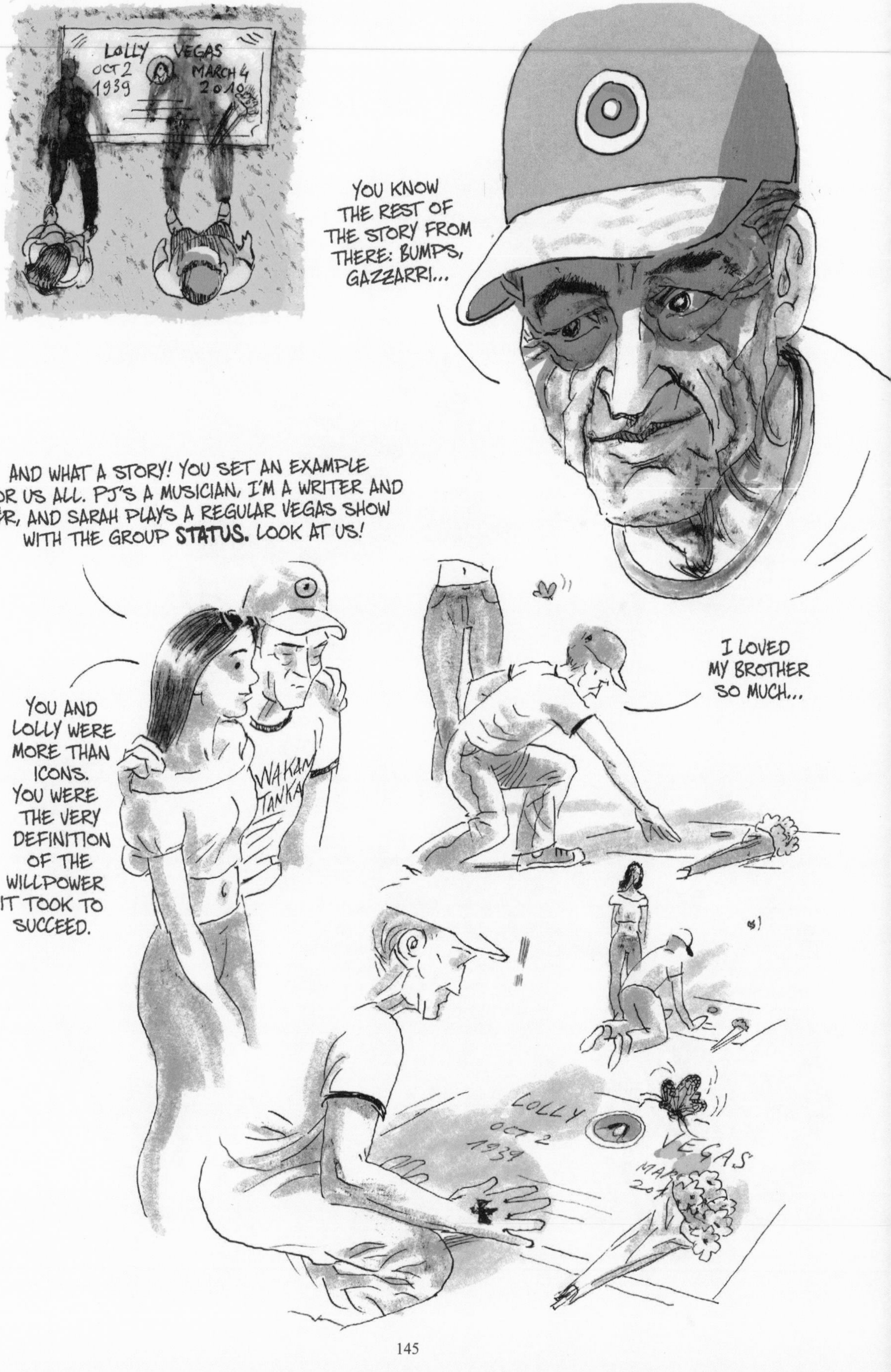
LOLLY VEGAS
OCT 2 1939
MARCH 4 2010
YOU KNOW THE REST OF THE STORY FROM THERE: BUMPS, GAZZARRI...
AND WHAT A STORY! YOU SET AN EXAMPLE FOR US ALL. PJ'S A MUSICIAN, I'M A WRITER AND A&R, AND SARAH PLAYS A REGULAR VEGAS SHOW WITH THE GROUP **STATUS.** LOOK AT US!
YOU AND LOLLY WERE MORE THAN ICONS. YOU WERE THE VERY DEFINITION OF THE WILLPOWER IT TOOK TO SUCCEED.
WAKAN TANKA
I LOVED MY BROTHER SO MUCH...
LOLLY
OCT 2
1939
VEGAS

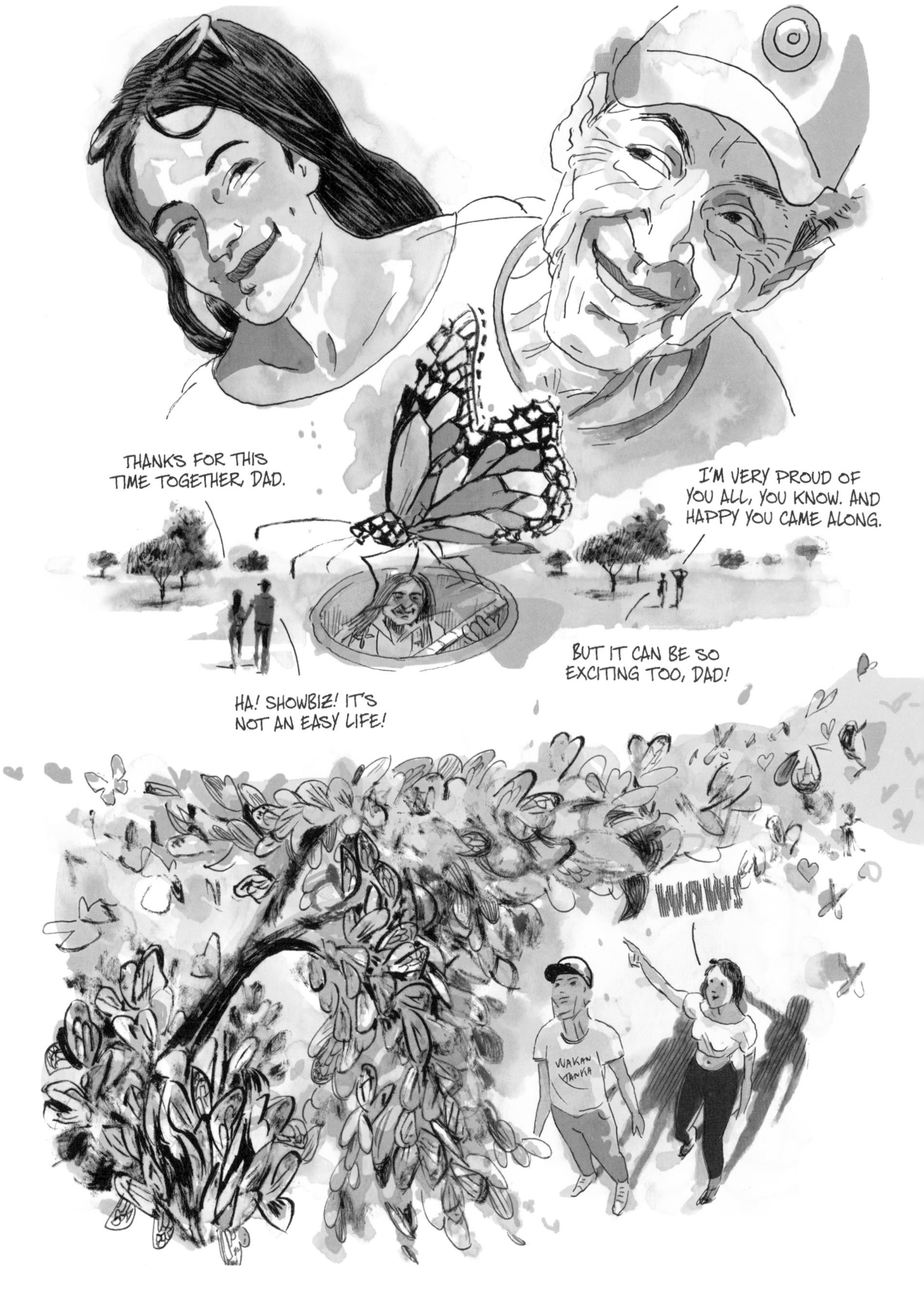
THANKS FOR THIS TIME TOGETHER, DAD.
I'M VERY PROUD OF YOU ALL, YOU KNOW. AND HAPPY YOU CAME ALONG.
HA! SHOWBIZ! IT'S NOT AN EASY LIFE!
BUT IT CAN BE SO EXCITING TOO, DAD!
WOW!
WAKAN TANKA

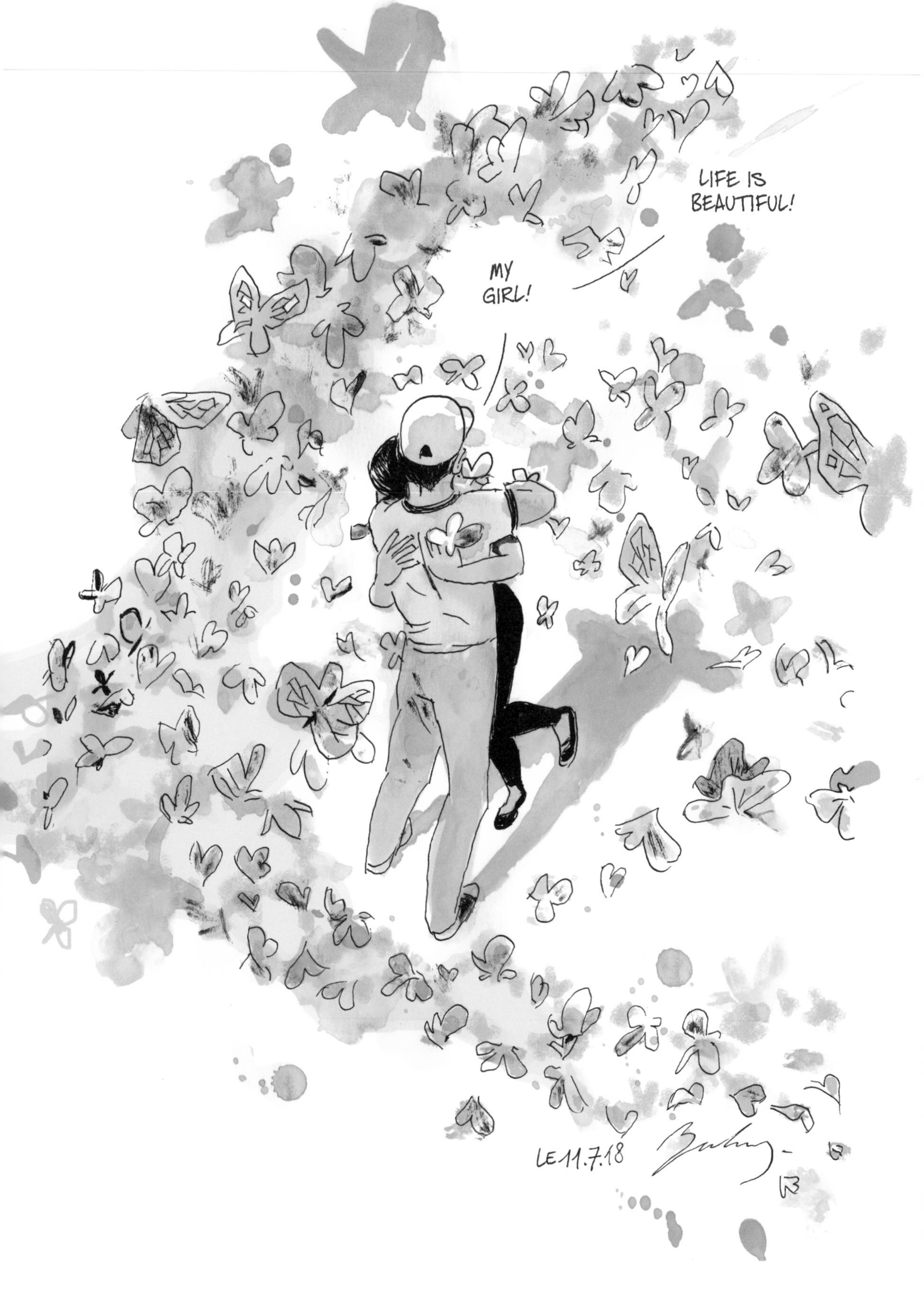
LIFE IS BEAUTIFUL!
MY GIRL!
LE 11.7.18

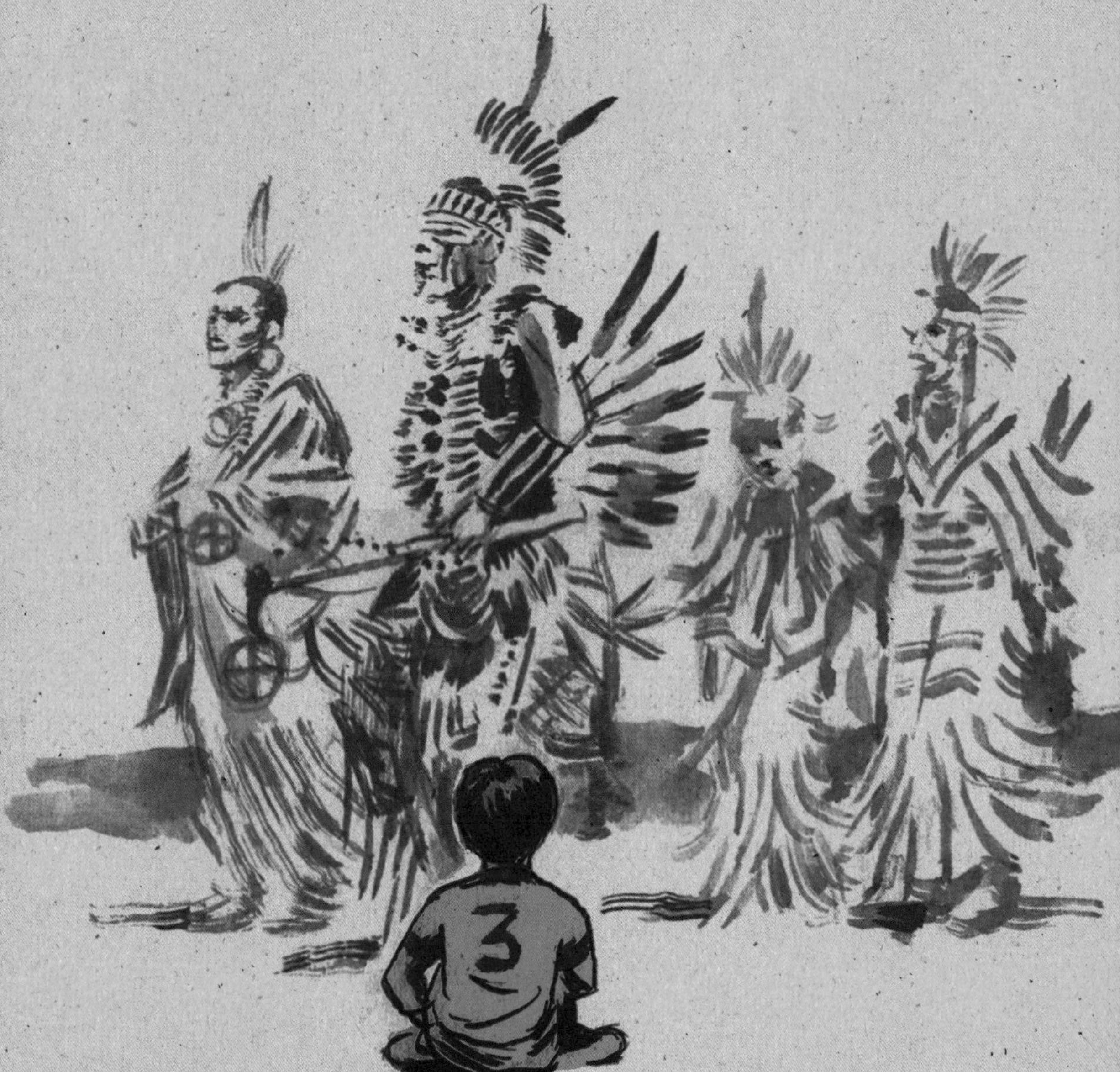

AFTERWORD

Once upon a time, in 1978, I was a student at the School of Decorative Arts in Strasbourg, France. New Wave was in its infancy; punk and reggae ruled the day. But I was all about prog rock. Discussions could grow heated, arguments turning into sparring matches. What with constructionism and the experimental Supports/Surfaces movement, classicists and people just going in circles, diverse and varied musical trends, we weren't short on things to fight about. Up till then, there'd been nothing new under the sun, and that was how things still were. I'd defend Yes and Gentle Giant tooth and claw against my friend Patrick, who hated everyone except the Sex Pistols. I'd call him a loser, he'd return the compliment, and everything was just fine.

There were also professors, old school vs. new, pre- and post-1968, of course. Lucien Leroy was a veteran drawing teacher, beloved by students and terribly talented. He asked us to draw a musical instrument; I drew my bass. Then we had to draw the same instrument aged and decrepit, which I also did. I killed a lot of trees back then. "You like bass? Rhythm? Talented musicians?" he said over my shoulder while I was mauling my beautiful bass. "Check this out!" And he handed me the Redbone album he'd brought in that morning just for me.

What an album! I loved it, cherished it, treasured it.

In the late '70s and early '80s, 45 rpms of hit records were easy to find, but albums were another thing altogether. It wasn't until the 1990s, and the start of the Internet, that I tracked down Redbone's whole discography and completed my collection. The Native American group might've been far away, but the Web brought them closer, though not that much information was available yet.

In 2002, I was playing bass in a rock group named Rowen, and naturally,

Pete DePoe and Christian, The Hague, 2008.

I wanted to cover "Maggie." That was when I really began digging online. Info was scarce and spotty, despite the group's major commercial hits in 1970s Europe.

In 2004, I created the site redbone.fr, a place to put everything I'd found out about the group. I scanned album covers and did my best to type out lyrics in English, since they weren't included in the albums. That was when I started corresponding with Sandra van der Maaden in Holland, who'd created the site redbone-europe.com at around the same time. Along with Ellen Bout and Maurice Heerlink, she'd put together quite a bit of information—different from my own, of course—and we traded what we had. Their goal was to organize a European tour for Redbone, which sadly never happened. Sandra was pivotal to me, because not only did she help me improve redbone.fr, but she also put me in touch with Pat Vegas and Pete DePoe. She has my warmest thanks.

Redbone had been a genuine hit machine across Europe, but even more so in Holland, where ten of their songs hit the charts, with five breaking into the Top 10. "We Were All Wounded at Wounded Knee" was No. 1 for five weeks! In France, Germany, the UK, and Norway, they had more songs in the Top 10. "The Witch Queen of New Orleans" was a sensation in France and Germany—richly deserved for a song like none other of its era. But weirdly enough, "Come and Get Your Love" never did as well as it had in the U.S. That exception aside, it only seemed

Pat Vegas, Christian, and Acela Cortese, Los Angeles 2017.

natural that fans appreciated the group more in Europe than America. Europeans had discovered an innovative group where Americans saw only a one-hit wonder, or even deliberately overlooked artistic expression from a cultural minority.

In 2008, I spent a day with Pete DePoe, who was living in Holland at the time. Pete is a wonderful person, charming and charismatic.

In 2010, I started corresponding with Pat Vegas. First by telephone, and then via email. We've been in touch ever since, and our long conversations helped me compile enough info to think about creating this graphic novel.

In 2017, while we were hard at work on this book, I met Pat Vegas and Acela in Los Angeles. They did me the honor of having me as a guest on their radio show. Those three days in their company are filled with moments I'll treasure forever. I also met Tony Bellamy's children Mellica and Tony Jr., as well as his widow DeVona. I'd like to offer them all my sincerest gratitude for sharing their memories and putting their trust in a Frenchman who'd come to comb over what for them was the distant past.

As of 2018, redbone.fr is still going strong, growing with every press article and tour date and photo and bit of trivia I can find about Redbone.

CHRISTIAN STAEBLER

INTERVIEW
WITH PAT VEGAS

What do you think of the story of Redbone as a comic?

First off, I'd like to thank this book's creators for such a fantastic piece of work. Thibault Balahy's drawings are amazing and surprising. They bring our history back to life. It's an honor for me to be depicted in a comic and to have my story told.

I was an avid comics reader as a boy, and I still have a collection of old issues I plan to pass on to my children. Even though this kind of graphic novel wasn't around back then, comics were part of our daily lives.

Do you think this graphic novel should be published in the U.S.?

Absolutely! This is where it belongs. And I can't wait to read it in English...

Redbone deserved a bigger place in American cultural history...

Ha ha ha! Things are changing. Slowly, but they've changed a lot since Redbone got its start. The recognition's there. Why, I just got back from Canada today—from the Indigenous Music Awards in Winnipeg, where I received the CBC Music Lifetime Achievement Award for my body of work. Native American culture is finally getting recognition, even if that recognition can vary by era. Last October, Redbone also played the first Indigenous Peoples Day in L.A. Los Angeles joins a long list of cities like San Francisco, Berkeley, Denver, Seattle,

Anchorage, Portland, Albuquerque, Minneapolis, and Santa Cruz in replacing Columbus Day with Indigenous Peoples Day on their local calendars. Last year, the county Board of Supervisors voted to reimagine Columbus Day and adopt Indigenous Peoples Day as the county's official holiday.

We were honored to participate in the festivities, and my son PJ joined me onstage. He's been standing in for my brother these days on the songs where Lolly used to sing lead. PJ's a born singer with a tremendous voice.

Pat and his son PJ in concert in L.A., 2018.

Where does your political involvement come from? What drove you to stand up for Native American identity?

My father and his father lived on the Hopi reservation, and the way people on reservations were treated always upset and enraged me. I didn't like it, and I remember feeling that rage ever since I was a little boy. I was full of resentment—I felt like I had to do something. We started speaking up when people from AIM reached out to us because they were fighting for the same things. They were trying to inform people, tell them how Native Americans were treated. So that was when we joined forces. Most of the money we earned our first two years went to AIM to support their cause. We worked for almost nothing those first two years. We were friends with people like Russell Means and Dennis Banks. We were really close with those two. There was also John Trudell, Floyd Red Crow Westerman…

Can you be open about your roots today, no longer needing to pass as Mexican?

Now, the word "Mexican" is already problematic! It's like saying "Texan," or "Philadelphian." Everyone we call Mexicans were in fact Native Americans. The Spanish came and took over Mexico, then the Germans came after them, and finally the French, and they all married Indians.

My family were Papago, Indians from America. My mother was born right here in America; she was born in Texas, and she was Papago. And my father was Papago, so we're Papago Indians. But my father's family lived in Sonora, Mexico. They were there looking for work. But they couldn't find any, so they came back to the Papago reservation, where they couldn't find any either. So they went to Coolidge, Arizona, where they found some at last. My grandfather on my father's side got involved with a woman from the Hopi reservation. So when it came time to register the whole family, he did so with the Hopi reservation, but it says "Papago" right there in the ledger. He registered as Papago but lived on the Hopi reservation with his girlfriend. It's kind of confusing. But you had to find a way to survive. So yeah, things have changed a lot.

INTERVIEW CONDUCTED BY CHRISTIAN STAEBLER
OCTOBER 28, 2018

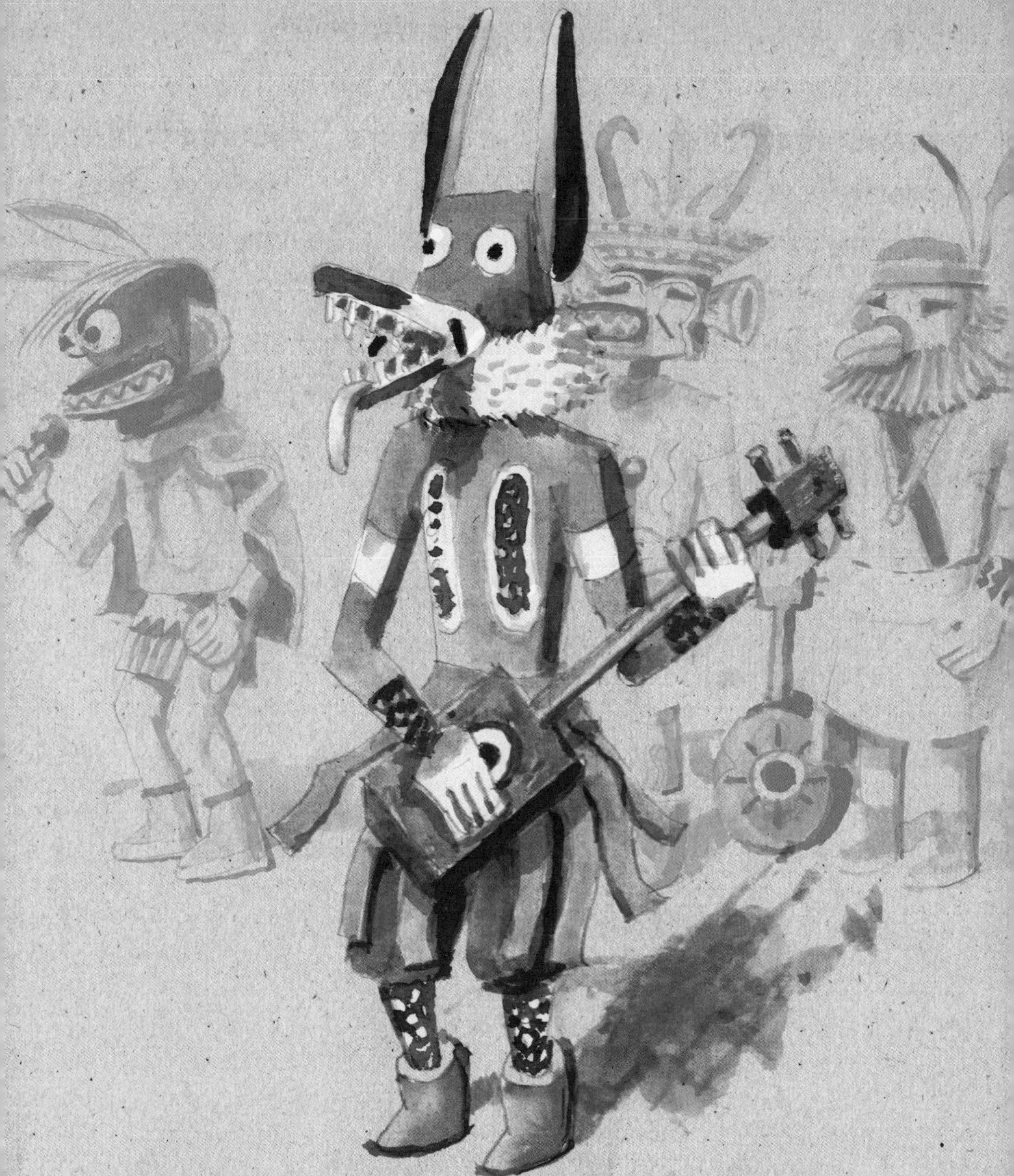

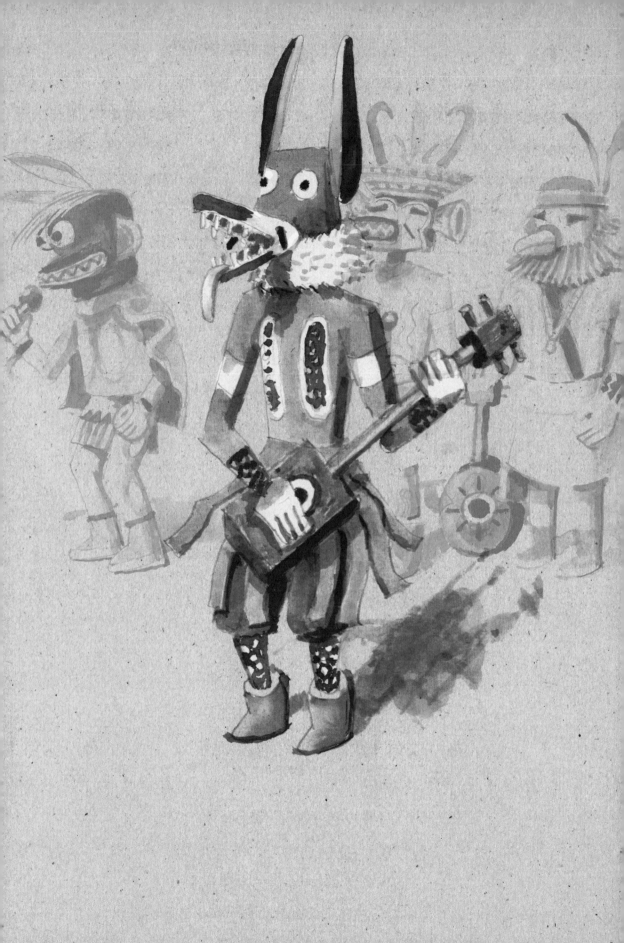

BIBLIOGRAPHY

GENERAL REFERENCE:

- *Native Americans,* Arlene B. Hirschfelder (Dorling Kindersley Pub., 2000)
- *La Terre des Peaux-Rouges* [Land of the Redskins], Philippe Jacquin (Découverte Gallimar, 1987)
- *Treaty between the United States of America and the Navajo tribe of Indians: with a record of the discussions that led to its signing, Navajo Tribe of Arizona, New Mexico & Utah* (KC Publications, 1968)
- *We Are Still Here: A Photographic History of the American Indian Movement,* Dick Bancroft & Laura Waterman Wittstock (Minnesota Historical Society Press, 2013)

ON REDBONE:

- *Come and Get Your Love: A Celebratory Ode to Redbone,* Pat Vegas & Jim Hoffman (Rehbon Publishing, 2017)
- *King Kong Pete: Redbone and Beyond,* Pete DePoe & Jim Hoffmann (King Kong Beat Publishing, 2017)

ON AIM:

- *Where White Men Fear to Tread: The Autobiography of Russell Means,* Russell Means & Marvin J. Wolf (St. Martin's Press, 1995)
- *Ojibwa Warrior: Dennis Banks and the Rise of the American Indian Movement,* Dennis Banks & Richard Erdoes (University of Oklahoma Press, 2004)
- *The Thunder Before the Storm: The Autobiography of Clyde Bellecourt,* Clyde Howard Bellecourt & Jon Lurie (Minnesota Historical Society Press, 2016)

ON AMERICAN INDIAN BOARDING SCHOOLS:

- *Away From Home: American Indian Boarding School Experiences, 1879-2000,* Margaret Archuleta (The Heard Museum, 2000)
- *To Win the Indian Heart: Music at Chemawa Indian School,* Melissa Parkhurst (Oregon State University Press, 2014)

DISCOGRAPHY

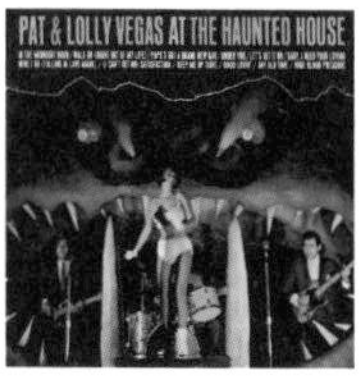
PAT & LOLLY VEGAS AT THE HAUNTED HOUSE

1966 – PAT & LOLLY VEGAS AT THE HAUNTED HOUSE

A pre-Redbone album with a few '60s classics and six original songs by Pat and Lolly to discover. All the ingredients that would make Redbone a success are already here. Another great pleasure? Hearing them cover "(I Can't Get No) Satisfaction" and "In the Midnight Hour."

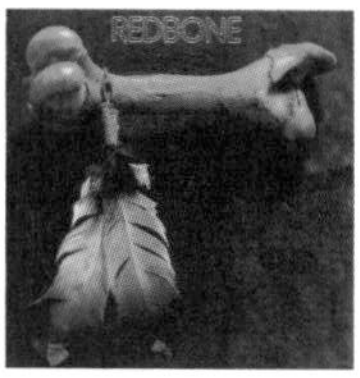
REDBONE

1970 – REDBONE

This first album is musically accomplished in every way. Filled with ancient rhythm, piercing melodies, and funky guitar solos before their time, this unprecedented double album sets itself apart from other music of the day. Listen to "Crazy Cajun Cakewalk Band" or "Danse Calinda" for perfect examples of their early style. Maybe their most timeless album because of its "roots" sound. Long instrumentals side by side with virtuoso improvisation complete the ensemble.

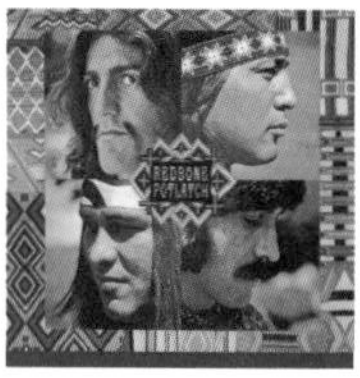

1970 – POTLATCH

This second album has their first big hit: "Maggie." A hit song isn't the same thing as a good song, but this one knocks it out of the park. Shorter songs and no instrumentals: Redbone was aiming to conquer the airwaves. But for all that, they never lost their special sound. Their first message songs are also on this album, like "Alcatraz" and "Chant: 13th Hour." The two brothers with their exceptional voices share lead duties.

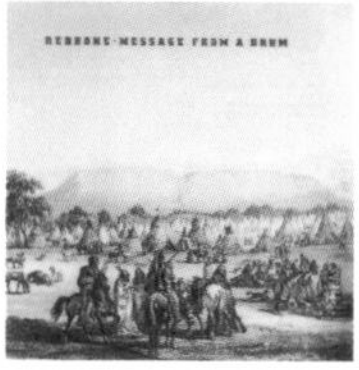

1971 – MESSAGE FROM A DRUM

The third album has their second hit: "The Witch Queen of New Orleans," maybe one of the finest songs in rock history. But this album is so much more than that. The magnificently swirling, scorching guitar solos sweep you away on wings of musical feeling, especially the track "Emotions." Their first arrangements for a string orchestra.

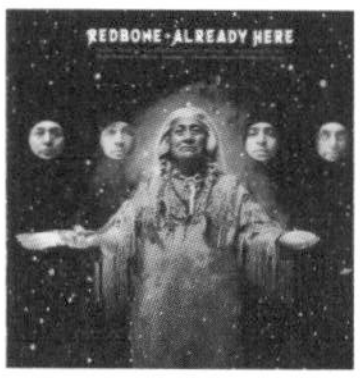
REDBONE·ALREADY HERE

1972 – ALREADY HERE

On this fourth album, the musicians have found their sound and continue to pursue it. Some songs stick in your head and stay with you, filling you with energy and happiness. "Poison Ivy" is a must, on the order of "Maggie," and was also very popular.

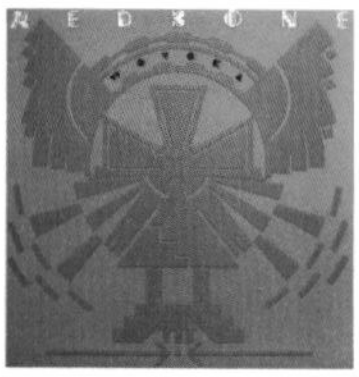

1973 – WOVOKA

This fifth album is their most famous, and deservedly so. It blends very "pop" songs with Native rhythms and roots. The result is a total gem. There's still strange and atmospheric music, almost like free jazz, to be found ("Liquid Truth" and "23rd and Mad"), right next to their biggest popular hit, "Come and Get Your Love." The use of the latter in 2014's *Guardians of the Galaxy* only enhanced the album's legendary stature. It's also the first to feature both Butch and Pete.

1974 – BEADED DREAMS THROUGH TURQUOISE EYES

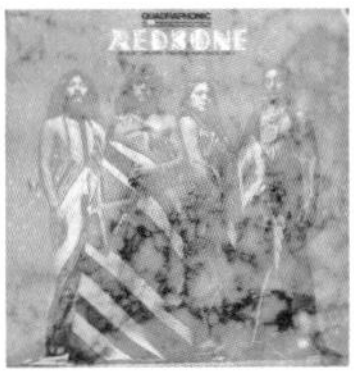

This sixth album was far more commercial than the previous ones. But oddly enough, none of these songs became hits, even if "Suzi Girl" and "One More Time" deserved to. Should this be read as a consequence of their outspoken political views? However, several atypical tracks for the group pop up, such as "Cookin' with D'Redbone." With the recent CD in 2017, six additional songs not on the initial release fill out the album. Yet another occasion to discover Redbone's greatest hits from their finest era.

1977 – CYCLES

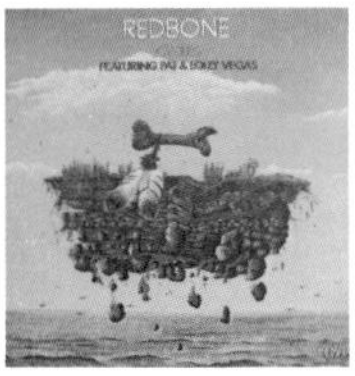
REDBONE

This seventh album was the group's last studio recording for three decades. Pat and Lolly are both present, of course, but they're the only ones from the group's golden age. More disco in feel, this is an underrated record. It deserves to be rediscovered, for it has some true gems ("Gamble," "Don't Say No"). A special mention goes out to the bass line on "Dancing Bones." But of course, all of Pat Vegas' bass lines were incredible. They seem simple, but they're so hard to imitate...

1977 – LIVE

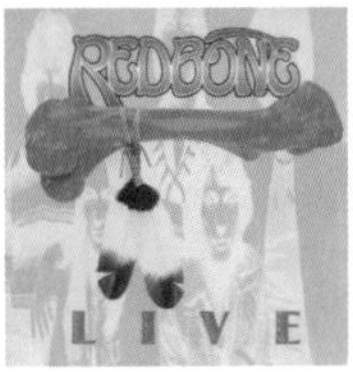
LIVE

The group's first live album was recorded the same year as *Cycles*, but went unreleased till 1994. This album shows their power, virtuosity, and magic. It's a fine testament to who they were at the end of their first era. The few existing videos depict a group with impressive power, rhythm, and musical sense.

2005 – PEACE PIPE

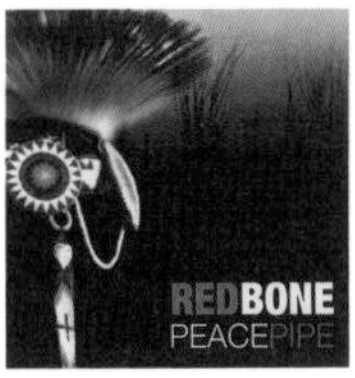
REDBONE
PEACEPIPE

It is a genuine pleasure to hear Pat's voice on a recent record. Powerful, perfectly judged, with splendid vocal harmonies. It almost feels like this album was recorded right after *Beaded Dreams Through Turquoise Eyes*. Super arrangements for violin, a good balance between rock and softer songs.

2017 – BUFFALO BLUZ

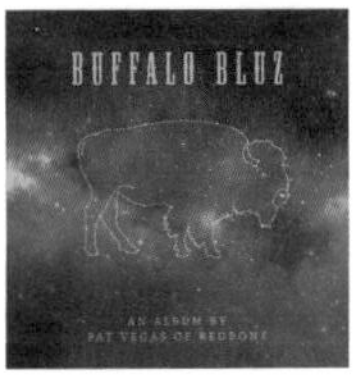
BUFFALO BLUZ

A new Pat Vegas recording that explores his most personal themes, a collection of powerful songs, new compositions and a few older interpretations. "Humpty Dumpty," "CC Rider," "Thorns Over Rose," and "The Pessimist" are unmitigated successes. Pat told me that he was after the very essence of a Redbone song. It seems like he found part of that here.

2018 – PJ Vegas – ON MY WAY

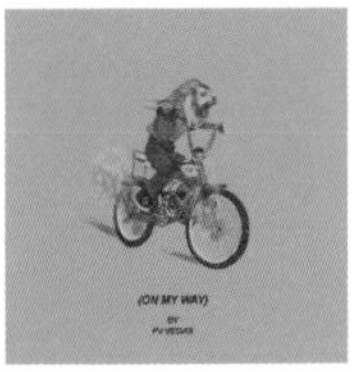

The son of Acela Cortese and Pat Vegas, PJ Vegas has for a few years now been producing danceable hip-hop music tinged with blues and rock that combines melancholy and powerful, yet peaceful rhythms. Peerless production, lovingly shaped sounds, and chiseled melodies make this five-track album worth a careful listen.

WOVOKA
JACK WILSON